The
PATH
of the
JUST

The
PATH
of the
JUST

Moshe Chaim Luzzatto

translation and commentary by
Yaakov Feldman

JASON ARONSON INC.
Northvale, New Jersey
London

10 9 8 7 6 5 4 3 2 1

Library of Congress Cataloging-in-Publication Data

Luzzatto, Moshe Hayyim, 1707–1747.
   [Mesilat yesharim. English]
   The path of the just / Moshe Chaim Luzzatto : translation and
commentary by Yaakov Feldman.
      p. cm.
   Includes bibliographical references and index.
   ISBN 1-56821-596-7
   1. Ethics, Jewish—Early works to 1800.   I. Feldman, Yaakov.
II. Title.
BJ1287.L83M33   1996
296.3'85—dc20   95-18663

Manufactured in the United States of America. Jason Aronson Inc. offers books and cassettes. For information and catalog write to Jason Aronson Inc., 230 Livingston Street, Northvale, New Jersey 07647.

CONTENTS

Translator's Introduction   ix

PART I: INTRODUCTION   1

Introduction to Part I   3

  Author's Introduction   5

  1   An Explanation of Man's Duty in the World   12

Summation of Part I   21

PART II: CAUTION   23

Introduction to Part II   25

  2   An Explanation of the Trait of Caution   27

  3   The Subdivisions of Caution   30

  4   The Means of Acquiring Caution   34

  5   Matters That Cause the Loss of Caution and
      How to Resist Them   42

Summation of Part II   47

PART III: ENTHUSIASM   **51**

Introduction to Part III   53

6   An Explanation of the Trait of Enthusiasm   55

7   The Subdivisions of Enthusiasm   61

8   The Means of Acquiring Enthusiasm   65

9   Matters That Cause the Loss of Enthusiasm and
     How to Resist Them   67

Summation of Part III   71

PART IV: INNOCENCE   **73**

Introduction to Part IV   75

10   An Explanation of the Trait of Innocence   77

11   Aspects of the Trait of Innocence   81

12   The Means of Acquiring Innocence   105

Summation of Part IV   107

PART V: ABSTINENCE   **111**

Introduction to Part V   113

13   An Explanation of the Trait of Abstinence   114

14   The Subdivisions of Abstinence   123

15 The Means of Acquiring Abstinence   125

Summation of Part V   128

PART VI: PURITY   131

Introduction to Part VI   133

16 An Explanation of the Trait of Purity   134

17 The Means of Acquiring Purity   140

Summation of Part VI   143

PART VII: PIETY   145

Introduction to Part VII   147

18 An Explanation of the Trait of Piety   148

19 The Subdivisions of Piety   154

20 The Evaluating Needed for Piety   172

21 The Means of Acquiring Piety   177

Summation of Part VII   181

PART VIII: HUMILITY   185

Introduction to Part VIII   187

22 An Explanation of the Trait of Humility   188

23   The Means of Acquiring Humility   198

Summation of Part VIII   203

Part IX: Fear of Sin   205

Introduction to Part IX   207

24   An Explanation of Fear of Sin   208

25   The Means of Acquiring Fear of Sin   215

Summation of Part IX   218

Part X: Holiness   221

Introduction to Part X   223

26   An Explanation of the Trait of Holiness   225

Summation of Part X   231

Index   233

Translator's Introduction

Most people seriously misunderstand *The Path of the Just*, as they do so much of *musar* (an untranslatable term that is usually rendered as Jewish "ethics," or "morals" and the like, but which would be best explained as being the science of Jewish humanism, transcendentalism, growth, and possible holiness all in one). Observant Jews, as a rule, either assume *musar* is a series of stringent "do not do's" said soberly and darkly, which they decide they could do without; or they assume it is a discipline that comes from an age of discipline, and hence it is no longer a force in their lives.

Most nonobservant Jews have never heard of *musar* and look for what it offers in non-Jewish literature that tells them how they can fully be the best they can be. And if they do find out about *musar* and read *The Path of the Just* they find they are shocked by it and horribly oppressed by its "impossible demands." As such it has been suggested that *musar* not be studied in our age, as it is "highly misunderstood" and "tends to be harmful." But I disagree. I believe our age cries out for its study.

This is such an alternately excellent, frightening and effervescent age, and the Jewish nation is smack in the middle of the mélange of good and evil that characterizes it.

We enjoy privileges now we never could before. We are physically safe as we have not been for so long (we tend to forget how life-threatening it was to be a Jew); numerous sophisticated Torah-study institutions have opened in our communities after we thought the tradition and its wisdom would die out; for the most part we no longer suffer from the wracking poverty that was so

ingrained in us; we enjoy the benefits of a network of organized and professional Jewish community organizations; and we have easy and open access to
Israel, which is our own. Like other peoples we enjoy the long life, health, and
high quality of life the modern era affords us, as well as the mass of information that contributes to intellectual growth.

Unfortunately, though, like other people, we suffer dread and fear in the
face of nuclear war (God forbid), and we can see only too well the deep mire
into which Western civilization has fallen and seems doomed to live. But our
people suffers from its own, unique problems.

The greatest problem we Jews have to contend with today, though it is
not recognized as such yet, is the loss of our memories and dreams. We have
forgotten who we are, what we do, where we would like to be, what our unique
national power and genius is, and what it is that makes us continue to go forward in history.

Once we had character and vision. If we got lost or sidetracked, we had
only to close our eyes and hear ourselves out again, and we would go right on
course to the goal we all recognized (and either followed or openly disavowed
but recognized nonetheless). But we have lost that. Like a singer in the midst of
a great din and rumble, we cannot hear our keynote, and we are dumbfounded.

We have lost our dreams and memories, for one thing, because we have
lost our sense of self. The Jewish nation has lost touch with its true self, the
part that pants and pulses inside of it and is fecund with remarkable possibility.

And the other reason why we no longer have our dreams and memories
is because we have offered them upon the altar of creature comfort and wealth.
We suffered so in the past, when we could so barely survive, that now at this
more fortunate juncture we have confused comfort and existence with wonder
and vision; we have settled for wealth and power and have abandoned ourselves.

It is time we realized that, thank God, we no longer have to gather our
forces together against the bitter cold or against a maniacal enemy, and that we
have been given an equitable life and comfort at last. It is time we heard ourselves out again and allowed ourselves the luxury of vision and the return to
presence of mind and contemplation. We are to be encouraged to once again
breathe in and go forward in accordance with our dreams.

But what was it we dreamt of? What constituted our vision? Where did
we clearly see ourselves heading?

Though we may not sense it in ourselves or in our brethren just yet, and
though it is out of synch with many of our current drives, the primordial Jewish dream—the view we had of the best of all lives and the advantage we hoped
to enjoy over all other peoples—was the life of piety and righteousness. We

dreamt of a life of goodness, rather than "the good life" so many others envisioned. Deep inside ourselves we knew and expected that the only thing that would fulfill us and satisfy our souls was a life of righteousness.

To be sure, we have always had our thieves and our evildoers, and we have unfortunately only rarely as a people lived up to so lofty a dream as that, but we have always had the dream, and we have always *longed* to live it out even as we failed in the mission.

The Path of the Just is just the work to remind us of that dream, and to have us return to our unique ways. It can fill our souls' lungs with bellowing wind again and give us life. So why has it been said that the reading of *musar* in general, and of *The Path of the Just* in particular, is dangerous and out of the question in our time? I cannot be sure, but I would like to offer an explanation which I humbly assume I am capable of offering because of my background.

I am a *baal teshuvah*, a Jew who became observant later in life. I was not raised a halachic Jew, and gave it no thought until the age of twenty-six, when *The Path of the Just* was recommended to me. As I was not yet at all leaning toward assuming an Orthodox lifestyle but was only studying it, the work neither intimidated nor tempted me.

Time passed, I grew, I started to study in *yeshivah*, and I once again read *The Path of the Just*. By that time it mattered, and it was woesome. I would read it and shudder. It convinced me—because of the way I was reading it, and, I believe, because of the English language terms within it—that the Jewish life of observance was dour, brittle, and noisy. Consequently, I was frightened and wondered if I had perhaps chosen a deadly path. So I stopped reading the book, ignored it, and continued happily along in my studies and practice.

As the years passed and I became more settled in my practice and self, as well as in Hebrew comprehension skills, I read it again. I noticed then that in the original it was a lovely work and not at all intimidating, and I wondered why. As a writer, I assumed that was so because nothing translates as well as its original—especially when the original was written by a master craftsman like Moshe Chaim Luzzatto. But I thought otherwise after a time. That was not the issue, I discovered. When I compared the original with the English I again felt uneasy about the work. Again, it seemed to be so very sober and "correct." So the fault was not that of style.

It occurred to me then that the vocabulary and the very subject matter seemed to have a decidedly *un-Jewish* tone to it in English, and smacked of repression and the like, simply because the terms used to express the original thoughts were terms used in very un-Jewish English-language works (terms such as, "piety," "control," "caution," "sin," "retribution," etc.).

What was missing to my mind was the Jewish passion for the holy and the pull toward rectification and betterment—the Jewish vision and dream mentioned above. In translation, *The Path of the Just*—a text of Godliness, Jewish spiritual excellence, service to the world, wealth of character, delight in one's having found the foundation of it all—seemed to be an ominous tract of denial and burdensome responsibility. And I came to believe that was perhaps the reason why some counseled against the study of *musar* in our age.

I came to see that *The Path of the Just* yearned for a commentary and new English translation that would attempt to indicate its original magic, vision, and broad wisdom. And so I took it upon myself to translate it and comment upon it in such a light (never meaning to impugn the previous translations, God forbid; only to add to them).

I can now only hope that *The Path of the Just* will no longer be seen as the "Puritan tract" it has often been taken to be, and that it will instead be seen to be the text for the Jewish life of excellent goodness and piety, of saintliness and holiness it really is. The whole point of this translation and commentary has been to underline that fact, and to once again bring *The Path of the Just* to the foreground of Jewish wisdom literature.

The Path of the Just is indeed a difficult work. That cannot be left unsaid. But it is an eminently precious one, nonetheless. If we will derive nothing else from the reading of this book other than the sense that the *tzaddikim* (righteous) are not "born that way" but that they become *tzaddikim* only after profound dedication, reverence for and love of God, and that *that* is their holiness, we will have accomplished a lot. So this book can in fact be seen as a text for the study of the ways of the holy people which all of us—capable ourselves of following that path should we decide to—are privileged to inspect and consider on our own.

I have taken some liberties with the work. In the original, the book is divided into twenty-six chapters. While I have retained those chapters, I have also divided the book into ten parts. Nine of those parts correspond to the nine traits the author dwells upon, and the tenth (which is the first in the translation) corresponds to introductory material (Luzzatto's introduction and the work's first chapter). And I changed the third person voice Luzzatto used throughout the work to the second person so that the reader would sense that he or she is being included in the practical advice being offered, as I believe that is how Luzzatto himself would have written in our day.

I have also included an introduction to each part, which acts as an overall presentation of the contents of the chapters involved in that part, and which

attempts to Hebraize the English terms as much as possible by citing the connotations the original would indicate. I then commented upon particulars within the body of the translation which called for explanation and focus. And, finally, I included a synopsis of the main points of each part in abbreviated and accessible form for the reader's use in his or her understanding and practical application of the principles in this book.

I wish to thank Rabbi Zalmen Weiss for his painstaking assistance and wise counsel in the course of this work. All that is meritorious in it is to be attributed to his advice, and all the errors herein are the translator's own.

I also wish to thank my parents, Irving and Sally Feldman, for their encouragement and assistance, as well as Dr. and Mrs. S. Morris Goldberg and Mrs. Melba Klein for theirs. I thank my wife, Sara Riva Feldman, for her love, her encouragement, her assistance, and for her wisdom, as well as for Nechama, Aryeh, and Dina, our precious legacy.

And I thank the Almighty for the strength and the abilities to do whatever I have done, and I ask of Him that He allow me the same in the future.

Note on the Typesetting of This Book

With the exception of his footnotes, material written by the translator has been set within ruled boxes. This way, the reader can easily distinguish between the translator's commentary and Luzzatto's own words.

The
PATH
of the
JUST

I

INTRODUCTION

Introduction to Part I

Part I comprises two chapters: the author's introduction and the book's first chapter, which acts as a rationale for the entire work.

As a work of *musar*, *The Path of the Just* is to be seen as a textbook of worship and character development with analyses, explanation, and exercises. Each part of the book discusses a trait that follows on the heels of the one preceding it and that is necessary for the acquisition of the one following it. Each trait is thoroughly analyzed as to what it is, how it is acquired, and what keeps one back from acquiring it.

But before the author can get to all that, he must introduce the notion of serious, well-considered concentration upon worship and character development. It is Luzzatto's understanding that such study is in a sorry state because it is overlooked or poorly carried out. It is also his understanding that it is incumbent upon us. He lays that incombency upon the well-known Torah verse that reads (Deuteronomy 10:12), "And now, Israel—what does God your Lord require of you if not to revere God your Lord; to go in all of His ways, to love Him and to serve God your Lord with full heart and soul, and to keep all of God's commandments and statutes. . . ."

Luzzatto spends the greater part of the rest of his introduction arguing that we spend so very much of our precious and limited time on the study of things that are either irreligious or irrelevant to personal development.

It should be stated at this juncture that he is not saying that an observant Jew should not study the arts and sciences; rather, that too much time is spent on their subtleties when such time should be spent on the subtleties of God-reverence. In other words, the study of the arts and sciences in and of itself is not spiritually spurious—the *over* study of them is, as is the overconcentration upon things which are more clearly religious by nature but nonetheless tangential, such as *pilpul* (finely tuned analyses of things impractical).

The point is made that the best way the reader can remain inspired is to regularly and diligently review this book, and the remainder of the introduction is an impassioned plea for the concentration upon what is precious and holy in an orderly and intelligent manner, based upon the aforementioned verse in Deuteronomy.

The first chapter, while still introductory in effect and purport, is nonetheless different. It is an enrapturing, concise, and brilliant statement of that greatest theme of all religious literature: the meaning of life. In it he tells all: who we are, what our task is, and where and how we are meant to accomplish it. One can ask for nothing else.

Read seriously and devoutly, the first chapter can change one's life. It can fill one in on the very point of it all, and give one the impetus to carry on (which is the author's intention). It is meant to fill the reader with an elemental thrust and determination, and to give him the "what for?" for the difficult road ahead that is the living out of this book.

This chapter is meant to remind the reader of priorities and to lend him a sense of the perspective of eternity. It is a rah-rah from on high—very high. It is a reminder of one's true nature and makeup, and it is a recognition of the potential in the hearts of all to live up to their souls' grand expectations. It is also a recognition of the impediments, but it is an explanation for the need for such as well.

What we have here is a holy man's understanding of the vast and whirling universe and our place in it.

Author's Introduction

I have not written this text to teach people what they do not already know, but rather to remind them of what they do know and are well aware. For what will be found in the great majority of what I have to say are things that are already known, and about which there is no doubt, but because they are so well-known and the truth of them is so self-evident, they are often hidden or completely forgotten.[1] The advantage to be

---

1. Luzzatto is making a bold assumption here: that the reason we do not follow through on the ideas expressed in *The Path of the Just* is because they are so obvious and so common.

Instead it seems the real reason is that most people are either lazy or they're frightened, confused, or put off by such things, as Luzzatto himself says in the ninth chapter of the book. In fact, that is just why they might expend so much energy upon the subtle studies he will soon mention—to avoid the matter. (Even the Torah scholars who would delve so deeply into impractical study, as he is about to point out, could be guilty of that as well, using it as an "escape," so to speak.) After all, it is quite normal to avoid change—physical as well as spiritual—even if the change is a necessary part of the process of development, which everyone seems to want. And *The Path of the Just* requires change and development.

(It should be said, however, that that is not his point here. At this juncture Luzzatto means to bemoan the fact that so many intellectuals do not delve into the matter of God-reverence because they believe it to be too simpleminded and unworthy of their time.)

In addition to that, it should be pointed out that our age asks questions about spiritual struggle and personal development that were not asked by Luzzatto's generation: "Why? To what end?" and what would once have been heretical, "What's in it for me?—what do I get out of it?" Those are serious questions that must be addressed. If they are not, the process demanded by the book will never be gone through in our time.

In his first chapter, Luzzatto tells us what we have to look forward to if we complete the task ahead of us. It is, he tells us, what we were created for in the first place: the ability to "delight in God and enjoy the radiance of His divine presence." We are assured that it is "the true delight, the greatest enjoyment of all." In chapter twenty-six he tells us that "the holy

gotten, therefore, from the reading of this book will not come about with a single reading of it. It is quite probable that the reader will find little if anything in his first reading of it that he would not have known beforehand. Its advantage comes in the reader's review and meticulousness. That way he will recall what he might have off-handedly forgotten, and place upon his heart an incumbency previously unrevealed.

You will notice, if you reflect upon the state of things as they now are, that the great majority of intelligent, enlightened, aware, and informed people expend a great deal of their energies on reflection upon and examination of the minutiae of the vari-

---

. . . are considered to be 'walking before God in the land of the living' while they are in this world"; and that when one will have attained holiness, "a spirit from on high will descend upon you, and the Creator will dwell upon you as He does to all of His holy ones." So what we are being promised is the felt Presence of the Divine, a sure involvement in Godliness, an evolution to the angelic. It is the end of woe and the ever-presence of bliss.

It (intimacy with the Creator, "the true delight, the greatest enjoyment of all") is what it is we have been wanting all our lives without knowing it: it is the fulfillment of all of our dreams—of even the most unholy.

That can be explained thusly: When the body and the person crave, they generally crave things of the world, physical things or subtle personal things. They may crave food or love or power or wealth. But, we assume, only the body and the person *can* crave. "After all," we reason, "what would the soul want?—it is already a part of the Divine, and has all that it needs in its being!"

The truth of the matter is that if the soul could be said to crave anything it would be what it already has—made manifest in the person it "occupies." The soul yearns for its inherent power, love, and wealth. But the body and the person misunderstand that craving and try to make it manifest in material terms.

In other words, the soul yearns for its inherent wealth (for it is wondrously wealthy), and the person takes that to be a yearning for material wealth; the soul yearns for its natural power (for it has vast amounts of power), and the person takes that to be a yearning for material power, and so on.

What we are looking for in our essential beings is delight. But we look for it in the wrong places. The person and the body look for it everyplace but in God, where delight can only be found. In fact He is indeed "the true delight, the greatest enjoyment of all." We know that in our very core but forget it moment by moment. It is what we are looking for and yearn for.

It is the great response to the questions, "Why?" "To what end?" "What's in it for me?" and "What do I get out of it?" It is truly the fulfillment of all of our dreams.

But our age seems to have forgotten. That is because we have lost sight of the fact that there is holiness. Having "lost" God (of course, one never loses God, but only loses cognizance of God), we have "lost" His couriers as well. We have forgotten our Holy Ones—those who have lived only for intimacy with God and for the simple doing of His will made manifest to them. We have forgotten the fact that there are individuals who are truly as gifted in piety and matters of the life of the spirit as others are in the arts and sciences.

Holiness is a category of humanity we have decided to suspend in disbelief. To benefit from that great delight we must remember and take seriously the very core Jewish notion of holiness and association with God.

ous sciences, and upon subtle scholarship, each according to his own inclinations and personal bents. There are those who very much concern themselves with the questions of cosmogony or physical science; others, with astronomy or mathematics; and yet others with art.

Some others especially enter upon the matter of holiness, that is, the learning of the holy Torah. Of those, there are some who involve themselves in the give-and-take of talmudic argumentation; others, in homiletics; and others, in the deciding of practical law. Yet, there are few of them who would dedicate their research and study to the means of attaining wholeness in Divine service, on love of and reverence for God, on the attachment to Him, or on all the other matters of piety.

This is not so because these matters are not of the utmost importance to them. For were you to ask, they would each surely say that these were the essentials, and that there could never be found a true sage who would not concentrate upon these matters.

But as a result of their not delving into them (as they are so "obvious" and "simple"), they see no need to reflect upon them at great length. Consequently, the studying of such matters and the reading of the holy books concerning them would be left in the hands of those of a less subtle mind, those tending to be more coarse. It would be this sort of person who would tend to be diligent in these matters, not ever abandoning them.[2]

It has reached the point where when one sees someone attempting to make himself pious, one cannot help but assume that he is of a coarser nature. The results of such assumptions are detrimental to both the sage and the nonsage. It results in neither attempting true piety, which comes to be a rare and precious thing in the world.

True piety is consequently lacking in the wise as a result of their lack of investigation into the matter, and in the unwise as a result of their lack of same. It has come to appear to most that piety is dependent merely upon the recitation of many Psalms and long, convoluted confessions; upon difficult fasts; and upon ablutions in ice and snow[3]—none of which sits well with reason or the intellect.

---

2. Luzzatto seems to be intimating that, one way or another, the study of things divine *will* be carried out in the world, but that unless the wise occupy themselves with it, others will. This stands to reason. The urge to attach onto God is very human. At times it is done well, but mostly it is not. It is Luzzatto's aim that such knowledge, such natural inclinations, will be more successfully carried out by those more constitutionally suited for it, as it involves a subtle internal process of analysis.

3. Such acts are insufficient because they are external: they occupy the body and the person, not the mind and soul (which are one and the same thing). They are a *materialistic* perception of things needed for the soul and are equivalent to force-feeding a child who is starving for love and attention.

This is not to say that the recitation of Psalms is an inherently mindless act. Said with faith and the knowledge that they are being heard by God, like prayer, the recitation of Psalms is enriching. What Luzzatto is referring to is the mindless tumbling out of dozens and dozens of Psalms in the hopes that "something" will be carried out in the process.

True, favorable and desired piety is very different from our conception of it. (It is very easy to understand why, for what does not occupy one's mind does not penetrate into it.) Despite the fact that the upright have set the beginnings and foundations of piety into their hearts, they do not busy themselves with it, so they might very well see instances of it and overlook them. It might pass before them and they would not know it.

Matters of piety, God-reverence and love, and purity of heart are not so ingrained in your heart that you would not have to find the means of acquiring them. They are not just come upon nonchalantly like natural processes such as sleep and wakefulness, hunger and satiety, and so forth. In truth, you have to foster means and devices to acquire them. And there is no lack for things to keep them back from you (just as there is no lack for ways to hold back the deterrents).

As that is the case, how could it be that you would not have to spend time in the profound study into the truth of these matters to know how they are acquired and maintained? And how should this wisdom ever enter your heart if you do not ask for it?

The need for the perfection of service and its necessary purity and innocence (without which it is not at all desirable, but rather disgusting and reprehensible, and [1 Chronicles 28:9] "God searches all hearts and understands the inclinations of everyone's thoughts") has become self-evident to the wise. How shall we respond on the day of reproach if we will have slacked off in our study of these matters, and abandoned a thing in our midst so profound as to be the very essence of what God asks of us?

Can it be that we would toil and labor in the study of things not at all incumbent upon us to study, such as *pilpul*, which could bear no fruit,[4] or laws that have no practical application in our days—while our great obligation to our Creator is abandoned to habit or left aside as elements of a religion of rote?

If we neither consider nor investigate the true nature of God-reverence and its ramifications, how can we hope to attain it, or to rescue ourselves from the vacuity of things of this world which have us forget it?[5] Will it not be entirely gone and forgot-

---

4. Again, it should be pointed out that, like the recitation of many Psalms, *pilpul* is not an inherently unrighteous sort of thing. It can in fact be an act of worship and devotion when it is done for the sake of concentration upon the pure, the abstract, and the transcendental. Luzzatto's contention is that it should nonetheless be carried out in a proper proportion of emphasis.

5. It is the contention of this book that this world is a shallow thing; that true reality, which is associated with closeness to God, can only be experienced in the "World to Come." But there are two understandings of the World to Come in the tradition. The first is the one Luzzatto makes use of here, in *The Path of the Just*, when he means it to refer to the place the righteous go after their death, also known as "the Garden of Eden." And the second is the one he uses in "The Way of God," which refers to the existential state of being the world as a whole will evolve to at a point in time. The latter is preceded by the messianic era and the resurrection of the dead. It is in both places that, as it is stated in the first chapter, one "delight[s] in God and . . . enjoy[s] the radiance of His Divine presence."

ten despite our acknowledgment of a responsibility to it? And if we do not try to set Divine love in our hearts by the use of all things that would bring it to us, how will it be found within us? How will attachment to God and longing for Him and His Torah come to us if we pay no heed to His greatness and exaltedness, which inevitably result in that attachment? How are we to purify our thoughts if we do not attempt to clear away the blemishes that the human condition places upon us? How are our personalities, which need so much rectifying and setting straight,[6] going to be rectified and set straight if we do not apply ourselves to the task with a great persistence?[7]

If we would only investigate the matter honestly we would arrive at the truth and we would do ourselves a favor (and others as well, by teaching it to them and improving them too). Solomon was referring to this when he said, "If you would search for it as you would for silver, and desire it as a hidden treasure, then you would understand God-reverence . . ." (Proverbs 2:4–5). He does not say, ". . . then you will understand philosophy," ". . . then you will understand astronomy," ". . . then you will understand medicine," ". . . then you will understand law," or ". . . then you will understand *Halachah*"—but rather, ". . . then you will understand God-reverence." So you see that in order to attain God-reverence you must search for it as you would for silver and desire it like a hidden treasure. This is from amongst the things that have been taught to us from our ancestors, and what is accepted axiomatically by members of our faith.

Can time be found for the study of all things, but not this? Why can we not set aside some period of time to at least look into the matter, if the rest of our limited time demands of us other studies or considerations? It says in Job 28:28, "*Hen* (behold) God-reverence is itself wisdom." Our sages said (*Shabbat* 31b), "'*Hen*' implies one, as we find in the Greek language 'one' is '*hen*.'" So reverence is wisdom—*it* alone is wisdom; and what does not involve study cannot be referred to as wisdom. The fact is that profound analysis rather than fantasy and weak logic is called for to arrive at the truth in all of these matters, as is certainly the case in the acquisition and full comprehension of them.

But that is not to say that this world is worthless. It serves the high purpose of allowing the opportunity for arriving at the World to Come more prepared for it. What it is oftentimes is cumbersome and counterproductive. It too easily allows for error. (See beginning of chapter one.)

6. Human, we necessarily suffer blemishes in character or personality. They are neither permanent nor intrinsic, but they are here with us. They too serve their purpose. And they are especially excellent when they are transcended. In fact, without them, transcendence itself is not possible. So they are our potentials for perfection.

7. The clear implication is that we can set them straight if we decide to. It is in our hands. We are the heroes if we manage to do it, and the villains if we do not. Our tradition does not allow for the luxury of blaming others or circumstances. It hands us our capabilities.

If one would reflect upon the matter he would find that true piety is not dependent upon those things the fools who make themselves out to be pious think it is, but rather upon true wholeness and profound wisdom. This is what Moses our teacher taught us when he said (Deuteronomy 10:12–13), "And now, Israel—what does God your Lord require of you if not to revere God your Lord; to go in all of His ways, to love Him and to serve God your Lord with full heart and soul, and to keep all of God's commandments and statutes. . . ."[8] Herein are included the preferred subdivisions of the perfection of Divine service: reverence, walking in His way, love, wholeheartedness, the keeping of the *mitzvot*.

"Reverence" refers to reverence for His exaltedness—that you be in a state of reverence before Him comparable to what you would experience being before a great and awesome king; that you be abashed before His greatness; and that, as a result of His greatness, you be aware of every move you make before Him—especially when speaking to Him in prayer or Torah study.

"Walking in His ways" includes all manner of character correction and reparation. This is what our sages referred to when they said (*Shabbat* 133b), "Just as He is compassionate, you are to be compassionate; just as He is gracious, you are to be gracious, and so forth." The point of this is that all of your traits and actions are to be just and ethical. Our sages have stated the principle thusly (*Avot* 2:1): "[Do] all that is attractive and has its doer appear attractive," that is, do all that directs you toward the true, good end—the strengthening of Torah and the institution of universal brotherhood.

"Love"—that a type of love of God be set in your heart that would lead you to do what satisfies Him as energetically as you would do the same for your mother or father. It should bother you if God is unsatisfied, either because of yourself or someone else, and you should want that thing for God and derive a great joy in obtaining it for Him.

---

8. Immediately preceding these verses we find Moses reminding the Jewish nation of when he had received the second set of tablets, upon which the Ten Commandments were rewritten. He says in the name of God (Deuteronomy 10:2,11), "I will write upon the tablets the words that were on the first tablets that you broke, and you shall place them in the ark. . . . [Then you, Moses, shall] rise up in procession before the people. Let them come and occupy the land that I swore to their fathers that I would give to them."

The subject of this part of the Torah is rectification and progression. It speaks of the recognition of past error—even grave and serious error like the making of the golden calf, which caused Moses to break the first tablets—and going on from there to greatness and the fulfillment of ultimate goals.

This is the great and significant lesson of *The Path of the Just*: that as humans we make mistakes, we "blemish" our beings. As such we erect golden calves of one sort or another daily, sometimes purposefully, other times inadvertently. Yet we have it within us to undo and go on. We can "rise up in procession" and "occupy the land" after all. The way to do that is to "revere God . . . , go in all of His ways, . . . love Him and . . . serve [Him] . . . with full heart and soul, and . . . keep all of [His] commandments and statutes . . ." (Deuteronomy 10:12–13).

"Fullness of heart" means that your service to God should be done with the purest of intentions—only for service to Him, for no other reason whatsoever. Included in this must be a service of the heart not in conflict, but full, and not as an act of rote, but rather one of your full self.

"Keeping all of God's commandments" is as it implies—keeping all of the Divine commandments in their fullness and with all of their conditions.

Indeed, all of these principles require great explanation. I have found that our sages (of blessed memory) have ordered these principles in a different, more particularized way—according to the levels required to aspire to, and in their correct order. This is in a *beraita* found in various places in the Talmud, including the chapter entitled "Before Their Festivals" (*Avodah Zarah* 20b), and it reads: "From this Rabbi Pinchas Ben Yaer derived that Torah study brings you to caution, caution to enthusiasm, enthusiasm to innocence, innocence to abstinence, abstinence to purity, purity to piety, piety to modesty, modesty to fear of sin, fear of sin to holiness, holiness to holy spirit, and holy spirit brings you to the resurrection of the dead."

I have based this book upon that *beraita* to teach myself and to remind others of the necessary conditions in Divine service in the appropriate order. And I will explain in each section the particulars and gradations, the means to attain them, as well as their respective deterrents, and how to avoid those.

Now I and whoever else may care to do so can read this book so that we might learn how to revere God our Lord and not forget our duties to Him. And that which the coarseness of our natures tries to remove from our hearts will be brought back to us by the reading and studying of this work, which will remind us of our obligations.[9]

May God be with our hopes and keep us from stumbling, and fulfill within us the desire of the poet who was the beloved of his God (Psalms 86:1): "Teach me, God, Your ways so that I may walk in Your truth. Unify my heart that I may revere Your name." Amen, may it be His will.

---

9.   Human nature becomes coarse when it concerns itself overmuch with material matters and forgets its spiritual source. When the individual reminds himself of matters of the spirit he is loosened and refined. One way of reminding ourselves of the spirit (and it is incumbent upon us to remind ourselves of it) is to study the holy works that discuss it, such as this one.

1

An Explanation of Man's Duty in the World

The very foundation of piety and the root of thorough Divine service are that your duty in the world, as well as what it is you are directing your sights and proclivities toward in your lifelong labors, become clear and self-evident.[1]

Our sages (of blessed memory) have taught us that we were created to delight in God and enjoy the radiance of His Divine presence.[2] This is the true delight, the greatest enjoyment of all.[3]

---

1. A "foundation" is something that precedes the edifice which is built upon it in time (piety, in this case), keeps it secure in its place, and ensures its existence; a "root" is also something that precedes the thing itself (in this case, "complete Divine service") in time, but it has it fed from things deeper than itself and keeps it well nourished.

What Luzzatto is saying is that you must foster a serious and well-thought-out understanding of just what your duties in the world are and where you are headed before you can ever hope to be securely, solidly, and healthily pious or effective in your Divine service.

When your notions of such things are based upon those kinds of foundations and roots they become "clear and self-evident" because they are not befuddled and swayed by one thing or another.

2. "Delight" in God and "enjoyment" of His Divine presence are radical pleasures and ecstasies, and they are our lot.

Notice the sensuality of the expectations. As profound physical satisfaction is the closest we get to Godliness in this world (though such satisfaction may also be very, very subtle and take the form of high emotionality and intellectuality, it is nonetheless physical), Luzzatto is forced to use such imagery to explain his intention. If he were to use spiritual-type imagery it would not go far to explain the "delight" and "enjoyment" we can expect to find.

3. See note 1 to the Author's Introduction.

But in truth, the place for this pleasure is the World to Come,[4] as it was created, readied, and prepared for just such a pleasure.[5]

The road that will take us to our desired destination is this world. Our sages were referring to this when they said (*Avot* 4:16), "This world is like a vestibule to the World to Come."[6]

The means to bring you to this goal are the *mitzvot* which God has commanded[7];

---

4. See note 5 to the Author's Introduction for a description of the World to Come.

5. Just as what is pleasurable in one place may not be so in another (for example, one would not enjoy an otherwise delicious hot meal in an overheated, humid house), so too for this, the pleasure of all pleasures, there is a place especially prepared for its enjoyment.

6. After we are told that "we were created to delight in God and to enjoy the radiance of His divine presence. . . . But in truth, the place for this pleasure is the World to Come," we might justifiably wonder what this world is. We might think it serves no purpose whatsoever and is absurd and futile.

But Luzzatto is quick to let us know that this world *does* have meaning and is in fact quite necessary in the scheme of things: it alone is "the road that will take us to our desired destination." A road may be redundant, annoying, unattractive, or burdensome, but it is always essential. It is the thing without which whatever might happen could not.

And like a "vestibule," it is the place in which one readies oneself.

Once there was a man who was to meet with the powerful and wealthy chairman of the board of a huge corporation on a Monday morning. For weeks before he prepared his speech and arranged his thoughts. The day before he redoubled his efforts and did all that he could to fight off fear. And on the morning of the meeting he was set.

He arrived at the building, signed in at the security guard's desk, rode the elevator to the penthouse, and stepped up to the appropriate secretary. He announced himself and was told that the chairman would see him shortly, wouldn't he please make himself comfortable.

He reviewed his notes and breathed shallowly. He noticed that he was nervous and wanted nothing more than to not be so. Suddenly, the secretary announced that the chairman would see him now, and that he had only to walk through that vestibule to get to his office.

It was in the walk through the vestibule that he most significantly gained his composure and set the tone with which he was to approach the chairman with his request. That was where the very success of the mission was to be accomplished. It was the moment that summed up all of his efforts, without which all would have been in vain.

That vestibule is this world. Yet while in relation to the World to Come it is a vestibule, it must be said, though, that in effect—in the way we experience it in our day-to-day lives—this world is nonetheless significant and fecund with meaning.

7. Notice the progression here, if you will: We should realize we are heading in a certain direction and have a purpose (to "delight in God and enjoy the radiance of His Divine presence"); after our appetites are whetted for that we are told that there is only one place to live out that purpose (the World to Come); then we are assured that there is a road set specifically for that goal (this world); and now we are told that there are means within this world to bring us to this goal—that there is steam for the locomotion toward the ultimate end while on the path (the *mitzvot*).

and it is only in this world that these *mitzvot* can be done.[8] That is why we were placed in this world in the first place: so that we might reach the place set for us—the World to Come—by the use of the means prepared for that task. Then we will bask in the good we will have acquired through these means. Our sages were referring to this when they said (*Eruvin* 22a), "Today (was created) to do them (the *mitzvot*); tomorrow to receive the reward for them."

If you delve further into the matter you will find that true spiritual wholeness is nothing other than the clutching onto God. King David referred to this when he said (Psalms 73:28), "As for me—closeness to God is my good," and (Psalms 27:4) "I only ask one thing of God, this I request: that I might sit in God's house all the days of my life." For this alone is the true good; all else we might consider to be good is mere smoke and emptiness.

It is only fitting that you toil and strive at the beginning to be worthy of this good, that is, that you try to clutch onto Him with the things that will enable you to do this—the *mitzvot*.

The Holy One (blessed be He) has placed mankind in a situation where there are many things to hinder closeness to Him. These are the mundane desires which, if followed, would have you draw away from the true good. You have in fact been placed in the midst of a mighty battle wherein all worldly happenstances—for the good or for not—are trials. The poor have their trials, the wealthy theirs. As Solomon has said (Proverbs 30:9), "Lest I grow full, scoff, and say 'Who is God?'; lest I grow poor and steal. . . ." There are times of tranquility, then times of tragedy, but all in all, you find you are surrounded by war.

You will only be the full man worthy of clutching onto your Creator if you are truly a warrior, victorious in your battles from all sides. Then will you go from the vestibule of this world into the palace of the World to Come, enlightened by the light of life. According to the degree you conquer your *yetzer hara* and your desires, distance yourself from the things that distance you from the good, and try to clutch onto Him, will you succeed and be joyful in Him.[9]

---

8. The fact that the very means to bring you to your ultimate goal can only be found here in this world once again indicates the great importance of this world.

It should also be pointed out that while there is certainly a this-worldly aspect to the performance of *mitzvot*, what Luzzatto is saying here is that *mitzvot* are primarily means to an end, and not ends in themselves. All too often we seem to forget that and perform *mitzvot* without the necessary understanding, sensitivity, or perspective. In truth *mitzvot* are mighty and Godly things. Again, they alone are the very things that will enable us to bask in the light of the divine. That should be remembered.

9. Drama is based upon conflict and resolution. If all goes well with a hero for a long while, there is nothing to observe and grow from: there is nothing captivating and wondrous. But if the hero suffers setback or defeat and manages nonetheless to advance and carry on, we have the makings of theater and high drama.

To this point, all has been well and straightforward. We had only to resolve to follow

Reflecting upon the matter you will see that the world was created for our usage. But we stand in the midst of a great balance: should we be attracted to the

---

the path with our eyes set ahead and we could be assured of it all. But where would be the grand conquest and heroism we would only want of one who would directly delight in God? Where would the conflict and resolution of the holy effort be? To allow for heroism and ultimate achievement, God created stumbling blocks along the way: the urge to abandon the great challenge and to settle for less.

The Baal Shem Tov tells the story of a great king who was a master of illusion. One day the king decided to use his powers of illusion to erect a series of walls around his castle. He had posters placed on the outermost wall that stated that he would be offering a reward for whoever would accept a challenge.

All one had to do to win great wealth and power in the kingdom was to climb over the many walls and greet the king. However, it was pointed out, the king had placed moats between each wall. And he had placed ferocious beasts there, as well as armed guards with orders to slay anyone making the attempt. Most people in the kingdom were simply too frightened to even attempt the challenge, but a few hardy souls decided to do so.

The king then decided to place pots of gold just past the third wall on the way to the palace. That way those who would have been so successful as to have made it to that point would be faced with a decision: should they go on in the hopes of completing the task and winning the great wealth and position promised to the victor, or should they settle for the small though respectable prize that faced them now? Each one of them decided to settle for the small but safe prize.

Just then, the king's young son was returning from a sojourn out of the kingdom. "Where have these walls come from?" he wondered. When he approached the outermost one he read the sign. "I love my father too much and want to see him too much to care for the walls and the threats along the way," he said. So he leapt over each one, braved the moats, beasts, and soldiers, and stood before his father.

The king snapped his fingers and undid the illusion, and in an instant the walls and all that went along with them were gone. He loved his son the prince for his great effort and bravery, and passed on to him the promised wealth and position.

The pleasures and attractions of this world are like the small pots of gold that were found by the hardy souls just past the third wall. They seem to be worth settling for. And there is a pull within us to take them and forget the challenge and the dream. That pull is often perceived as being the voice of wisdom and sense, but it is in fact the voice of delusion and defeat.

That pull is the *yetzer hara*, usually translated as the "evil inclination." But that is an inadequate translation as most people are simply not inclined toward evil. They can perhaps be accused of being inclined toward spiritual mediocrity, but not evil (with notable exception). The *yetzer hara* should rather be understood as being the urge to remain attached to the earth and things mundane (which, in fact, is "evil," because it is a substitute for the yearning for closeness to God); and its opposite, the *yetzer hatov* (usually translated as the "good inclination") should be understood as being the urge toward Godliness.

When one overcomes his urge to remain attached to the earth and things mundane he has won a great battle, and merited to see the king. He has jumped the high walls, fought off

world[10] and distanced from our Creator, both we and the world with us would be damaged; but if we would master ourselves and clutch onto our Creator, and make use of the world's things to help us in our Divine service, both we and the world with us will be elevated.[11]

---

all threats, and not settled for the small rewards. Just such a challenge is presented to each one of us in our lives, and the success of our mission is dependent upon our efforts and determination to "see the king."

10. That should read, "should we be *exclusively* attracted to the world and distanced from our Creator. . . ." It is the attraction to the world and what is in it to the exclusion of God Himself or Godliness *in* those things that separates us from Him. One could be attracted to things because of God's essence in them and draw closer to God. That is in fact the essential relationship one should have with such things.

11. The suggestion that we "master ourselves" seems to be odd and to smack of self-denial and repression. It is almost as if he is saying we are to control or stifle ourselves, which implies the disallowance for growth and self-fulfillment or -expression. This then is one of those phrases that makes for a misunderstanding of the book.

What Luzzatto is saying here is very clear when seen in its true light. It is the statement that if you want to enjoy the presence of God you have to block out the presence of certain other things which prevent the presence of God. We have an equation here: be more attracted to the world than to God, and you and the world suffer in that you do not enjoy the presence of God; master yourself, clutch onto God, have the correct perspective on the place of things in relation to God, and you and the world will enjoy the presence of God. And holiness will be dominant in the world. But what is holiness, and why want it?

Less than three months after the Jews came out of the desert they were approached by Moses with the information that they were soon to see God and receive the Torah. God told Moses that he was to say to the people in His name (Exodus 19:5–6), ". . . If you will listen carefully to My voice and keep my covenant you will be a . . . kingdom of priests and a holy nation."

There was an immediate reaction to that (Exodus 19:7–8): as soon as Moses "approached and called to the elders of the people, and . . . placed all of these things that God had commanded him before them . . . the people responded in unison, saying, 'We will do all that God has said!'"

It has been asked what it was within the promise that they would be a "kingdom of priests and a holy nation" that especially charged them up with such an unqualified vow of submission? What indeed is it to be holy and dedicated to God (as one would expect of a priest)? Does that not involve a lot of self-denial, a lot of "self-mastery"?

It may be because of the promise stated at the beginning of the book that the holy will enjoy the radiance of God in the World to Come. But at this point, when we are being told that we have to "master ourselves" to do that (in fact, the gist of the "Path of the Just" involves just that), we have to wonder if we can so "delay gratification." Is there anything we can enjoy *now*, in this world, thanks to our self-mastery?

To be sure, there is real and immediate pleasure in many of the *mitzvot*. No one can deny the delight and satisfaction that comes with the full keeping of the *Shabbat* and the Holy Days; nor can anyone deny the need within the heart to pray daily; and no one can overlook

All created things enjoy a great elevation when they are used by the "completed" person—the one who is made holy by God's holiness. Our sages were referring to this when they spoke of the great light that the Holy One, blessed be He, has hidden away for the pious (*Chagigah* 12a): "When the Holy One, blessed be He, saw the light that He had stored away for the pious He rejoiced, as it is said (Proverbs 13:9), 'There is a light for the pious, and He shall rejoice.'" Regarding the stones in the area where Jacob spent the night and which he placed under his head, our sages of blessed memory said (*Chullin* 91b): "Rabbi Yitzchak has said that this comes to teach us that all the stones gathered in one spot saying, 'Let the pious one lay his head on me!'"[12]

Our sages were stressing this point when they said about the verse (Ecclesiastes 7:13), "Behold the work of God . . ."[13]: "When the Holy One, blessed be He, created Adam He placed him in the Garden of Eden and had him roam from tree to tree and said to him, 'See how lovely and praiseworthy all My works are! And all I have created I have created for you. See to it that you do not ruin or destroy my world!'" (*Kohelet Rabbah* 7).

The point is this: We were not created for our situation here in this world—but rather, for that in the World to Come. But our situation here is the means to attain to the one due us in the World to Come, which is our goal.

Many teachings of our sages can be found in this same vein, likening this world to a place and time of preparation, and the next world to one of rest and the ingesting of the already-prepared. This is what they meant by (*Avot* 4:16) "This world is like a

---

the joy of sitting in the *sukkah* during the Sukkot holidays, and so forth. So there *are* immediately fulfilling aspects of the observant life.

But there are other, even more gratifying, this-worldly delights involved in holiness as well. They involve the inner peace, tranquility, and inexplicable presence of mind enjoyed by the holy. Those things only come about after a great deal of effort and "self-mastery," but they come about.

The truth of the matter is that we *all* have it within us to assume that presence of mind, but we mostly dare not. We are like the psychotic who keeps knocking his head against the wall and thrashing his body against the floor and refuses to take the medication that will ease his "demons" but will necessarily temper his energies. We are afraid of a sanity that will take away what we have grown used to and identify as our very being—our fears, worries, and illusions—when it has nothing whatsoever to do with ourselves, but is rather a poisonous bile.

The holy ones see us thrashing ourselves about and causing ourselves pain and they want to suggest a medication. It too will ease "demons" but will necessarily temper energies. But with it will come the sanity that is holiness and a relationship with God. The medication is "self-mastery"—a substitution of holy inclinations for the drives and urges that have us whirl about in our madness.

12. This indicates the elevation experienced by even the inanimate things in the world when the holy ones make use of them.

13. The verse continues with, ". . . who can make straight the crooked?" and makes reference to the fact that we can either straighten the world out or make it crooked.

vestibule . . ."; (*Eruvin* 22a) "Today (was created) to do them (the *mitzvot*); tomorrow to receive the reward for them"; (*Avodah Zarah* 3a) "One who struggles on the Eve of the *Shabbat* will eat on *Shabbat*"[14]; and (*Kohelet Rabbah* 1) "This world is like the shoreline, and the World to Come is like the sea," as well as by many other expressions like them.

In truth you could not believe that we were created for our situation here in this world. After all, what is our life here in this world? Who is truly happy or tranquil in this world? "The days of our lives are seventy years; with strength, eighty years. And the best of them are filled with toil and foolishness" (Psalms 90:10). We suffer from all sorts of woes, illnesses, pains and inconveniences—and after all that, death. Not one in a thousand finds that the world fills him with true contentment or peace of mind. And even if that rare individual were to live to one hundred, he would nonetheless eventually be taken away from the world.[15]

Not only is that so, but if in fact the purpose of our life was to meet the needs of this world, it would not have been necessary for God to have breathed into us a soul so exalted and distinguished—a soul greater than the angels themselves. Nor would He have placed within us a soul which finds no gratification in the things of this world.

This is what our sages were referring to when they said (*Kohelet Rabbah* 6:7): "It is written (Ecclesiastes 6:7), 'And the soul too will not be fulfilled.' To what is this to be compared?—to a city-dweller who married a princess and who, though he

---

14. That means to say that one cannot expect to reap profits without having toiled.

The traditional *Shabbat* is a lovely, peaceful thing. It involves enjoying wine along with a candle-lit, hot dinner on Friday night, and a slow, full lunch the next afternoon, followed by a long nap. There may then be a walk, some reading or conversation, or a combination of all, but it is nearly always topped off with the last leisurely meal of the day at dusk. The soul is at ease on *Shabbat*, as is the whole of the being.

But the Eve of *Shabbat*, Friday, is a hectic and chaotic time. The day is filled with tasks: researching, shopping, and preparing for the *Shabbat* meals, and cleaning the house. There are things to ready and set up because they will not be done on the *Shabbat* (because of the spiritual nature of the day), and it must be fully accomplished by a sure and well-defined time not open to interpretation—sundown.

So when the Talmud tells us that "One who struggles on the Eve of the *Shabbat* will eat on *Shabbat*" it means to say that one cannot possibly revel in the ease and readiness of the *Shabbat* unless one has struggled to prepare for it completely. That is to say, one cannot fully bask in the light of God in the World to Come unless one has toiled in this world in preparation for that light.

15. Students of existentialism have come to the understanding that the world is narrow and dark. They have noticed a meaninglessness. But they have not made this, the most sublime leap. They have not recognized the absurd and then come to recognize or be told of the metalogical which is the basis of this chapter. The man or woman of faith would recognize life's absurdity and not deny it, but would find solace in the higher reality that is the World to Come.

may bring her the best in the world, can never impress her for, after all, she is a princess. Such is the situation of the soul. Even if you were to supply it with all of the pleasures of the world it would not be affected by them. And why?—because it is one of the celestials."

Our sages have likewise taught (*Avot* 4:22), "You were conceived against your will, and born against your will." For the soul does not love this world at all—it in fact abhors it. Certainly the Creator would not have created something whose purpose went against its nature and which it abhorred.

But rather, the sole purpose of our creation was to be our situation in the World to Come. That is why we were given such a soul. For *it* is fitting for Divine service; by means of it can we accrue our reward, in the proper place and time. For it is obvious that the soul should not abhor this world, but rather love and desire it.

Now that we understand this, the need for stringency in keeping *mitzvot* and the preciousness of the Divine service presented to us should be obvious. For they are the means to bring us to true wholeness. Without them we would attain nothing.

However, as is known, a goal is attained only by the combined power of the means used to attain it. That goal will be affected both by the strength of that power and by the way the means themselves have been used. So when the inevitable time comes for the joining of all of these means it will be found that any small deviation in them will alter the effect in a clear and certain manner.

At this point it becomes clear that we must do the *mitzvot* and serve God in a most precise manner—in as precise a manner as we would weigh gold or pearls if we were jewelers, because of their great value. Because the results of them are true wholeness and an eternal, incomparable preciousness.

It has thus become clear to us that the main purpose of our having been placed in this world was to keep the *mitzvot*, to serve God, and to withstand spiritual trials,[16] and that the only appropriate pleasures to be gotten from this world are those which aid and assist in these tasks—that give you enough ease and peace of mind to set your heart to the service that has been placed upon you.[17]

---

16. "Withstanding trials" is another troublesome expression. It suggests pain, woe, and flagellation. But it should be understood in light of what was said earlier on in the chapter, that "you have . . . been placed in the midst of a mighty battle wherein all worldly happenstances—for the good or not—are trials. The poor have their trials, the wealthy theirs. As Solomon has said (Proverbs 30:9), 'Lest I grow full, scoff, and say "Who is God?"; lest I grow poor and steal. . . .'"

That is to say, trials are often not what we think they are. In fact, pleasantness and personal comfort may themselves be our trials, that is, they may try our willingness to accept the delight of God in our lives rather than the delight we may be experiencing. "Withstanding trials" refers to accepting and living by the ultimate truth as defined in this chapter rather than by other standards of truth.

17. What he is saying is that you *can* derive pleasure from things of this world, but only to the end that they will make your spiritual path easier and less cumbersome.

It is only fitting that all of your inclinations be directed exclusively to the Creator—that there be no goal in any of your actions, large or small, other than that of getting closer to Him and eradicating the barriers that separate you from Him, which are the matters of this world and what is dependent upon them. This should be done to the point where you are drawn after Him as iron is to a magnet; that you run after, take hold, and not let go of all you can determine will be a means to drawing close to Him. And that you run away from whatever you determine will deter you from this as you would from fire.[18]

This is being referred to when it is stated (Psalms 63:9), "My soul clings to You; I am supported by Your right hand." That is, our whole coming into the world was for this purpose alone—to attain to this closeness by rescuing our souls from all that distracts and waylays them.

We have to investigate the particulars of this principle in the correct order, from beginning to end, now that its truth has become clear and self-evident to us. We will do this in the order Rabbi Pinchas Ben Yaer has set for them in his statement we have already quoted in our introduction: caution, enthusiasm, innocence, abstinence, purity, piety, modesty, fear of sin, and holiness. With heaven's help, we will now explain each and every one.

---

18. When metal is drawn to a magnet it becomes magnetized; when something is drawn to fire it is destroyed. In both cases, the object drawn in is nullified and changed. But the metal nullified by the magnet *benefits* from the nullification, while the object nullified by the flames loses all.

So too, when one is drawn toward God, he becomes Godly. In fact, the faster he holds onto the "magnet," the better, and the sooner the separation the sooner the loss. But the more one avoids contact with the "flame" (those things that separate us from God) the better off he is.

Summation of Part I

The Author's Introduction

1. *The Path of the Just* was written to remind people of what they already know, not to teach them new things. It would be best read several times so that what is familiar could make an impression, and the reader could thereby be reminded of his obligations.

2. There are many people who dedicate their lives and studies to the various arts and sciences, and some others to the theoretical or practical aspects of Torah, but few dedicate themselves to the study of the love and fear of and attachment to God, or to piety.

3. That has resulted in fewer intellectual people dedicating themselves to those matters, and incorrectly so. Everyone suffers as a result of that, both the wise and the unlettered: the wise because they do not attempt true piety, and the others because they do not attain it.

4. Matters of piety call for investigation and thought and the acquisition of specific tools and devices. It is not what we might think it is. Among other things, it is not putting oneself through acts of mortification.

5. We often place great effort upon things within Torah that are not at all incumbent upon us and serve no practical purpose, while our very real obligations to God are either left abandoned or carried out by rote.

6. Fundamentally, the acquisition of piety involves the following five traits:

a. *reverence* ("that you be in a state of reverence before Him comparable to what you would experience being before a great and awesome king"),

b. *walking in His way* ("all of your traits and actions are to be just and ethical"),

c. *love* ("It should bother you if God's desires are not fulfilled, either because of yourself or someone else, and you should want them to be and derive a great joy in ensuring that they are"),

d. *wholeheartedness* ("one's service to God should be done with the purest of intentions"), and

e. *the keeping of the mitzvot* ("in their fullness and with all of their conditions").

7. The tradition words this in an orderly, step-by-step manner when it says (in the words of Rabbi Pinchas Ben Yaer, *Avodah Zarah* 20b), "Torah study brings you to caution, caution to enthusiasm, enthusiasm to innocence, innocence to abstinence, abstinence to purity, purity to piety, piety to modesty, modesty to fear of sin, fear of sin to holiness, holiness to holy spirit, and holy spirit brings you to the resurrection of the dead." This book is an explanation and analysis of that statement.

Chapter 1

8. The first thing to do to perfect your service to God is to come to understand your purpose in life, and to know your ultimate goal. Your ultimate goal is to delight in God and bask in His Presence. But that can only be done in the World to Come.

9. The only way to get to the World to Come is through this world; and the only things that will give you the means to get through this world to the World to Come are the *mitzvot*. Your purpose in life is to go through that process.

10. But we have been placed in an environment that runs counter to that end. It comprises things and sensations that draw us away from our goal, and we must constantly struggle with them. Yet the more difficult and successful the battle, the greater the ultimate joy.

11. Logic would surely suggest that we were not ultimately created for our situation in this world of woe and despair. If we were, would it have been necessary for us to have so lofty and magnificent a soul, which derives no pleasure from this world? Such a soul was placed within us for its place in the World to Come.

12. We can now understand why the *mitzvot* are to be done in a precise manner. They are the means to get us to our end, and are often demanding so as to be most effective. They should be precious to us.

13. Since it is now clear that our purpose in this life is to keep the *mitzvot*, serve God, and withstand spiritual trials, it is only fitting that all of our inclinations be directed toward God, and that we avoid all things which run counter to that goal. The rest of this book will be a study of the particulars of this process.

II

CAUTION

Introduction to Part II

The second part comprises four chapters (2–5) and concerns itself with the acquisition of the trait of "caution." The chapters are entitled, "An Explanation of the Trait of Caution" (chap. 2), "The Subdivisions of Caution" (chap. 3), "The Means of Acquiring Caution" (chap. 4), and "Matters That Cause the Loss of Caution and How to Resist Them" (chap. 5).

The essential teaching of *The Path of the Just* is that we are each one of us capable of greatness—not heroism, perhaps, but greatness. We have it within us to erect forces for reparation and great abundant good. We ourselves can bring on redemption by our small and pedestrian good deeds as much as the large, brave, and mighty can do so by their brave and large deeds.

But we are also capable of great destruction. We must admit to ourselves that we can keep back redemption by our small and pedestrian *bad* deeds as much as the out-and-out evil and terrible can with their horrible and mean deeds. Therein lies our considerable power as human beings.

What is called for, as our age knows only too well, is reparation and perfection. We can no longer allow for the evil and terrible. When they are unleashed in our world, they are all-consuming and eternal. An age that has seen Hitler and the atomic bomb has no doubts about the fact that single individuals and tiny things matter very much; an age that takes the teachings of psychology seriously knows very well that the human situation is the sum total of both large and small drives and motivations.

What Rabbi Luzzatto is addressing in *The Path of the Just* is human perfection. He asserts it is possible. But he is also wise enough to warn us that it is neither immediate nor guaranteed, and that it calls for effort.

The first small step in human perfection is the acquisition of the trait of caution, which involves self-mastery, self-control (chap. 2). The way to come to self-mastery is by means of self-analysis and, when necessary, change (chap.

3). And you only come to change through Torah study, the realization of what is incumbent upon you in this world (chap. 4), and the avoidance of certain common pitfalls (chap. 5).

Rabbi Luzzatto does not define caution, but we can infer that he understands it to mean a deliberate consciousness of your self and your ways, and a reparation of both. In the Hebrew, "caution" does not carry along with it the connotations of delay, unwillingness, irresolution, intimidation, or cowardice as it does in English. The word is *zeherut*, and it is synonymous with "shining" and "peering out," and in a related form (*zy'hara*), it is used for the moon (see *Targum Yonatan*, Deuteronomy 4:19). As such it connotes watching and overseeing, and hints at a separate presence above things observing, which is symbolic of the self watching itself and taking note.

2

An Explanation
of the Trait of Caution

The point of caution is that you should be cautious in both your actions and your interests; that is to say, conscious and aware of whether your actions and methods are for the good or not.[1] You should not abandon your soul to the threat of destruction, God forbid, nor simply go blindly about in your accustomed way, in pitch black.[2]

This is certainly what common sense would dictate. We have the sense to rescue ourselves by running away from what would destroy our soul; would we possibly want to conceal from ourselves the means of our rescue? There could be no greater degradation or foolishness than this.

---

1. We have to define terms here. Your *actions* are the things you have already gotten to the stage of doing one way or another, after either having thought them out or not. Your *interests* are those things you tend toward and may or may not carry out. Your *methods* are the ways you carry things out from the interest to the action stage.

Consciousness is usually a nebulous and vague cognizance of the existence of something or other upon which you may or may not act. *Awareness* is a closer, more intimate cognizance of that thing or person.

So what Luzzatto is saying here is that you are to be both acutely and even vaguely aware of what you *tend* to do (your interests) and *how* you do it (your methods), so that you will finally come to do only beneficial things.

Being "vaguely" aware of these things is mentioned because that nudging, nebulous, not-quite-yet-definable consciousness of your inclinations, methods, and actions is the first and necessary step towards self-analysis.

2. When Luzzatto speaks of "abandoning" your soul or going about "blindly" he is speaking about one and the same thing: not being in control of your growth and destiny. When we are passive and undemanding of ourselves we "abandon" our souls to come-what-may, and leave ourselves open to destruction, God forbid.

But when we master ourselves and proceed on with open eyes we allow for perfection and wonder.

One who would act in this way hasn't the native intelligence of the animals or beasts who just naturally watch out for themselves by fleeing from all that is likely to threaten them. One who goes about in the world without reflection upon whether his path is for the good or the bad is like a blind man who walks upon the shoreline, where the threats of danger are great, and harm is more likely than not.[3] In truth, being blind from birth or by decision (by willfully closing your eyes) is one and the same thing.[4]

The prophet Jeremiah would complain about the evil ones of his generation who would be afflicted by this trait of closing their eyes to their actions and not giving thought to whether they should abandon or continue them. He said about them (Jeremiah 8:6), "No one repents of his wrongdoing to say, 'What have I done?' Every one of them turns about in his course like a horse rushing headlong into battle." That is to say, they would rush about in their way without setting aside

---

3. Much *musar* literature and the like infer or say outright that when you transgress you are evil and should be punished as an evil person, as justice demands that you be, and there is justice in the world.

But Luzzatto is saying something else here. It is that when you transgress, you *endanger* yourself—you suffer as a natural result of that transgression, and that is your punishment, that is what you should watch out for. But he does not say that you are to be taken as an "evil" person necessarily (though especially transgressive—people *are* evil—and suffer especially, whether we or they know it or not).

It must be kept in mind (as we will find in chap. 4) that when it comes to ethics and matters of divine service there are people who react best to lofty and noble concepts, those who react to concepts that speak of personal gain or loss, and those who react most advantageously to talk of hell-fire and brimstone and nothing else (which is the multitude). Luzzatto addresses just that point in chapter four, and offers advice specific to just those sorts of people.

The advice that is being offered here, that you should be careful how you go about in the world, as "the threats of danger are great, and harm is more likely than not," is for those who react best to concepts that speak of personal gain or loss. It does not speak of punishments and reparations that would have to be made, nor does it apparently speak of transcendence and God (though it should be kept in mind that because the greatest threat to the soul is separation from God, and that issue is being addressed here, too, the loftier souls are being warned as well, according to their perspective).

The differentiation of Luzzatto's perceived "audience" must be kept in mind when we study this work. We must recall that there will be times when he will address the baser fears and anxieties, and other times when he will address the loftier, more transcendent drives, depending upon the circumstances and the point he wants to make.

4. We make decisions day in and day out, moment by moment. We decide one moment to not care about one thing or another, and another moment we decide to care about something else. We likewise decide to see one thing or another one moment, and to not see something else some other time.

We are constantly *deciding* ourselves into one sort of life or another. We can decide to be righteous as well; that is our right and our capability.

time for themselves to examine their actions or methods, and they would fall into evil ways inadvertently.[5]

Relentlessly burdening yourself with tasks so that you haven't the time to reflect upon or consider where you are heading is in fact one of the devices and guiles of the *yetzer hara*. It knows that if you were to concentrate upon your ways for just an instant you would certainly repent of them, and a strong regret would grow within you that would lead you to utterly abandon your sins.[6] This is one of the suggestions the evil Pharaoh had when he said (Exodus 5:9), "Make the men's work more burdensome! . . ." His intentions were not only that he would not leave them time to plot against him. He meant to destroy any chance of self-reflection by loading them down with relentless, unending labor.

This is in truth the advice of the *yetzer hara* to us. It is a crafty and sly fighter. The only way you can escape from it is with great wisdom and reflection. This is what the prophet exhorted when he said (Haggai 1:5), "Pay attention to your ways"; what Solomon said in his wisdom (Proverbs 6:4–5), "Allow neither sleep to your eyes nor slumber to your eyelids—save yourself like a deer from the hand of the hunter. . ."; and what our sages meant when they said (*Mo'ed Katan* 5a), "All who are deliberate in their ways in this world will merit to see the salvation of the Holy One (blessed be He)."

Obviously, even if you do enjoy mastery over yourself, without God's help you could not save yourself, for the *yetzer hara* is mighty. As it is written (Psalms 37:32–33), "When the evil person looks to the righteous and wants to kill him, God will not abandon him. . . ." If you are in control of yourself, God will rescue you and save you from the *yetzer hara*. But if you are not, God himself will certainly not oversee your doings. After all—if you will not have compassion upon yourself, who will? This is what our sages were referring to when they said (*Berachot* 33a), "It is forbidden to have compassion upon those who simply will not understand," and when they said (*Avot* 1:14), "If I am not for myself, who will be?"

---

5. Luzzatto is suggesting that when you do not set aside time for the consideration of your actions you will *inevitably*, though inadvertently and unconsciously, fall into evil ways.

You may reason that you cannot be blamed for inadvertent and unplanned actions, but we are not speaking of blame here. The point of the matter is that you will have certainly done certain things with undesirable consequences, and that is our concern—though it goes without saying that the lack of planning is itself wrong, even though that is not the point here.

6. The tradition enunciates four steps in the *teshuvah* (repentance) process: at first you are to abandon the transgression, then you are to verbally admit your guilt to God, regret ever having done it, and finally you are to take it upon yourself never to commit such a transgression again. All but the second step (verbally admitting your guilt to God) are alluded to here.

3

The Subdivisions of Caution

If you want to master yourself,[1] you will need to involve yourself in two kinds of self-analysis. The first concerns the consideration of what is the true good you are to choose and the true bad from which you should flee. The second concerns the consideration of your own actions to determine whether they are good or bad. This latter one can be further broken down into two categories: while active and while not.

As to while you are active: you should not do anything without considering it in light of this notion. And as to while you are not active: you should recall your past actions and consider them in light of this notion as well to determine if there is some bad therein to be removed, or good that should be continued and fortified. If you do find some bad, then you should reflect, and come up with devices that will allow you to flee and be purified from it.[2]

Our sages had us know about this matter by telling us (*Eruvin* 13b), "Man would have been better off not having been created than being created. But now that he has been created, let him examine his actions. Others are of the opinion that he should *feel* his actions."

We see that these two terms are in fact two very good and beneficial warnings. Generally, one who examines his actions would inspect them so as to reflect upon

---

1. At the end of the previous chapter Luzzatto said that ". . . even if you do enjoy mastery over yourself, without God's help you could not save yourself, as the *yetzer hara* is mighty. . . . [But] if you *are* in control of yourself, God will rescue you and save you from the *yetzer hara*." So he begins this chapter with the process of self-mastery, as that is the preliminary step in the conquering of the *yetzer hara*.

2. How can you "come up with devices that will allow you to flee and be purified from" past transgressions? That is like not doing a past act retroactively! Luzzatto addresses just that issue in chapter four when he discusses repentance. He says there that repentance is "the uprooting of the will" to transgress, which is "equivalent to uprooting the act itself," and that "your transgressions will be retroactively turned around and uprooted from existence by your pain and regret for what has happened."

them and see if there could be found anything that he should not do—that does not correspond with God's *mitzvot* and laws. For all that would be found to be in this category should be removed from the world.

But *feeling* one's actions includes even the good ones and involves inspecting and observing them to see if there is any underlying motivation that is not good, or if there is any part-bad that you might be forced to extricate and remove. This is like feeling a garment to see if it is good and strong, or weak and shabby. You should carefully "feel" your actions to determine their motivations this same way so as to stay pure and clean.

The principle of the matter is that you should delve deeply into all of your actions and examine all your ways and not leave yourself with bad habits or traits, or, certainly, sins or transgressions. I believe it is as necessary for you to sift through and analyze your ways each and every day as it is for successful businessmen to constantly evaluate their businesses to be sure they do not suffer loss, and that you set aside particular times to do this so that this sort of self-evaluation will not be a once-in-a-while kind of thing, but fixed. Such a practice promises great returns.

Our sages clearly taught us about the need for such self-evaluation. They said in regard to the verse (Numbers 21:27), "Therefore the rulers said, 'Come, let us account for things'"—"Therefore the rulers said over their *yetzer hara*'s: 'Come, let us evaluate matters of the world, that is, the loss incurred in the doing of a *mitzvah* against the gain, versus the gain in sinning as against its loss'" (*Baba Batra* 78b).[3]

The veracity of this advice can only be truly seen and internalized by those who have already freed themselves from the stronghold of their *yetzer hara* and have mastered it. One who is still bound and imprisoned by it cannot come to see or recognize the truth of this statement, as he is literally blinded by his *yetzer hara*.[4] He is like someone who is walking in the dark and cannot see the many stumbling blocks before him.

Our sages said (*Baba Metzia* 83b), "'You laid down darkness and there was night' (Psalms 104:20) refers to this world, which is likened to night." How profound a statement of truth this comes out to be when you plumb the depths of it! Night's darkness can cause two major errors of sight: it can either cover your eyes so that you cannot see what is in front of you, or it can confound your sight so that you might, for example, believe a pillar is actually a human being, or vice versa.

---

3. From this statement we see that Luzzatto's idea of self-evaluation is rooted in recognizing the price you pay for your actions, not in dwelling upon your "badness" or "lowliness."

He is once again not addressing the multitude of people who *would* dwell upon their "low" state, nor is he addressing the elite and altruistic. He is again addressing those who react best to the ideas of personal gain or loss. (See n. 3, chap. 2). But it should be pointed out that reward and punishment can be understood from many levels, and the fact that it is being brought up by those who rule over their inclinations should be taken into account as well.

4. Why does he speak of being *literally* blinded rather than figuratively? Because when you are bound and imprisoned by the *yetzer hara* you can no longer see the things around you for what they are, so that what is far from Godliness often times appears to be close, and vice versa.

Such is the case with the coarseness and materiality of this world. It is the darkness of night to the mind's eyes, and can cause you to err in two ways: first, in that it does not allow you to notice the stumbling blocks along the way. Gullible people trustingly walk along as a result of this, fall, and are lost without even experiencing an initial fear. The verse says regarding this (Proverbs 4:19), "The way of the evil ones is like darkness; they do not know how they will stumble"; and (Proverbs 22:3) "The clever man sees evil and hides, while the fools pass through it and are punished"; as well as (Proverbs 14:16), "The idiot passes through trustingly"—for, in their opinion, their minds are as clear as can be, and they fall before they can at all catch sight of the stumbling block.

The second type of error[5] is more serious than the first. It has you misinterpret things so that what is in fact bad seems to be truly good, and vice versa. Your wrong actions are reinforced as well as a result of this. It is not enough that the truth is hidden from you and you cannot see the bad right in front of your face: you come to establish "great proofs" and "evidence" to substantiate your incorrect logic and false perceptions.

This is the great wrong that can envelop you and bring you to the pit of doom. The verse refers to this when it says (Isaiah 6:10), "The heart of this nation has grown fat; its ears have become heavy, and its eyes have turned aside. . . ." And all this is so because they have been immersed in darkness and have come under the sway of the *yetzer hara*. But those who have come out from this state of imprisonment see the truth for what it is and can advise others about it.

We can liken this to a huge garden maze that would be set up for fun (as was done in the homes of the well-to-do in the past), made up of row after row of walls, with identical small paths between them to confuse and confound. The goal would be to reach the center rotunda. But some of the small paths would be straight and lead directly to the rotunda, while others would divert and lead far away from it.

The game player could not see or know whether or not he was on one of the direct paths. They would all be similar and seem to be no different from each other to the eye of the beholder unacquainted and unfamiliar with them, never having entered into the maze before or reached the rotunda, its goal.

But the person who would have already reached the rotunda could see all the paths before him and pick out the direct from the diverting ones. He could warn the others and say to them, "That's the one you should take," and anyone who chose to trust his word would reach the goal, while whoever would not trust him and would follow his own hunches would certainly stray behind, get lost, and not reach it.

---

5. The "second type of error" being referred to here is the one caused by the previously mentioned "coarseness and materiality of this world," that comes right after not noticing the stumbling blocks along the way (see the previous paragraph).

This is the situation in our case. One who has not mastered his *yetzer hara* is in the middle of all of the maze's paths and cannot choose between them. But one who has mastered it—who has gotten to the rotunda, who has gotten past the paths and can clearly see all the choices—is eligible to counsel whoever is willing to listen to him. That is the person we should trust.

What in fact is the advice they give us? "Come, let us account for things. Let us evaluate matters of the world." They have themselves already been tried and come to see and know that this alone is the true path that can direct you to the desired good.

The point of the matter is that you should constantly, consistently ponder, as well as set aside specific time to be alone so as to consider what is the true path you must take according to the rules of the Torah. Then you should contemplate your actions and decide if they are in agreement with this or not. In this manner you will find it easy to purify yourself from all bad and to set your ways straight. As the verse says (Proverbs 4:26), "Consider the path of your feet and all your paths will be set." And (Lamentations 3:40), "Let us seek out our ways and examine them, and then we can return to God."

4

The Means of Acquiring Caution

Generally speaking, what brings you to caution is Torah study, which is what Rabbi Pinchas said at the beginning of his *beraita*—"Torah brings you to caution."[1] But what brings it about in particular is the reflection upon the seriousness of the Divine service incumbent upon us, and the extent of Divine judgment.

---

1. There are two kinds of Torah study being addressed here: general, all-inclusive Torah study, being the study of both the homiletic/ethical and the legalistic types of materials; and the study of the homiletic/ethical in particular.

But as Luzzatto asks in his introduction, "Can it be that we would toil and labor in the study of things not at all incumbent upon us to study, upon *pilpul* which could bear no fruit, or upon laws which have no practical application in our days—while our great obligation to our Creator is abandoned to habit or left aside as elements of a religion of rote?" He is intimating that too much time is spent by those who are so blessedly fortunate to have the time to learn the holy Torah on impractical and academic-type matter.

Much of the Talmud discusses the purpose of life and our relationship with the Creator, and much of it reveals the history of the decision-making processes of practical Jewish law (*Halachah*). Needless to say, we are to study those legalistic sections of the Talmud so that we might better understand why we do what we do, but then we must cease and desist. We must then consult contemporary books of Jewish law to determine what our Divine practice is to be, then go on with it, and leave the in-depth and profound study of the legalistic sections of the Talmud to our great decisors of *Halachah*.

Jewish practice is quite straightforward and laid out as such in the many books we are fortunate to have. But the "whys" and "to-what-ends" are so demanding, and life is so short that we sell ourselves short by the avoidance of such issues we seem to be privy to. The irony is that the very most important and fulfilling questions of all are discussed in the talmudic literature, albeit quixotically and calling for thought and concentration. But we tend to overlook that in our drive to analyze and ruminate upon the "means" to the great end (which is attachment to God), the *mitzvot*. Let us study the *mitzvot*, do them in a knowledgeable and wonderful way, and go on with our great mission.

This realization can be acquired by concentrating on the tales told in the holy books, and studying the sayings of our sages which speak to this. But there are various people at various levels of understanding: those who fully understand, those of somewhat lesser understanding, and the great majority of people. So there is specific advice regarding such realizations for each of those people.[2]

The advice for those who fully understand will be to foster a cognizance that wholeness alone is the thing that should be longed for, nothing else; that nothing is worse than the lack of wholeness and what keeps it back from us. After this is explained, and it likewise becomes clear to them that the means to wholeness are good deeds and good personality traits, they would certainly never want to diminish or make light of them.[3] It would have already been clear to them that if these means would be

---

2. See notes in chapters 2 and 3 respectively.

This comes to tell us that the Torah is understood in different ways, according to one's readiness and ability to accept it from its Source, God.

The very essence of Torah, which is contained in the first two of the Ten Commandments, ("I am the Lord your God who brought you out from the land of Egypt, out of the house of bondage," which speaks of accepting God as God, and, "You will have no other gods before Me," which speaks of rejecting all persons and things as God), says enough for those who would understand and could endure its fullness. But it does not say enough to lesser souls. Such people require more statements and more mundane explanations.

And yet others could not be satisfied with such hints and allusions which, while wordier and more blunt than the clear and pure utterance of the first two Commandments, do not quite say enough to those people to act as counselor and advisor for the practical life. Hence, they require a more enunciated and "mundane" explanation.

So much of Torah is presented in that way—bluntly and tersely for those who only need to hear the utter truth in order to follow through (Luzzatto's people of "full understanding"); a bit more parabolically and variously to those who need more encouragement ("those of somewhat lesser understanding"); and laid out fully and in a directive manner for those who will only follow that (the great majority of people).

All these three ways of revelation are, needless to say, true, and all are Godly, but each is necessary if it is to work for the particular group it is directed towards. And that is so because they will only listen to it, and it is ultimately only important that the Torah be listened to and followed.

3. He is saying here that "wholeness alone is the thing that should be longed for, nothing else." But in the first chapter he says that "we were created to delight in God and enjoy the radiance of His Divine presence. This is the true delight, the greatest enjoyment of all." He also says here that "the means to wholeness are good deeds and good personality traits," and he says in the first chapter that "the means to bring you to this goal are the *mitzvot* which God has commanded."

We see from this that "wholeness" (i.e., the perfection and completion of self and capabilities) and the delight in and enjoyment of God are one and the same. We see as well that *mitzvot* and good deeds and personality traits are one and the same too (aside from the fact that the *mitzvot* bring us to the performance of good deeds and the assumption of good personality

diminished or weakened or would be without their full, required strength, they (the people of full understanding) could not obtain true wholeness—it would be lacking in them to the extent that their strivings would be lacking, and they would be unwhole.

This would be a great sorrow and misfortune for them. They could not help but choose to increase in good deeds and traits, be stringent in all their conditions, and never rest or cease from worrying that perhaps something could be missing that might otherwise bring them to the wholeness that they so desire. King Solomon was referring to this when he said (Proverbs 28:14), "A man who is always afraid is fortunate," which our sages (*Berachot* 60a) explained as referring to fear of matters of a Torah-nature.[4]

The ultimate degree of this level is referred to as "fear of sin," a most auspicious level of attainment. You should always be afraid and concerned that perhaps some trace of sin could be found within you that would draw you away from the wholeness it is incumbent upon us to strive for. Our sages commented upon this in the form of a parable (*Baba Batra* 75a): "We learn (from this) that everyone burns over the dwelling-place of his friend"—not because of envy, which comes about from ignorance (as I will explain later, with the help of Heaven); but rather because a person sees himself as missing some element of wholeness that he can obtain as easily as his friend. Realizing this, a person of full understanding will certainly not fall short in his understanding, and will be cautious in his actions.

The advice given to those of lesser understanding will be based upon their level of comprehension, and will concern itself with respect, which they so desire.

---

traits). That is to say that the point of all of the *mitzvot* is to bring one to good deeds and good personality traits. That is certainly obvious in the case of those *mitzvot* that you do for another person, such as charity, kindness, love, hospitality, and so forth. But how is it so in the case of the more ritualistic *mitzvot*, such as prayer, keeping kosher, observing the *Shabbat*, and so forth? They too are meant to foster good deeds for others and to evoke good personality traits within us: they teach us various lessons in faith and trust in God, satisfaction with our lot, recognition of the good, and so forth, which themselves make for good personality traits. But such notions are only for those who "fully understand." Others will disagree with it or misunderstand it, and claim that it either says something it does not or that it has dangerous ramifications.

4. You might think that people of "full understanding" would not worry about or be afraid of anything, and that that would define the state of being "full of understanding." To be sure, those sorts of people do not worry about the same things we worry about nor does their worry have the same detrimental effect ours does, but they do not worry any *less* than we do.

Worry is a state of being that comes about when you are unsure of your future and realize that you cannot know its outcome. All humans suffer from it, and that should not be denied. The full-of-understanding are not inhuman or angelic; they are full of understanding, no more and no less. The advantage that they enjoy is that they have come to realize the nature of things and our roles in life, and they are able to sublimate their natural human fears into fears about things that matter. We worry about and fear for things that do *not* matter, and that is what has us suffer and grope in the dark.

It is obvious to all thinking people that the division of spiritual levels in the world of truth, that is, the World to Come, is based upon the performance of righteous acts. And that one who is greater in such things than his friend will be exalted above him, while one who is lacking in them will be "lower." As that is so, therefore, how can we hide our eyes from our actions, or diminish our efforts, if in the end—when we can no longer repair what we have damaged—it will cause us sorrow?

But there are fools who only want to have it easy. They say: "Why should we burden ourselves with all this saintliness and abstention? Isn't it enough that we're not bad and doomed to *Gehinom*? We're not about to exert ourselves to get into the Garden of Eden. If we don't get a big portion, we'll get a small one, and that will be just fine for us. We don't plan to burden ourselves with all this."

We would ask them just one question: Could they so easily stand seeing one of their friends honored and glorified more than they, ruling over them, as can happen in this ever-changing world? Or, even more so, could they stand seeing one of their servants or some pitiable, low pauper doing so and not be pained by or seethe in the sight? Certainly not. As we know, all of our efforts are rooted in having dominance over whomever we are able to, and on placing ourselves in a higher position.

Such is the nature of the jealousy of one person over another: if you see your friend in a position superior to yours while you yourself remain static, you will endure it (because you must—there may be nothing you can do to change it) but your heart will wither within you.

So if you find it so hard to be in an inferior position in relation to illusory and unreal characteristics, and to suffer a kind of inferiority that is only external, as opposed to a "superiority" that is vain and untrue—how would you ever be able to endure seeing yourself being inferior to people to whom you are now superior in the place of true, valued, and eternal superiority, the World to Come?[5]

Though you cannot yet recognize that situation and its worth, and so you do not concern yourself with it, you will certainly recognize the truth of it in its time, to your embarrassment and everlasting great sorrow.

An easy-going nature such as this, which they adapt for themselves to make their Divine service easier, is a rationalization of the *yetzer hara*, and not anything based on truth. There would be no need for rationalizations if they would see the truth of the matter; but as they do not care about it, and instead keep on going their own ways, the rationalizations will remain with them until it will be too late—when they can no longer repair what was ruined.

King Solomon was referring to this when he said (Ecclesiastes 9:10), "Do whatever is in the powers of your hand to do, for there is no action, accounting for, knowledge. . . ." That is, what you hold off doing until the power the Creator has given to your hands—which is the power of free choice (given you your whole life, and through

---

5. This means to say that if you care about your relative worth in a relatively worthless world, imagine how much you will care about it where it truly matters.

which you are free and commanded to act)—has left you, you cannot do in the grave or in the netherworld. For by then you will no longer have the power to do it. If you do not increase in righteous acts in your lifetime, you cannot do so afterward; if you do not account for your actions here, you cannot do so then; if you do not make yourself wise in this world, you cannot do so in the grave for (*Ecclesiastes* 9:10), "there is no action, accounting for, knowledge or wisdom in the netherworld, where you are going."

The advice for the great majority of people would follow along the lines of detailing rewards and punishments that are based upon the gravity and extent of the law.[6] In truth we should constantly be shivering and trembling. Who could endure the great day of judgment? Who could be accounted righteous before his Creator, whose observing eye is exacting upon everything, great and small? As our sages said (*Chagigah* 5b) about the prophet's statement (Amos 4:13) "'And He tells one his conversation'—Even one's small talk with his wife is related to him at the hour of judgment"; as well as, in reference to Psalms 50:3, *U'svevav nis'ara me'od*[7]: "This comes to teach us that the Holy One (blessed be He) is exacting with His saints to a hairsbreadth."

Even the patriarch Abraham—the Abraham beloved of his Creator, referred to as (Isaiah 41:8) "Abraham My beloved"—could not avoid judgment on the small things about which he was not particularly careful. He said (Genesis 15:8), "How will I know?" and the Holy One (blessed be He) said (*Yalkut* 1:5), "By your life, you shall surely know that your descendants shall be strangers."[8] And because he made a covenant with Abimelech without the express command of God, the Holy One (blessed be He) said, (*Yalkut* 1:21), "By your life, I will delay the joy of your sons by seven generations."

---

6. This is not to say that the notion and particulars of reward and punishment are unknown to the full of understanding or those of lesser understanding, or that they are not real and ever-present. As Luzzatto says immediately following this statement, "In truth we should constantly be shivering and trembling. Who could endure the great day of judgment?" What it says is that the vast majority of people *dwell* upon reward and punishment (mostly punishment) and define their Divine service by it. Such an attitude—while valid, needed and productive in many cases—is nonetheless less holy and advanced.

7. *U'svevav nis'ara me'od* is usually translated as, "And it storms wildly around Him." But it can be translated, in a less literal sense, as "And those who surround Him are very much 'haired,'" which accounts for the talmudic statement to follow, "This comes to teach us that the Holy One (blessed be He) is exacting with His saints to a hairsbreadth."

8. Abraham asks in Genesis 15:8, "How will I really know that it (the land of Canaan) will be mine?" That indicated a lack of faith on his part, as God had just promised him that indeed the land *would* be his. The statement in *Vayikra Rabbah* 11:5, "By your life, you shall surely know that your descendants shall be strangers" means to say that since you said, "How will I really know. . . ," you will come to know something else: (*Vayikra Rabbah* 15:13) ". . . that your descendants shall be strangers in a land that is not theirs for four hundred years."

Because Jacob was angry with Rachel when she said to him (Genesis 30:1), "Give me sons," the Midrash (*Bereishit Rabbah* 71:10) says that the Holy One (blessed be He) said to him, "Is that how you answer the oppressed? By your life, your sons will stand in front of her son." And because (with the best of intentions) he hid Dinah in order that Esau should not take her, and because he withheld some good from his brother, God said of him alluding to Job 6:14, "'He keeps back goodness from his friend'—Since you would not have her marry a circumcised man, she will marry an uncircumcised man; and since you did not allow her to marry in a permitted fashion, she will marry in a forbidden way" (*Bereishit Rabbah* 80:3).

Because Joseph said to the chief steward (Genesis 40:14), ". . . but remember me in conjunction with yourself," two years were added on to his imprisonment. And, as our sages said (*Bereishit Rabbah* 89:3), because he embalmed his father without the express permission of God, or (according to another opinion) because he heard his brothers say, "Your servant, our father" and kept still, he died before his brothers (*Bereishit Rabbah* 100:3).

Because David referred to words of Torah as mere "songs" he was punished by stumbling, as a result of Uzzah's words, and having his joy confounded (*Sotah* 35a).

Because Michal reproved David for dancing in front of the Ark of the Covenant, she was punished by not having any children other than the one she died bearing (2 Samuel 6:20 ff).

And because Hezekiah showed the treasury to the ministers of the Philistine king, his sons were sentenced to be eunuchs in the court of the Babylonian king (2 Kings 20:14 ff).

There are very many other such examples.

We are told in tractate *Chagigah* (5a) that whenever Rabbi Yochanan would reach the verse (Malachi 3:5), "I will draw close to you in judgment and will be a quick witness against the sorcerers, against the adulterers, against those who swear falsely, and against those who oppress the hired man in his wages, the widow and the fatherless . . . ," he would cry, "Is there any remedy for a servant whose light and heavy actions are weighed equally against each other?"

Certainly the intent of his statement is not that the punishment should be equal for both. As is known, God repays actions in kind, measure for measure. But the point is that actions are weighed, and the trivial ones are weighed just as are the more serious. For the more serious actions themselves will not forget the trivial any more than the Judge will hide His eyes from all of them in general, or from the more serious in particular. He will oversee and observe them all equally and at once, judging and appropriately punishing each one. This is what King Solomon was referring to when he said (Ecclesiastes 12:14), "God will bring every action before Him in judgment. . . ." For just as God does not leave unrewarded any righteous act, no matter how small, so does He not leave unjudged or unrebuked any sinful act, no matter how small. This disproves the statements of those fools who would say that God neither considers nor pays heed to the more trivial things in His judgments.

The principle is (*Baba Kamma* 50a): "Whoever says the Holy One (blessed be He) overlooks things will be overlooked by Him." Our sages have also said (*Chagigah* 16a), "If your *yetzer hara* tells you to sin and assures you that God will forgive you—don't listen to it."[9]

All this is clear and obvious, as God is the God of truth. This is what Moses our Master was referring to when he said (Deuteronomy 32:4), "The actions of the Rock are complete; all His ways are just. He is a trustworthy God, without wrong. . . ."

God desires justice. Would He conceivably bypass justice by overlooking blame more than merit? Therefore, if He desires justice, He must reckon with each person according to his actions and as befitting his actions, in a most exacting way, whether good or bad. That is to say, when the verse says that "He is a trustworthy God, without wrong; He is righteous and just" that means (as our sages say) that this refers to His actions toward both the righteous and the evil. Such is His way: He judges all and punishes for each sin, and that is that.

You might ask, "If this is so, where does His attribute of compassion come in if He must judge all things so exactly?" The answer to that is His compassion is the very thing that keeps up the world. Without it, the world could not at all exist. Yet His attribute of judgment is not to be denied.

According to the strict letter of the law, the sinner should be punished immediately, without any delay at all, upon the performance of a sin, and the punishment itself should be meted out with great anger, as we would expect in the case of one who rebels against the word of the Creator. There would seem to be no way of undoing this sin as, in truth, how can one rectify what has been ruined by the committing of a sin? If one would for example murder someone or commit adultery against someone, how in fact could these deeds be rectified? Can one undo what has already been done?

But in truth the Divine attribute of compassion obviates these points. It is what gives time to the sinner and disallows for his being immediately done away with upon sinning, or for the punishment to lead to utter destruction. As a great kindness, it allows for repentance for the sinner so that the uprooting of the *will* to do is equivalent to uprooting the act itself. That is, by the very fact that the penitent recognizes his sin, acknowledges it, reflects upon his bad actions, repents, regrets it as much as he would regret a vow made inadvertently, sincerely wishes he had never done that thing, is terribly pained in his heart that he had ever done such a thing, decides to abandon it, and runs away from it—such an uprooting of the thing from his will is likened to the rescinding of a vow and he is forgiven. This is what the verse is referring to when it says (Isaiah 6:7), "Your transgression will be turned around and you will be forgiven of your sins." That is, your transgressions will be retroactively turned around and uprooted from existence by your pain and regret for what has happened.

---

9. That is to say, if your *yetzer hara* tells you to sin and "assures you that God will *just naturally* and *automatically* forgive you—don't listen to it."

This is certainly a great kindness, and not an aspect of strict judgment. But it is an aspect of kindness that does not utterly deny judgment. It leaves something over. That is, now there is regret and woe instead of the will to do the sin or the pleasure derived from it. And the extension of time is not a pardoning of the sin but rather an "endurance" on God's part so as to open doors of reparation.

Such is the way of all Divine kindnesses. As our sages said (*Sanhedrin* 104a), "The son acquits the father" and (*Kohelet Rabbah* 7:27) "Part of a soul is equivalent to the entire soul," meaning that it is the way of Divine goodness to receive the smaller as it does the greater. But this does not in fact contradict or disprove the attribute of judgment. We have reason enough to recognize its importance.

But an unconditional pardoning or overlooking of sins is contrary to the notion of Divine judgment, for if there were no honest sense of law and justice it could not be found at all. But if one of the means of "escape" mentioned is not used by the sinner, judgment will certainly not return empty-handed. As our sages have said (Jerusalem Talmud, *Taanit* 2:1), "He withholds His anger but takes what is His."

We conclude that one who wants to open his eyes has no real excuse for not practicing self-mastery as much as possible, as exactingly as possible. The wise will certainly acquire the trait of caution if he tends to himself by these means.

5

Matters That Cause the Loss of Caution and How to Resist Them

There are three instances that cause the loss of and the resistance to this character trait: attendance to and overinvolvement in the things of this world, levity and mockery, and bad companionship.[1] Let us approach each one separately.

We have already spoken about the attendance to and overinvolvement in the things of this world: how your thoughts become bound by the fetters of the weight you place upon these things and it then becomes impossible to reflect upon your actions. When our sages noted this they said (*Avot* 4:12), "Reduce your concern with this world—concern yourself with Torah."

You must necessarily concern yourself with the matters of this world to earn your living, but overconcern—to the point where it looms so large that it leaves no room for Divine service—is not necessary. That is why we were commanded to set aside specific time for learning Torah.[2] This is especially crucial, we have already

---

1. These three traits indicate a progression. At first, and on your own, you may attend to and overinvolve yourself in the things of this world. After a while that causes you to lean toward levity and mockery, as the state of this world just suggests that and it can be best worked in with such traits—when one does not dedicate himself to Divine service. And finally, when one is full of levity and mocking, he tends to attract bad companionship—other people who act in a like way.

2. We certainly need to make a living to get by in this world, and we also need to escape from the work we do. The accustomed way of escaping is to do something inane and mindless. As a result of that, when we escape, we escape *downward* and we lower our sights. What Luzzatto would suggest is that we *raise* our sights, that we escape from the drudge and demands by going *upward* and studying Torah.

You need only study Torah in the mornings, before you leave for work, and in the evenings when you are free from all other obligations. That way you will have framed your day with Torah study and come to realize the fact that you are working to get by so that you may live comfortably enough for you to grow in spirit.

pointed out, to one trying to obtain the trait of caution. As Rabbi Pinchas has said, "Torah brings you to caution." Without it you could never at all obtain caution.

Our sages were referring to this when they said (*Avot* 2:6), "A person without Torah-knowledge cannot be a saint." This is so because when God created the *yetzer hara* He created the Torah to temper it, as it is said: (*Kiddushin* 30b): "I created the *yetzer hara* and I created Torah as a seasoning to it." It is apparent from the fact that the Creator created just this cure for this specific ailment that it would be impossible to thoroughly cure a person from the ailment any other way, and that anyone who thinks he can be saved otherwise is mistaken. He will realize his error at the time of his death, as he dies transgressing.

In truth the *yetzer hara* is powerful in us. And without our knowing it, it gets stronger and stronger, and controls us. We can try everything in the world, but if we do not try the remedy particular to it, Torah, we will never know of or sense its overtaking us until we die in our sins and our souls are lost.

This is like the case of the sick man who went to several doctors. Each doctor recognized his condition, and prescribed a particular medicine. But he, without ever having had any medical training, decided not to take that medicine, but rather another one that he thought might cure him. Needless to say, this man is doomed to die. The human situation is like that. No one other than God (Who has created it) is fully acquainted with the illness that is the *yetzer hara* or its inherent strength. And He has taught us that its cure is Torah. Who is it, then, that could disregard that and take what he wants to instead of it and survive? The thick darkness of materiality will surely continue to grow strong within him by degree, without his knowing it. He will find himself so very far from truth—so caught up in evil—that it would not even occur to him to search truth out.

But if this person were to engage himself in Torah, and were to keep its ways, commandments, and warnings, a renewed desire to stay on the good path would ultimately be kindled within him.[3] Our sages were referring to this when they said (*Chagigah* 1:7), "(God says) If only they would abandon Me and keep my Torah— the great light-giving within it would turn them around for the better."[4]

---

3. We have to be reminded of our role in life and of our mission. The thought of it does not just come naturally. In fact the nature of the daily life (which Luzzatto refers to here as "the thick darkness of materiality") is calculated to have us forget those things.

Also, you have to know you do not know something—be it truth or whatever—before you can search for it. If you do not know of your ignorance, it will never occur to you to remedy it. The studying and living of Torah is a sure and ready way to allow yourself to learn what you lack and how to obtain it, and it tends to further encourage you on in the spiritual path.

4. That is not to say, God forbid, that the study and practice of Torah is a way of avoiding God. What it means to say is that as long as there is Torah study, the light of the Torah will inevitably have the people return to God, even if they fall prey to idol worship, licentiousness, and so forth.

In the category of means to facilitate caution as well is the setting aside of specific time for reflecting upon your actions and rectifying them, as has been mentioned. Also, if you are wise, any free time you might have from your everyday concerns will not be lost. You would grab hold of it and not let go, and engage yourself in spiritual concerns and in rectifying your Divine service.

Although this—overinvolvement in worldly matters—is the most common cause of the loss of caution, it is also the easiest to escape from. But the second one—levity and mockery—is very difficult. Anyone who is sunk in it is sunk in a great sea from which it is very difficult to be rescued.

Mockery is ruinous to the heart. All sense and reason are gone when it is around. The lighthearted is like a drunkard or an idiot[5]: it is impossible to give counsel or direction to him because he will not take it. King Solomon said (Ecclesiastes 2:2), "I have said of levity that it is silly and have asked of happiness what it does."

Our sages said (*Avot* 3:13), "Levity and lightheartedness accustom you to promiscuity." Though any sensitive soul recognizes the seriousness of promiscuity and resists it because of the image already drawn in his mind of the profundity of the transgression and the degree of punishment incurred from it—nonetheless, slowly but surely, levity and lightheartedness could draw and pull him closer and closer to it, to the point where fear of the transgression eventually leaves, and he reaches the point of *nearly* committing the sin, and then does.

Why? Because just as the very condition required of the trait of caution is conscious taking-stock, the very essence of levity involves diverting your attention from all noble and profound thoughts, so the fear of Heaven does not enter into it at all.

Notice as well the difficulty and destructiveness of mockery. The person who mocks contends with rebuke and remorse like an oil-covered shield that resists and repels arrows that they might fall to the ground and not touch its wearer's person. By seeing or hearing something that might have it reflect upon or examine its actions, the heart can encourage and arouse itself to do good. But with only one act of mockery or a bit of levity a great amount of self-encouragement and self-rousing to righ-

---

It might also mean to say that God wishes people would stop concentrating upon abstract and academic notions of Him and would settle in on the practical aspects of a spiritual life as enunciated in the Torah. That would automatically bring them to Him.

5. This is not to say that a sense of humor in and of itself is harmful. In fact it may very well be the healthiest and most holy of perspectives to have. Humor is the ability to overlook what might be taken to be pain and to make it bearable and even valuable. It often indicates a mature distance from the un-Godly.

But mockery is an immature and bitter cackling, a sour, unrealized wish used as revenge. It is invariably at someone's expense and can never do good. And lightheartedness is an unsuccessful way of avoiding something that speaks to the very core of our selves and wants to be spoken back to. A lighthearted person *wants* to be drunk or idiotic and, tragically, sees that as an escape.

teous action can fall to the ground. Then the original urge for good would make no impression at all. And all of this would not be because of any kind of weakness or misunderstanding, but rather because of the nature of mockery to undo morality and the fear of Heaven.

The prophet Isaiah would screech like a crane about this. He saw that this trait in the people would not allow his moral rebukes to make an impression, and that all hope would be lost for the sinners he was addressing. He said (Isaiah 28:22), "And now stop ridiculing, because your bonds might tighten." Our sages have already proclaimed (*Avodah Zarah* 18b) that one who mocks brings trials upon himself. As the verse explicitly states (Proverbs 19:29), "It is only fitting that one who mocks be judged."

This is in fact as logic would dictate. One who busies himself with self-analyses and study does not have to suffer corporally for his sins: he would have already repented as a result of the thoughts of repentance borne in his heart after having read or heard moral teachings or rebuke. But the mockers—who do not occupy themselves with taking rebuke, as a natural result of their mockery—have no other means of reparation than Divine judgment. There is nothing in their mocking nature equivalent in power to moral teaching to eliminate such judgment.[6] And the true Judge is as serious in His judgment as the seriousness of the transgression and its ramifications. Our sages were referring to this when they said (*Avodah Zarah* 18b), "Mockery is difficult because it starts in trials and ends in destruction, as it is said (Isaiah 28:22), 'Therefore do not be mockers, lest your binding-ropes be strengthened, for I have heard words of utter destruction. . . .'"

The third thing that causes you to lose caution is a circle of friends, that is, a circle of sinful, foolish friends. The verse refers to this when it says (Proverbs 13:20), "A friend of fools will suffer harm." Often we find that even after the need for Divine service and caution become self-evident to a person, he might slacken off or overlook certain things relevant to it so friends might not ridicule him, or so that he might fit in with them. Solomon warned about this when he said (Proverbs 24:21), "Do not mix with *shonim*."[7] By this he means that if someone quotes the section of the Talmud that says (*Ketubot* 17a), "One should always join in with people," you should tell him that this refers to joining in with people who act like people, not like people who act like animals.

Solomon further warned (Proverbs 14:7): "Walk away from a foolish man." King David said (Psalms 1:1), "The man who does not walk in the council of the wicked, or stand on the road of sinners, or sit in the settlement of mockers is fortu-

---

6. This indicates that one way or another you will suffer as a result of your transgressions, your errors. The choice is yours as to whether you want to suffer through remorse and regret (which is the shorter path), or physically (the longer, more intense path).

7. *Shonim* is usually translated as "those who change constantly," but can also be understood to refer to those who *study*, that is, study incorrectly.

nate." Our sages have understood this to mean (*Avodah Zarah* 18b), "If he starts out walking[8] he will end up standing,[9] and if he stands[10] he will end up sitting."[11] David said (Psalms 26:4), "I have not sat with false men . . . , I have hated a congregation of evildoers."

A person should only purify and cleanse himself, and keep himself back from the ways of the great preponderance of people who are stuck in passing fancies. He should turn himself in the direction of the courtyard of God and His Tabernacle. This is what David concluded when he said (Psalms 26:6), "I will wash my hands in cleanliness and I will circle Your altar, God."

Should you find yourself in the company of someone who ridicules you, do not take his remarks to heart. Do just the opposite—ridicule and embarrass him. Just consider this: If you had an opportunity to acquire great wealth would you hold yourself back because of somebody's ridiculing? You should avoid destroying your soul because of a ridiculer all the more so. Our sages said (*Avot* 5:20), "Be as ferocious as a leopard, light as an eagle, swift-footed as a deer, and strong as a lion to do the will of your Father in Heaven."

And David has said (Psalms 119:46), "I will speak of Your testimonies before kings and not shame." He meant that even though for the most part the concerns and conversations of kings involved grandeur and hedonism, David (who was also a king) did not at all worry about being embarrassed and would discuss morals and Torah in their company instead of taking part in their usual stories of the grandeur and hedonism of people like themselves. After he had realized the truth, his heart was not seduced by such emptiness. As he explained it, he would (Psalms 119:46) "speak of Your testimonies before kings and not shame." In a similar manner, Isaiah said (Isaiah 50:7), "Therefore I have made my face like flint and knew I would never shame."

---

8. . . . in the council of the wicked.
9. . . . on the road of sinners.
10. . . . on that road.
11. . . . in the settlement of mockers.

Summation of Part II

Chapter 2

1. Caution is a twofold process: being cautious in your actions themselves and in your general interests, and considering whether what you are doing or are likely to do is for the good or not.

2. It only makes sense that a person would not expose himself to physical danger. The way to avoid threats to your *spirit* is by keeping your eyes opened and considering whether or not your actions should be continued or abandoned.

3. Doing that calls for the setting aside of time for the conscious and deliberate consideration of all of your actions and ways. Being too busy is one of the devices the *yetzer hara* uses to have you avoid such introspection. Wisdom and self-mastery are needed to counter that.

4. You simply cannot conquer the *yetzer hara* alone; you need God's help. He will help you if you will learn to master yourself.

Chapter 3

5. To master yourself you will need to consider what the good is that you would like to come to, and what the bad is you would like to avoid. That is determined by Torah. And you will need to scrutinize your actions and determine whether they lean toward that good or toward the bad.

6. You will also need to come to the point where you do nothing without taking that into consideration, and without reflecting upon your past actions, too, to determine under which categories they fell.

7. The way to do all that is to arrange a daily, scheduled routine of self-

analysis and consideration of the spiritual loss incurred by the performance of a transgression as opposed to the temporal gain.

8. You must realize that because of the darkness we fall under the sway of (which is caused by the *yetzer hara*) we often rationalize bad habits and explain them away.

Chapter 4

9. There are two things that ultimately bring you to a state of caution: Torah study, and a realization of what is truly incumbent upon us in this world and the extent of Divine judgment.

10. As to that realization, there is advice along those lines to be given to those who would fully grasp the truth of things, some for those of lesser understanding, and particular advice for the multitude. For not all people assimilate the truth the same way.

11. The advice for those who would understand it would be to come to the realization that all that matters is wholeness, and the only way you can come to it is through good deeds.

12. The advice for those of lesser understanding will be based upon the fact that such people care about their relative worth. As your standing in the World to Come will be based upon the value of your good deeds in this world, it would behoove you to do as many things of value as possible while in this world.

13. The advice for the multitude will be based upon a recounting of the rewards and punishments for our actions, a reminding of the Day of Reckoning and the fact that none can avoid it, as well as the assurance that God judges *all* of our actions, large and small.

Chapter 5

14. There are three things that would have you *not* acquire the trait of caution: overconcern for things of the world, levity, and keeping bad company.

15. The warning against overconcern for things of the world implies that you care enough about matters of the world to get by in it, but not enough to remove yourself from Divine service. The means of giving yourself the proper balance of concern for matters of the world is the study and living out of Torah.

16. It is to your disadvantage to be lighthearted, as when you are, you are often beyond reason and cannot take advice. Caution requires careful analysis, while lightheartedness is the essence of avoidance and not taking things seriously.

17. The Torah tells us that "bad will befall the friend of bad people" (Proverbs 13:20). This is so because people will often avoid acts of piety so as not to be ridiculed by friends. Do not keep company with people who follow all the whims and fancies of the day.

III

ENTHUSIASM

Introduction to Part III

The third part comprises four chapters (6–9) and concerns itself with the acquisition of the trait of "enthusiasm." The chapters are entitled, "An Explanation of the Trait of Enthusiasm" (chap. 6), "The Subdivisions of Enthusiasm" (chap. 7), "The Means of Acquiring Enthusiasm" (chap. 8), and "Matters That Cause the Loss of Enthusiasm and How to Resist Them" (chap. 9).

As you will notice, the chapter titles for enthusiasm perfectly match those of the trait of caution. But that is done purposefully. As Luzzatto himself says (chap. 8), caution and enthusiasm "are very similar. The only difference between them is that enthusiasm relates to positive *mitzvot*, and caution to negative ones."

From this point on in the book, Luzzatto not only dwells upon the subject at hand, but ventures out onto relevant, though admittedly nonessential sidelines. While these tend to serve to illustrate the main theses, they also address other issues in Jewish thought the author feels it is necessary to dwell upon at the moment.

The diversions in this part include forays into the analyses of: laziness, errors in Torah-study that come about from sloppiness in thought (chap. 6); the danger of delaying, fostering a desired emotion externally through movement (chap. 7); the realization of the good God does for us all no matter what our station in life (chap. 8); the place of work, the notion of just "passing through" this world and accepting things for what they are, and the logical extent of trust in God (chap. 9).

Luzzatto offers a definition for enthusiasm: "It is the eagerness to do and complete *mitzvot*" (chap. 6). But the Hebrew for it, *zerezut*, connotes other things as well, such as: strength, vigorousness, quickness, readiness, instigation, valiancy. It is related to "harnessing" and "saddling" (see Targum Onkelos to

Genesis 14:14), and as such it alludes to bravely and intensely gathering together all of one's qualities for one end—the doing of *mitzvot*, in this case. *Zerezut* does not carry with it the negative connotations of excitation, agitation, tumult, frenzy, fidgetiness, or militancy as the English word "enthusiasm" might.

Included in this part is the first caveat that what is being asked for is often quite difficult, and that that should be kept in mind while you are doing your best. As it says (chap. 6), "In truth human beings are just that—humans, and not angels. It is therefore impossible for us to have the might of the angels (who are always enthusiastic to do God's will). Nonetheless we should strive to get as close to this level as we possibly can."

6

An Explanation
of the Trait of Enthusiasm

Enthusiasm follows caution. But while caution has to do with *not* doing, enthusiasm has to do with doing. As it is written (Psalms 34:15), "Depart from evil and do good."[1]

The meaning of enthusiasm is self-evident: it is the eagerness to do and complete *mitzvot*.[2] Our sages put it this way (*Pesachim* 4a), "The enthusiastic do *mitzvot*

---

1. The quote from Psalms should be read in context. It starts out by asking, "Who desires life? Who loves his days and wants to see good in them?" It then tells us that it is "one who guards his tongue from speaking evil and guards his lips from speaking falsely." The way to do that, the Psalm continues, is to "depart from evil and do good; search for peace and pursue it" (verses 13–15).

We see from the fact that Luzzatto is quoting from this verse that he is pointing out to us that one who "desires life" (i.e., life in the World to Come) and wants to see good in his days (this also alludes to the World to Come, which contains the true good, closeness to God) should "guard his tongue from speaking evil and guard his lips from speaking falsely" (i.e., should be introspective and analytical, and above all *honest* with himself about his faults). Only then will he come to "depart from evil."

But that is not enough. While it is vital and holy to depart from doing evil, and honest introspection is the best way to do it, it is as important to move on from there in a new, positive vein and actively "do good." Those are the two steps in finding and producing peace both internally and in others: by quietly "searching" for it within and vociferously "pursuing it" without.

2. Our age is an enthusiastic one in many ways. God knows we are productive, bold, innovative, and willing to take risks. We have gone further out into space than has any age before us; we have risked life and limb in the conquest of dread diseases; and we have fought the good cause on principle many times over, and have thought nothing of personal loss.

Yet Luzzatto says in chapter 7 that "enthusiasm is the one great trait of perfection that is presently lacking in human nature."

eagerly." It takes as much conscientiousness and determination to take hold of the *mitzvot*, so that you can gain rather than lose merit, as it does to save yourself from the snares of the *yetzer hara*, so that it does not control you and become entangled in your affairs. For just as the *yetzer hara* tries by any means to have you fall into the nets of sin, it also tries to have you lose the chance to do *mitzvot*. If you slack off and become lazy instead of encouraging yourself to pursue them and take hold of them, you will surely be left empty-handed.

Man is by nature very "weighed down" by an earthiness and coarse materiality. That is why he does not want to exert or burden himself. But if you want to merit to Divine service you have to fight this nature and be self-motivated and enthusiastic. For if you abandon yourself to this "heaviness" you will not succeed in your quest. Our sages counseled us to be as "ferocious as a leopard, light as an eagle, swift-footed as a deer, and strong as a lion to do the will of our Father in heaven" (*Avot* 5:20). And they included Torah study and the performance of righteous deeds as the things that need prodding (*Berachot* 32b). The Torah itself clearly warns us to "be strong and very courageous in keeping and observing the whole Torah that Moses, My servant, has commanded you" (Joshua 1:7). One who wants to turn around his nature needs a lot of prodding.

Solomon warned us repeatedly about the detrimental nature of laziness and the great loss that comes from it.[3] He said (Proverbs 6:10–11), "A little sleep, a little slumber, a little crossing of your arms to nap, and all of a sudden poverty and want come along like an armed soldier." He meant that even though the lazy person does not set out to do harm, he does it inadvertently by being inactive. He also said (Prov-

---

It seems that he is saying something else that we must take note of that will also help to explain the thrust of this section, as well as the rest of the book. It can be seen by how he defines enthusiasm: "the eagerness to do and complete *mitzvot*," which he describes as being "self-evident."

In other words, he is concerned with a *spiritual* enthusiasm, while we are concerned with material enthusiasm. We are not enthused about spiritual progress. We may give it lip service—in a Machiavellian sort of way, when it is to our material advantage—but we are not enthused about it. We would never relate enthusiasm with the doing of the *mitzvot*, God's will. It is in no way "self-evident" to us that the two are related.

But we are being told here that if we are to be perfected and to dwell in the presence of God we are going to have to come to be enthusiastic about doing His will.

3. The Hebrew word for laziness is *atzlut* (with an *ayin*) and it is phonetically related to the word *aitzel* (with an *aleph*), which denotes being by the side of something. As such, *atzlut* is taken to mean "standing on the outside" or "considering oneself as being exempt from something."

The error in laziness therefore is not so much in the not doing of what should be done, though that is certainly harmful, but in the *assuming that you would never have to*, and acting relaxed and free as a consequence. That assumption and the subsequent inaction cause the great loss Luzzatto speaks of.

erbs 18:9), "One who slackens in his duties is the brother of the destroyer," meaning that even though that person is not himself the destroyer doing the harm, you should not think that he is innocent: he is the destroyer's brother, one of his kind.

Solomon evoked a common enough scene to illustrate and explain the detrimental nature of laziness. He said (Proverbs 24:30–34), "I went by the field of a lazy man and the vineyard of a foolish man, and behold they were grown over with thorns, and their surfaces were covered over with thistles. . . . I noticed it, considered it, looked closely and learned this lesson from it: a little sleep, a little slumber, . . . and all of a sudden poverty and want. . . ."

Aside from the literal meaning of the story, which is true enough and is what happens to lazy people, our sages arrived at an interesting interpretation of it (*Yalkut* to Proverbs 961): "'. . . and behold they were grown over with thorns' means that someone wanted to know the meaning of some concept in Torah and could not arrive at it; 'and their surfaces were covered over with thistles' means that because he did not trouble himself to arrive at the correct meaning, he adjudged something forbidden to be permitted or vice versa, and came to break down the fences (safeguards) established by our sages. What would be this man's punishment? As Solomon told us (Ecclesiastes 10:8), 'Whoever breaks down fences will be bitten by a snake.'"

The bad that comes from laziness does not come about in one fell swoop, but slowly and without notice. It comes in a sequence of one bad deed after another, until you find yourself sunk in evil. First it is only a case of not making the necessary effort, which results in not learning Torah as required for full understanding. This inadequacy in study would be followed by study lacking in understanding. As if that were not bad enough, misunderstanding of that section of Torah would continue, and things would become "clear" to the person that would in fact be against *Halachah*. He would wind up turning around the truth and destroying it, and going against the dictates of our sages and "breaking down the fences." His end would be destruction, which is the judgment against all who break down the fences.[4]

---

4. Three paragraphs back Luzzatto said that "even though the lazy person does not set out to do harm, he does it inadvertently. . . ." This paragraph comes to illustrate that. We might better understand it if we use a common example from contemporary experience.

Once there was a young woman who was always very bright as a girl. She came to find that by exerting herself just a bit she could accomplish as much as the other children in her classes and thereby please her teacher, and she would also have a lot of time left over to watch television. This realization excited her very much, because she wanted nothing more than to please and to relax by watching television.

So a pattern was established. If she could accomplish in one hour what the average child in class could accomplish in two or three, she would just work for the hour, then watch television. That seemed to work for a while, though there would be times when she would have to spend an hour and a half on her assignments. But at that point that did not bother her, because she wanted to be sure she did all of the work and pleased her teacher, and she knew she would be able to watch television soon enough.

Solomon said (Ecclesiastes 10:8), "I noticed it, (and) considered it—I thought it over and saw the great evil in it that was like a poison that spreads very, very slowly and is only noticed at death. And this is what I meant when I said (Ecclesiastes 10:8), '. . . a little sleep . . . and all of a sudden poverty and want come along like an armed soldier.'"

We see over and over again how, though people know of their obligations and what their duty is to their Creator, and it has become self-evident to them that they must rescue their souls, they will nonetheless disregard all this. Again, this would not be as a result of any lack of realization of their obligations, or for any reason other

---

After a while, the pressing need to put in the extra half hour "just to be sure" was no longer there and was replaced by a pressing need to watch extra television. After a while of that, the hour that was put into accomplishing the task at hand was put in begrudgingly and resentfully, and she tended to do it halfheartedly. She always told herself that if she really wanted to put in the effort (which she never did) she could do better than the other students.

While she was certainly able to keep up with the other students when she first came upon her realization, and was even able to exceed them effortlessly, that was no longer true. She found that she was now behind the better students in class, and she was even behind some of the mediocre but hardworking students. While that saddened her, she did not dwell upon it because she was still able to please her teachers with her occasional brilliant spontaneous moments, and she always managed to watch television.

The pattern continued for years. While she never failed in her subjects (something in her would never allow for that), she never excelled, and she always managed to bewilder teachers who started out the year expecting her to do well.

She graduated college minimally with an appropriate degree, found a job, and continued on in her pattern. But by that time she had lost all sight of her initial promptings. She forgot that she herself had made it her second nature to do as little as possible to win the minimum approval of an authority figure. And whereas she had "progressed" from just watching television to doing other, more adult diversionary things, there was still that urge, at this point that *need*, to do something other than what was expected of her.

As a result of that "natural trait of hers" she made a lot of mistakes at work. Inadvertently—she would never intend to do such a thing as she was a good person and meant only well (no one said otherwise)—she managed to overlook serious errors in her work that caused irreparable and serious damage to her company. She was fired.

"But, I never meant for that to happen," she would explain to close friends (and she had several, because she was warmhearted and kind), "and they don't have the right to fire me for human error. After all, who's perfect?!"

Poor soul. She never came to realize her part in her predicament. Because she was bright as a young child she came to believe that (as we used in our definition of laziness, *atzlut*, in note 3 above) she was "standing on the outside" and she considered herself "as being exempt" from effort and toil because she was gifted. One thing led to another, and after many years she caused great damage to herself and others as a direct result of that assumption.

In fact, being inclined to religion, she blamed God for her "bad fortune." And, being also inclined to politics, she fumed about the unfair and sad state of affairs in the world where someone like herself—a good person—could lose a job because of an innocent mistake on her part. This is the fate of the lazy person.

than the "heaviness" of laziness that overpowers them. So they say, "Let me eat a little," or "let me sleep a little," or "it's a hardship for me to go out of my house," or (Song of Songs 5:3) "I've already taken off my coat, so how can I put it on again?" or "it's very, very hot outside," or "it's too cold," or "it's raining"—or any other excuse or rationalization the lazy person may be full of. And for one reason or another, Torah is left aside, Divine service is left undone, and you come to abandon your Creator. This is what Solomon was referring to when he said (Ecclesiastes 10:18), "Because of lazy people the beams will collapse, and for idleness of the hands the house will leak."

But were you to ask the lazy person about his ways, he would retort with all sorts of sayings of the sages, scriptural passages, and logical explanations to prove (to his misguided mind) that he should have it easy and be left in his lazy ways. He cannot see that these rationalizations and ideas are not an outcome of his thinking the problem out, but that they spring forth out of his laziness. As it controls him, it inclines his thinking toward the direction of these rationalizations, so that he does not listen to the words of the sages or the people who truly understand. This is what Solomon bewailed when he said (Proverbs 26:16), "A lazy man is more sagacious in his own eyes than seven people who can give sensible answers." It does not sit well with a lazy person to think that words of reproof could conceivably be directed to him; he thinks that everyone is mistaken or stupid, and that he alone is wise.[5]

It is important that you know at this point that a major principle for fostering the trait of abstention is that every leniency in Divine service should be carefully and most thoroughly considered beforehand. For even though the leniency may seem to

---

5. This is an explanation of the tragic outcome of a life of laziness. It inevitably leads to error (as we have shown above in n. 4), but what is sadder than that is that it also *almost inevitably* leads to the loss of all hope for change because such a person comes to the point where "he does not listen to the words of the sages or the people who truly understand." That refusal leads to further error and destruction, God forbid.

That seems to be the tragedy of Luzzatto's and our age. As was pointed out (n. 2 above), he said that "(spiritual) enthusiasm is the one great trait of perfection that is presently lacking in human nature." As we stated, that can certainly be said for our generation as well. It has led to a basic and nearly all-pervading unwillingness to "listen to the words of the sages or the people who truly understand" and an offering of brilliant and "cogent" arguments against the religious life. Can it not be said of our age that we do not believe that "words of reproof could conceivably be directed" at us in these matters, and that we think that "everyone (in the past) is mistaken or stupid, and that (we) alone (are) wise"?

There is one way out, though, for a spiritually lazy person or society: sincere, honest introspection and change. That will surely be difficult for such a person or persons who are by nature not willing to make the effort. But it is the contention of the author and the writer of these lines that it is very possible and within our grasp. Granted, as Luzzatto puts it at the end of the chapter, "human beings are just that—humans, and not angels." But as he concludes, "nonetheless we should (and I would dare say *must*, for the sake of humanity) strive to get as close to this level as we possibly can."

be just and right, nonetheless it is very possible that it comes out of the advice of the *yetzer hara* and its deceiving ways. If, after all of that, your reasons for taking advantage of the leniency will be found to be just, then it is certainly correct. The point is that you need great prodding to strengthen and enthusiastically encourage yourself to do *mitzvot*, and to throw off the heavy laziness which holds you back. The angels were praised for this good trait. As it is said regarding them (Psalms 103:20), "(They are) mighty in energy, doing as He says, listening to the voice of His word." And, as it is written (Ezekiel 1:14), "The *chayot* dashed back and forth like lightning."

In truth human beings are just that—humans, and not angels. It is therefore impossible for us to have the might of the angels. Nonetheless we should strive to get as close to this level as we possibly can. King David used to praise his own share of this trait by saying (Psalms 119:60), "I hurried—did not delay—to keep Your *mitzvot*."

The Subdivisions of Enthusiasm

There are two subdivisions of enthusiasm. The first is in force before you begin to act on something, and the second is in force after you act on something.

The subdivision that is relevant to before acting on something is comprised of not letting *mitzvot* "spoil." When the time comes to do one, or when one presents itself to you, or when it first occurs to you to do it, you should hasten to take hold of it and do it and not allow a lot of time to pass by.

There is nothing more dangerous than delay. A deterrent to a righteous deed can come up with each moment of delay. Our sages warned us about how true this is in relation to the kingship of Solomon. David said to Benayahu (1 Kings 1:33–36), "Bring (Solomon) down to Gichon (to be appointed king in David's stead)", and Benayahu replied (1 Kings 1:37), "Amen. May God say so. . . ." Our sages commented thusly: "Rabbi Pinchas said in the name of Rabbi Channin of Tzippori, Is it not written (1 Chronicles 22:9), 'Behold, a son will be born to you who will be a man of tranquility'? But many adversaries may rise up against him between here and Gichon" (*Bereishit Rabbah* 76:2).[1]

That is why we were warned by our sages that when it is written (Exodus 12:17), "And you will guard the *matzot*" it means to say that you should not allow any *mitzvah* that comes within your grasp to spoil (*Mechilta*).

That is why they said (*Nazir* 23b), "A man should always be eager to do a *mitzvah*, for because a firstborn daughter preceded her younger sister in marriage she

---

1. That is to say, since it was foretold that Solomon would be king (as it is hinted at by the verse "Behold, a son will be born to you who will be a man of tranquillity") it seems unnecessary for Benayahu to pray at the moment when the prophecy was to be realized, "Amen, may God say so. . . ?" (*Perush Maharzu*).

The explanation as to why Benayahu did say so is that you can never know what can meet you on the road to your destiny, and the best way to insure success along the path is to take advantage of each moment to do God's will.

merited to bring forth four generations of Kings in Israel" (*Pesachim* 4a); "The enthusiastic are eager in *mitzvot*" (*Berachot* 6b); "You should always run to a *mitzvah*, even on the *Shabbat*"; "It is written (Psalms 48:15), 'He will guide us *al moot.*' That means to say 'as enthusiastically as young girls.' As it is said (Psalms 68:26), 'Among them are young girls beating tambourines (enthusiastically).'"[2]

Enthusiasm is the one great trait of perfection that is presently lacking in human nature.[3] One who strengthens himself and assumes as much of it as he possibly can will merit it in truth in the World to Come. The Holy One (blessed be He) will eventually give him his reward in exchange for the effort he put in at the time of his service.

The subdivision of enthusiasm that is relevant to *after* an act has begun refers to taking hold of a *mitzvah* and being in a hurry to complete it. The *mitzvah* should not be done that way because you are anxious to unburden yourself of it, but because you are afraid that you might not merit to complete it.[4]

---

2. *Al moot* is usually translated in the text as "until death," but it can be understood homiletically as meaning "as young girls." And how do we know "as young girls" refers to enthusiasm? By that fact that it is said, "Among them are young girls beating tambourines (enthusiastically)."

3. See notes 2 and 5, chapter 6.

4. As it is stated at the beginning of the chapter, there are two stages of spiritual enthusiasm: before you do a *mitzvah*, and after you have already begun to do it. Luzzatto says about the first stage, "When the time comes to do one, or when one presents itself to you, or when it first occurs to you to do it, you should hasten to take hold of it and do it, and not allow a lot of time to pass by" before you do. But after you have already begun doing it, you are to hurry to complete it, "not . . . because you are anxious to unburden yourself of it, but because you are afraid that you might not merit to complete it."

The notion of hurrying to complete a *mitzvah* because you are afraid of not getting something from it bothers us. But in fact, Luzzatto is saying something very different. It can be understood by seeing that from his initial statement we are being told that there are three moments when *mitzvot* present themselves:

(1) *seasonally* ("when the time comes to do one"), which would include the ceremonial *mitzvot*, such as the keeping of the *Shabbat* and the Holy Days, prayer, wearing *tefillin* (phylacteries, which are only worn in the daytime hours of weekdays), and so forth.

(2) *by happenstance* ("when one presents itself to you"), which would include the *mitzvot* that are done between one person and another, such as charity, kindness, visiting the sick, burying the dead, returning lost articles, conducting business ethically, and so forth.

(3) *upon inspiration* ("when it first occurs to you to do it"), which would include the *mitzvot* that are more emotional and heart-bound, such as love of or reverence for God, loving one's fellow, accepting upon oneself the "yoke of the kingdom of heaven," repentance, and so forth.

The performance of *mitzvot* within each one of these three "moments" is fraught with tenuousness. For example, the *Shabbat* may pass before you will have been inspired enough to take it on; the needy person may annoy you for one reason or another and thereby chip

Our sages continuously warned us about this. They said (*Bereishit Rabbah* 85:3), "Whoever starts a *mitzvah* and does not complete it will bury his wife and children"[5]; (ibid.) "A *mitzvah* is only attributed to the one who completes it."

Solomon said (Proverbs 22:29), "Do you see a man diligent in his work? He will stand before kings, and will not stand before commoners." Our sages said (*Sanhedrin* 104b), "this praise is attributed to Solomon himself because he hurried in the construction of the Temple and was not lazy about it and did not delay in it." The sages commented likewise about Moses for his having hurried in the construction of the Tabernacle (*Shir HaShirim Rabbah* 1:2).

You will find that all of the actions of the righteous are done eagerly. It is said about Abraham (Genesis 18:6–7), "And Abraham hurried to Sara's tent and said to her, 'Hurry!'"; and "he gave it to the young man hurriedly." It is said about Rebecca that (Genesis 24:20), "She hurried and emptied her flask." In a similar vein we find in the Midrash (*Bamidbar Rabbah* 10:5), "It is written (Judges 13:10), 'And the woman hurried. . . .'—this comes to teach us that all of the actions of the righteous are done hurriedly. That is, they would not allow a moment's delay either in the starting or completion of a *mitzvah*."

The man whose spirit is aflame in the service of his Creator will certainly not be lackadaisical in the doing of *mitzvot*. His movements would be as quick as fire, for he could not be at rest or still until he would have utterly completed the task.

Further reflecting upon the matter you will find that enthusiasm is an outcome of some inner incandescence. But enthusiasm itself can produce this incandescence. If you will examine your actions at the time of the performance of a *mitzvah* you will note that just as you yourself instigate external movements, so too can they instigate

---

away at your sudden altruism; or the passion of the moment of religiosity that would lead to loving God clearly and strongly, and so forth, may fizzle away in embarrassment or doubt.

Luzzatto's advice at such times is to seize the moment and complete the *mitzvah*. But he warns that you should not do so "because you are anxious to unburden yourself of it," that is, because you want to be sure you accrue "points" one way or another; but rather, you should hurry to complete it only "because you are afraid that you might not merit to complete it"— you are afraid the moment will fade because it is so fragile and tenuous, which it is.

What Luzzatto is offering here is advice that addresses a recognition of the preciousness of each moment. It is directed toward the person with the desire to use it most propitiously in the service of God.

5. This statement is not to be misunderstood as a cruel warning of a petty and vengeful God who is saying, "Do what I say or I'll kill your wife and children!" It should be understood for what it is: a statement of the possible fulfilling of a pattern of Divine Justice, because God acts towards you as you act (cf. *Sotah* 8b).

You may lose your wife and children—that is, you may be unable to completely fulfill the *mitzvah* of gladdening your wife, being fruitful and multiplying with her, as well as of raising and educating your children—because you did not complete some other *mitzvah* that was made available to you.

inner movements, to the point where they can consciously arouse your very yearnings and desires. But if you continue to accustom yourself to stilted body-movement, your spirit will also be trapped and extinguished. Experience attests to this.

As is known, the most desirable traits in service to the Creator are willingness of heart and longing of soul. King David praised his own good portion of those matters by saying (Psalms 42:2–3), "Like the hart pants after the water-brooks, my soul pants for you, God. My soul thirsts for God"; (Psalms 84: 3) "My soul longs and faints for the courts of God"; (Psalms 63:2) "My soul thirsts for You, my flesh longs for You."

The best advice for the person in whom this desire does not burn is that he consciously enthuse himself so that enthusiasm might eventually become second nature to him. External movement arouses the internal, and you certainly have more of a command over the external than the internal. So if you make use of what you have command over, you will eventually take control over what you do not. Great inner joy, desire and longing will come about as a result of your consciously igniting your movements. The prophet was referring to this when he said (Hosea 6:3), "Let us know—let us run to know God," as well as (Hosea 11:10) "They who will roar like a lion will go after God."[6]

---

6. What he means to say is that since "the man whose spirit is aflame in the service of his Creator will certainly not be lackadaisical in the doing of *mitzvot*," it would be to our advantage to be so "aflame." And since such enthusiasm comes from an inner element that can be purposely and consciously ignited from the "outside," it behooves us to learn how to do so.

The way to "consciously arouse your very yearnings and desires" is to do away with "stilted body-movements" which "trap and extinguish" your spirit—act excited, move excitedly, because "external movement arouses the internal." You will find that "great inner joy, desire and longing will come about as a result of your consciously igniting of your movements."

The Means
of Acquiring Enthusiasm

The means to acquire enthusiasm are the very ones, step by step, used to acquire caution.[1] Their concerns are very similar. The only difference between them is that enthusiasm relates to positive *mitzvot*, and caution to negative ones. When the great value of the *mitzvot*, as well as your great responsibility to them, becomes clear to you, your heart will certainly be aroused to Divine service, and you will not slacken in it.

What will strengthen this motivation will be your taking note of the very many good things that the Holy One (blessed be He) does for you moment by moment, and the great wonders He performs for you from your birth until your last day. The more aware you will be of these matters and the more you will reflect upon them, the more easily will you recognize your great debt to God who has been so good to you. And this will be the means by which you will avoid being lazy and weak in your Divine service. For while in truth you cannot repay Him for His goodness, you can at least acknowledge Him and do His *mitzvot*.

There can be no person, whatever his circumstances—be he poor or rich, healthy or ill—who will never have experienced some wonders or great good in his life. The rich and the healthy are already indebted to God for their wealth and good health. But even the poor person is indebted to Him. For, despite his poverty, sustenance has been provided for him by God in a miraculous, wondrous way, and he has not died of starvation. The ill person is indebted to God because he is actually strength-

---

1. "Generally speaking, what brings you to caution is Torah study. . . . But what brings it about in particular is the reflection upon the seriousness of the Divine service incumbent upon us, and the extent of Divine judgment." (chap. 4).

ened by the burden of his illness and his wounds, and He has not allowed him to sink into the pit. And this is the case with all other such things.[2]

There is no person who cannot recognize his debt to the Creator. He will certainly be aroused and enthused in his service to God by contemplating the good that he has received from Him, as I have already indicated; but he will be enthused even more so if he reflects upon the matter of how all of the good he enjoys, and all that he needs and finds to be essential is in the hands of God, and no other.[3] Then he will certainly not be lazy in his service to God, and will lack nothing that is essential for it.

You will notice that I have divided this section into the same three subdivisions I divided the trait of caution into, because their concerns are the same and one may be understood from the other. The advice for those who fully understand will be of the nature of cognizance of their duty and the value and worth of righteous deeds; for those of lesser understanding, the advice will involve cognizance of the World to Come and their place of honor therein—that they should not be shamed on the day of reward by seeing the level of good they might have attained but did not; and for most people the advice will focus upon this world and its needs, in the manner I have explained in chapter 4.

---

2. Luzzatto said in the first chapter that "the Holy One (blessed be He) has placed mankind in a situation where there are many things to hinder closeness to Him. These are the mundane desires which, if followed, would have you draw away from the true good. You have in fact been placed in the midst of a mighty battle wherein all worldly happenstances—for the good or not—are trials. *The poor have their trials, the wealthy theirs.* As Solomon has said (Proverbs 30:9), 'Lest I grow full, scoff, and say "Who is God?"; lest I grow poor and steal. . . .'" And here he says that "there can be no person, whatever his circumstances—be he poor or rich, healthy or ill—who will never have experienced some wonders or great good in his life."

We see from this that part of the "mighty battle" into which we have been placed is the test of our abilities to recognize the great wonders done for us by God. Could a wealthy person who has awakened himself to the boundless goodness of God ever "scoff and say, 'Who is God?'"; could a poor person who has done likewise ever steal?

3. Luzzatto is saying that there are *two* categories of things that are "in the hands of God, and no other": "all that [a person] needs and finds to be essential" *as well as* "all of the good he enjoys"—that is, God not only provides us with what we need, but also with things we can enjoy.

There are some who accept the fact that God provides the basics, but never come to realize that He also provides the niceties. They think those things come about through the machinations of the world and the work of our own hands, when in truth they come from God.

That is not to say we are not to *strive* for them, and that we should rest on our laurels awaiting. No—we must go at it and reach ever further. But we must also realize that ultimately it is God who provides and furnishes. Striving coupled with that happy realization is what makes for peace and acceptance.

9

Matters That Cause the Loss of Enthusiasm and How to Resist Them

The things that cause the loss of enthusiasm are the same ones that enhance laziness. The greatest of them are the yearning for relaxation, the dislike of inconvenience, and the utter love of pleasure.

The sort of person who lives this way is surely very burdened by the idea of Divine service. Someone who wants to enjoy his meals in comfort, to sleep through the night without interruption, or who would not walk if he could not do so slowly, and so forth, would find it difficult to wake up early to go to synagogue, or to interrupt his evening meal for *Minchah* services or for a particular *mitzvah* if the timing is not just so. He certainly would not hurry to perform *mitzvot* in general or to study Torah. Someone who regularly acts this way is not his own master and is not free enough to undo his actions whenever he might want to. His will is already bound by habits which have become second nature to him.[1]

Know that you were not placed in this world for relaxation, but for effort and toil. You should consider yourself to be a worker doing your work for your wages (as is mentioned in the Talmud, where our sages said of themselves [*Eruvin* 65a], "We are day laborers"), or you should consider yourself to be a soldier in rank who eats hurriedly, sleeps fitfully, and is prepared for movement at any time. It is said regarding this (Job 5:7), "Man was born for labor."

When you accustom yourself to this path you will find that the workload is lightened for you, because you will not lack for readiness and preparation.[2] Our sages

---

1. See note 4, chapter 6, which portrays a person who "is not his own master and is not free enough to undo his actions."

2. With the idea that this world is all we have comes the very logical and, with this

noted such a path when they said (*Avot* 6:4), "This is the path of Torah: you must eat bread with salt, drink small amounts of water, and sleep on the ground." This is the ultimate separation from relaxation and pleasures.[3]

Other things that cause the loss of enthusiasm are fear and anxiety about passing things and their consequences. At one point you might be nervous about cold or heat, another time you might worry about accidents, then another time about illness, and yet another time about the wind, and so forth. This is what Solomon was referring to when he said (Proverbs 26:13), "The lazy person says, 'There's a lion on the road' or 'There's a lion in the street (as an excuse).'" Our sages ridiculed this trait because of its clear connection to sinning, using the following verse (Isaiah 33:14) as proof: "The sinners are frightened in Zion; trembling has taken hold of the hypocrites." A great man said to one of his students who was frightened (*Berachot* 60a), "You're (obviously) a sinner!" As it is pointed out in Psalms 37:36, you should "trust in God and do good; live in the land and be nourished by your faith."

The point is you should consider yourself as "passing through" the world, but settled in your Divine service. You should willingly and contentedly face whatever greets you in this world, and take hold of whatever circumstances come your way. You should avoid relaxation and be drawn to work and effort, set your heart to trust in God, and not worry about consequences or happenstances.

You might argue that the sages warned that you must watch out for your well-being very carefully and not place yourself in danger—even if you are already a righteous person or someone who does a lot of righteous deeds.[4] They said (*Ketubot* 30a), "Everything is in the hands of Heaven but cold drafts." And the verse says (Deuteronomy 4:15), "Be very careful to watch yourselves." You should not consign yourself to trust in God's protection in everything, "even if it concerns a *mitzvah*," the rabbis added.

---

perspective, healthy idea that we deserve rest and pleasure. After all, if this is all there is, why burden yourself overmuch and why not drink from a full cup while you yet can?

But a Jew of faith believes, as Luzzatto has been stressing, that the World to Come matters, and that we are here to fulfill a particular role which involves "effort and toil." With such a perspective we are freed from oversensitivities to the inevitable vicissitudes of this world.

Also, if you consider yourself to be the boss, you worry about each and every detail; but if you consider yourself to be a "day laborer," you are responsible for your task in which you should excel, but you need not worry about it all. And if you need not worry about it all, can you be expected to require as much rest and relaxation? Hence, ironically, "when you accustom yourself to this path (which seems to be the more difficult and burdensome) you will find that the workload is (actually) *lightened* for you."

3. . . . *idle* relaxation and pleasure, that is. Relaxation and pleasure can be very spiritually beneficial, but only when done in the spirit delineated in chapter 1—that is, for the sake of your Divine service.

4. If you are a righteous person or someone who does a lot of righteous deeds you might consider yourself "safe" and naturally protected by Heaven, so you might risk placing yourself in danger.

You must know that there is fear, and there is fear. There is warranted fear and there is senseless fear; there is trust and there is naivete. God created man to be sensible and straightforwardly logical so that he could accustom himself to go the right way and guard himself from the things that might cause him harm (which were created to punish the evil). One who does not want to go along the ways of wisdom and is willing to expose himself to danger is not practicing trust in God—he is naive, and he is sinning and going against the will of God Who wants him to protect himself.[5] In fact, beside the dangers inherent in the thing he has done by not protecting himself, he could be culpable for his own fate by having actively committed a sin. And that will cause him to suffer punishment. This sort of self-protection is a form of concern that is warranted, sensible, and wise, and is referred to in the Torah where it says (Proverbs 22:3): "A clever man sees evil and he hides, but the fool passes right by it and is punished."

Senseless concern is when you compound one form of self-protection onto another, one fear or worry onto another to such a degree that you do away with Torah study and Divine service altogether. The factor to use in differentiating between the two types of concern is the one used by our sages when they said (*Pesachim* 8b), "Things are different where there is a possibility of danger." In other words, you must be cautious in a situation where threat is known of or obvious, but where that is not the case you do not need to be cautious.

Our sages said about such instances (*Chullin* 56b), "We do not assume a cause for suspicion when we do not see one"; as well as (*Baba Batra* 131a), "A sage should assume nothing but what he sees with his own eyes." This is also the essence of the quote from the Torah we mentioned earlier, that "a clever man sees evil and he hides." It is referring to hiding from the evil he sees—not from what *might* possibly happen.

This truly refers as well to what we quoted earlier on, that "the lazy man says, 'There's a lion on the road.'" Our sages bluntly interpreted this to be pointing out how unnecessary concern even holds a person back from doing righteous deeds. They said (*Devarim Rabbah* 8:7), "Solomon said seven things about a lazy person: Were people to tell him, 'Your Rabbi is in town and you should go learn Torah from him,' he would say, 'I'm afraid there may be a lion on the road.' Were they to say, 'Your Rabbi is in the vicinity,' he would say, 'I'm afraid that there might be a lion in the streets.' And were they to say, 'He's in your house,' he would say, 'If I would go to

---

5. This comes to teach us that the reason why there are harmful things in this world is so that the evil might be punished with them, even though these same harmful things can be dangerous to those who guard themselves properly.

Both of these acts—accustoming yourself along a certain path, and being on guard—require you to be "sensible and straightforwardly" logical, and require conscious effort and toil from you. And they alone will have the innocent avert harm. After all, "one who does not want to go along the ways of wisdom and is willing to expose himself to danger is not practicing trust in God—he is naive. . . ."

him I would find the door locked, and so forth.'" This comes to teach you that your worry does not cause laziness, but rather laziness causes you to worry.

Everyday experience attests to all this, and it is clear and widely known to the vast majority of people that this is the way of the ignorant. The thinking person should arrive at the truth and a clear understanding easily.

I have already explained the subject of enthusiasm in a manner I would consider to be sufficient to encourage you. The wise will be further wisened and will take in what they can. It is only right that enthusiasm should follow caution, for all in all a person cannot be enthusiastic if he was not first cautious. Someone who has not set it in his heart to be cautious in his actions, and to reflect upon service to God and its principles—which constitutes the trait of caution, as we have already said—will find it hard to be both enveloped by love and longing for Divine service and enthused with a yearning for his Creator. Such a person is still stuck in the attractions of the physical world and goes about doing the very things that just naturally keep him away from all this.

But in truth, after you will have opened your eyes to take a look at your actions and to be cautious in them, and to reckon the worth of *mitzvot* versus sins, as was mentioned, you will find it easy to keep from doing bad and you will yearn for and be enthusiastic about the good instead. This is clear.

Summation of Part III

Chapter 6

1. Enthusiasm is a conscientious and determined eagerness to do *mitzvot*.

2. You must be well motivated, enthusiastic, and strong to be successful in your Divine service, as we are by nature burdened with a corporeality and materiality that does not make it easy.

3. Laziness is the opposite of enthusiasm. Great loss, even harm, comes about because of it, though the lazy person may not intend it. The harmful results of laziness come about slowly and without notice, so that you suddenly find yourself steeped in it.

4. The lazy person is full of excuses and rationalizations for his ways. He will cite Torah, Talmud, and anything else to excuse himself. Inevitably he comes to be unable to hear the advice of others. As it is written (Proverbs 26:16), "A lazy man is more sagacious in his own eyes than seven people who can give sensible answers."

Chapter 7

5. In order to foster enthusiasm you should hurry to do a *mitzvah* as soon as it is made available to you, and hurry to complete it. One who is caught in the spirit and charge of service to God does not lack for enthusiasm.

6. While enthusiasm is the natural outcome of an inner incandescence, it can both instigate such an inner incandescence and *be* instigated as well. It is within your powers to do that. All you need do is *act* enthusiastic and it will eventually become second nature to you, as the external arouses the internal.

Chapter 8

7. Another way of acquiring enthusiasm is by recognizing the great good that God does for you moment by moment. There is not a person, rich or poor, healthy or ill, who is not the recipient of much of God's goodness and shelter.

Chapter 9

8. There are three things that especially cause the loss of enthusiasm: the desire for relaxation, an aversion to inconvenience, and an overlove of pleasure. Someone of that nature would certainly not be enthusiastic about going out of his way to do something required of him.

9. To counter such a leaning it is important to come to know that we were not placed in this world for relaxation, but rather for effort and toil. With this in mind, when you are asked to do something you will find it easy to do it, as you will be prepared for anything.

10. What also discourages the garnering of enthusiasm is overconcern for temporal things. To counter such a leaning it is important to come to know that while we are only passing through this world, our service to God is permanent. Trust in God in a sensible way (that is to say, do not take uncalled for chances), and do not dwell upon matters of this world.

11. In truth, it is only logical that someone would be cautious before he can be enthusiastic. And you will find that it is easy to be enthusiastic if you will first reflect upon your actions and then consider the full worth of *mitzvot*, which is the gist of caution.

IV

INNOCENCE

Introduction to Part IV

The fourth part comprises three chapters (10–12) and concerns itself with the trait of "innocence." The chapters are entitled "An Explanation of the Trait of Innocence" (chap. 10), "Aspects of the Trait of Innocence" (chap. 11), and "The Means of Acquiring Innocence" (chap. 12).

The excursions Luzzatto takes in this part (and there are very many—especially in chap. 11) include ruminations about a large number of forbidden acts and traits we must all be free of if we are to be "innocent," as well as a number of other concerns.

They include: the seduction of the heart, clouded vision, the removal of mortal desires from the heart, meticulous moral scrutiny (chap. 10); thievery (on the job, in advertising, unconscious thievery, in the form of deceit in weights and measures, and in usury), promiscuity (in open illicit sexuality, in more socially acceptable illicit sexuality, in profanity, and in fantasizing), unkosher foods (why they are desirous, and what they do to the spirit), perverse interpersonal relations (including verbal abuse, purposely ill-advising, tale-bearing and slander, hate and revenge, grudge-bearing, vain oaths, lying, desecrating God's name, and conducting business on the *Shabbat*), arrogance (with its various subdivisions and motivations, and its tenuous relationship with false modesty), anger (with its various subdivisions and motivations, and how to avoid it), jealousy (the foolish and shortsighted nature of it), and coveting or desiring (possessions or personal glory) (chap. 11); as well as study as a means of meticulousness and expertise (chap. 12).

Herein begins a more difficult and sublime part of the book. The expectations thus far have been reasonable, civil and the least to be expected of a Jew. From here on in begin the expectations of deeper, fuller and more pious changes. That is evidenced right off by the statement in the tenth chapter that, "only someone who has been thoroughly cleansed of all the nagging remnants of sin and transgression (which for the most part is the requirement for innocence) is *fitting to see the face of the King, God.*"

"Innocence" is not defined in the body of the part, but we may infer its meaning. The term for it is *nekiyut*, which can be translated either as innocence or cleanliness, clarity, bareness, expiation, and dignity or respectability (see *Sifra* on *Kedoshim* 4:2). As such it implies a certain freedom from things (transgressions), and a regality that comes with purity of self.

It does not carry with it the negative connotations of helplessness, ignorance, artlessness, or naivete. In fact, it is based on power, knowledge, skill, and cunning.

Included in this part is another caveat. In the tenth chapter it is written: "In truth it is very difficult to foster this trait. Our natures are weak, our hearts are easily swayed, and we allow ourselves things which bring us to error." But feelings of hopelessness that may come about because of that warning are done away with practical instructions as to *how* this trait can be acquired, at the end of the twelfth chapter.

10

An Explanation
of the Trait of Innocence

The trait of innocence is obtained when you are utterly free from all bad traits and sins—not only obvious, well-known sins, but also those the heart is often seduced into believing are not sins but which prove to be so upon reflection.[1] (This seduction

---

1. How can anyone be "utterly free from all bad traits and sins" when it is written (1 Kings 8:46), "There is no man that does not sin" and, as Luzzatto notes later on in the chapter, the Talmud tells us that (*Baba Batra* 165a) "all (people) succumb to some small measure of slander"?

We can only come to the answer to that when we reflect upon *The Path of the Just* as a whole. To this point we have discussed two traits: caution and enthusiasm. They are two sides of the same coin and fairly easy to come to. After all, it is certainly within the realm of the possible to reflect upon our ways and inclinations, change them when they are off-course, and bolster them when they are on-course.

But from this point of the book onward we start to approach the transcendental. This part (very nearly there, but not quite) would involve us in meticulous extrication of subtle things through crisp and directed insight, and through the ruthless doing away with our rationalizations for them. Mention is made of the difficulty of the task, comparisons are made with the state of the angels, and we apparently have to be assured at the end of the part that we can do it.

The next part, abstinence, the other side of innocence's coin, draws closer to that transcendence, because it is "the beginning of saintliness" (chap. 13). Its bywords are those of our sages, which read (*Yevamot* 20a): "Sanctify yourself through those things permitted to you," and it involves avoiding all things—even those the Torah permits—which may cause bad to come about (even if there is no bad whatsoever connected with them at the time). As such, it is concerned overall with doing more than what the law of the Torah would minimally demand, and striving for a blemishless relationship with God's world.

After this begins the part of the book that *is* transcendental, and that addresses the one who wants to be holy. To this point we have met with reasonable though uncommon de-

comes about as a result of the heart still being affected by physical desires. Because it has not been completely purified it is drawn into seeing certain things as being permitted which are not.)[2]

---

mands; henceforth we meet with the lofty and angelic. To now we have been asked to face ourselves and our errors and have been made to own up to our pettinesses; from now on we are past that and come full-face with the boundless soul. Only those deepest and grandest parts of ourselves that truly yearn for delight in God and for a view of the Divine Countenance are addressed now.

Luzzatto had a right to demand our cooperation to this point because the Torah demands it of us. From now on he does not have that right. We now enter into the realm of a "volunteer corps" of sorts. The "corps" devolves around the acquisition of the following traits: purity, piety, humility, fear of sin, holiness, Holy Inspiration, and Resurrection of the Dead. Come see what is asked of a member of this corps.

Purity concerns itself with "purify(ing) your heart and mind so that even that small bit of pleasure that you take from the world will not be taken with the intention of enjoying pleasure or fulfilling desire . . . (but only) for the good that will result from it in terms of wisdom and Divine service" (chap. 16). This obviously speaks of a selfless and God-focused relationship to the world which is not everyone's path.

Piety goes further along in that vein, demanding an active and enthusiastic compassion for all, and an open and nearly indiscriminate willingness to do good (chap. 19). This trait far bypasses personal growth and calls for a change of essential self.

Humility follows that same train of thought (change of essential self), and requires (chap. 22) "that you should not consider your own needs for whatever reason whatsoever." Taken in another light, it can be seen as an unhealthy sort of demand. But taken as the next step in the process of ultimate Godliness it is starkly logical and frankly saintly.

Fear of sin discusses the sort of person who intimately and engrossingly senses the presence of God in this world and is affected by that in all ways.

And holiness addresses (chap. 26) "those who constantly attach themselves to God" and who are "'walking before God in the land of the living' while they are in this world."

As we are told (chap. 26) "from there you can grow to an even higher level, 'Holy Inspiration,' where your intellect will rise above all human capabilities. That will allow you to enjoy a yet higher form of attachment to God. Then the keys to the 'Resurrection of the Dead' will be passed on to you. . . ." This is by far the ultimate in human attainments.

So, to come back to the subject at hand, when Luzzatto tells us here, at innocence, that we must be "utterly free from all bad traits and sins" we are not to take that literally. We know that to be true for several reasons. First off, it is too soon for that—there is so much more to be wrestled with in our journey and we cannot be expected to be free of all sin just yet. Also, Luzzatto has already written at the beginning of chap. 3, "you should delve deeply into all of your actions and examine all your ways and not leave yourself with bad habits or traits, *or, certainly, sins or transgressions.*" We know we are not to assume that all of us will attain this because later on in this chapter he says that "great effort is required to reach the ultimate in this trait (innocence)," and what could be more ultimate than doing away with *all* sin and *all* bad traits?

How can we even be expected to do away with sin later on, you might ask, taken the aforementioned statements (1 Kings 8:46), "There is no man that does not sin" and (*Baba*

The vision of the person who is thoroughly purified from this affliction—cleansed from any tinge of bad that physical desires might have left behind—is utterly clear, and his sense of discrimination is sharpened. His longings are not directed toward anything material. Should he at all sin he would recognize it as being bad and separate from it.[3] Our sages referred to these spiritually whole people who would so purify their actions that there could not be found even a nagging remnant of bad as "Jerusalem's innocent of understanding" (*Sanhedrin* 23a).

You can see now the difference between caution and innocence. For even though they are similar, they are different. The person who is cautious is cautious in his actions and sees to it that he does not sin where sin is clear and obvious to all. But he still has not mastered himself. His heart would naturally be drawn to or tempted by things whose bad qualities are not quite so obvious. Though he may try to conquer his *yetzer hara* and subdue his desires, he will not have succeeded in changing his nature or removing physical desires from his heart. He will have managed to overpower them and to go in the ways of wisdom instead, but they would continue to do all they could to dissuade and undermine him.[4]

First you must earnestly accustom yourself to be enthusiastic until you are cleansed from obvious sins, then further accustom yourself in Divine service and strengthen your love and desire for God. Force of habit in that will separate you from all mundane things, and see to it that your mind will take hold of true wholeness of spirit. In the end you will be able to obtain complete innocence, and what would have been the fire of physical desires would be extinguished by the strengthening of Godly desire.[5] Only then will your sight be clear and refined, as referred to above,

---

Batra 165a), "all (people) succumb to some small measure of slander"? The answer would have to be that since one who is innocent may yet err and consequently sin, "innocence" is the *desire* to do what is right.

We have a long way to go in the fulfillment of this book's promise of holiness and saintliness, *and we are under no halachic obligation to fulfill it.* (And that must be kept in mind at all times from now on.) But even if we will have not proven worthy of following the journey to its completion, we will have gone a long way in living up to our true selves and will have gained insight into the might and power of our holy ones. That is no small feat and brings glory and majesty into our lives in its own right.

2. A seduction is the powerful drawing of someone toward something. Everything is capable of seducing someone toward it—if that person is inclined toward that thing in the first place. So it is not surprising that someone whose heart is still affected by physical desires would be drawn toward more such things. The secret is to have the heart drawn toward higher-than-physical desires, and it will just naturally be "seduced" by those higher things.

3. That is to say, should he at all sin he would recognize it *for what it is* and separate from it.

4. The cautious person would have won a battle, or even a whole slew of them, but he would not have managed to win the war. The innocent would have won the war.

5. . . . what would have been the fire of physical desires would be *replaced* by the strengthening of Godly desire after you will have gone through this process.

and you will not be undermined or even approached by the darkness of physicality. Your actions will be cleansed of it all.

King David was pleased to find this trait in himself. He said (Psalms 26:6): "I will wash my hands in innocence and go round the Tabernacle of God." In truth, only someone who has been thoroughly cleansed of all the nagging remnants of sin and transgression is fitting to see the face of the King, God. One not so prepared can only be abashed and embarrassed before Him. As Ezra said (Ezra 9:6), "O God, I am abashed and ashamed to lift my face, God, to You."

Great effort is required to reach the ultimate in this trait. Obvious and well-known sins are easy to avoid, as it is clear to all that they are bad; but the kind of meticulous scrutiny required for innocence is difficult. People often rationalize that certain things are permissible when they are not, and that tends to cover over sins, as we said. This is what our sages were referring to when they said (*Avodah Zarah* 18a), "The very sins that people dash under their heels are the ones that surround them at the time of judgment"; as well as (*Baba Batra* 165a), "Most people commit sins of theft, some commit acts of promiscuity, but all succumb to some small measure of slander"—and this is so as a result of the subtle nature of small acts of slander, which causes people to trip over them without recognizing them.

Our sages tell us (Introduction to *Eichah Rabbah* 30) that King David would be careful to thoroughly cleanse himself of all this—so much so that he would go off to war securely, asking of God (Psalms 18:38), "May I chase my enemies and over-take them, and not return until I will have destroyed them?" This is exactly what Yehosophat, Assa, and Chizkiyah could not do, because they were not cleansed from this trait, as David himself pointed out when he said, (Psalms 18:21), "God will reward me according to my righteousness; He will repay me according to the inno-cence of my hands"; as well as (Psalms 18:25), "God will repay me according to my righteousness; according to the innocence of my hands in His eyesight," referring to the aforementioned innocence. Then he goes on to say (Psalms 18:38), "For with You I will run upon a troop. . . . I will chase my enemies and overtake them." And he proclaimed (Psalms 24:3–4), "Who will go up to God's mountain? And who will arise in His holy place?—one of clean hand and pure heart."

In truth it is very difficult to foster this trait. Our natures are weak, our hearts are easily swayed, and we allow ourselves things which bring us to error.[6] But one who does obtain this trait will have reached a very high level, as he will have proven himself to have withstood and been victorious in a mighty war. We will now go on to enunciate the particulars of this trait.

---

6. We find that Luzzatto says at the end of chapter 11, "I cannot deny that there is something of a struggle necessary to go through to obtain this kind of innocence." But he then goes on to tell us how: "set it in your heart to be one of those people who has this good trait . . . (and), with just a little practice, it will come to you with much more ease than you might have imagined."

11

Aspects of the Trait of Innocence

There are many aspects of innocence—as many as there are negative *mitzvot* (365 in number).[1] But in essence, to be innocent is to be cleansed of even the offshoots of sin, as I have already stated.

Even though it is always the *yetzer hara* that has you sin, there are some sins that your personality may be drawn to and would tend to rationalize reasons to allow. It is in those instances that you will especially need help in subduing the *yetzer hara* and in cleansing yourself of sin.

---

1. There are two types of *mitzvot* in the Torah: 248 "positive" and 365 "negative." The positive *mitzvot* (*mitzvot asei*, literally, "do *mitzvot*") are those which we are asked to actively involve ourselves in and accomplish. They include keeping the *Shabbat*, prayer, wearing *tzitzit*, studying Torah, and so forth.

The negative *mitzvot* (*mitzvot lo ta'asei*, literally, "do-not-do *mitzvot*") are things or actions we are asked to stay away from and actively or passively avoid. These include (to use the examples in this chapter) not stealing, not acting licentiously, not eating unkosher food, not engaging in slander or talebearing, and so on.

The point of the positive *mitzvot* is to direct ourselves toward God as much and as often as possible—to busy ourselves with the processes of spiritual evolution and the honing of the soul. The point of the negative *mitzvot* is to keep us away from elements that draw us away from God and debilitate our senses of the holy.

The positive *mitzvot* fall under the rubric of accepting God as our God (the first of the Ten Commandments). We do that by acting in a way that indicates we accept God as our God, that is, we follow His commandments. It is, after all, not enough to claim to believe in God: you have to act on that belief and be changed by it, or else it is not really a belief.

And the negatives fall under the rubric of having no other gods (the second of the Ten Commandments). We refuse to accept other gods by avoiding things which tend to draw us to them in a godlike and nearly all-powerful fashion. These two venues are the essential mother lode elements of all of Torah.

Our sages pointed out (*Makkot* 23b) that "in terms of forbidden acts, people are especially drawn to thievery and promiscuity."[2] Yet we know that most people are not blatantly dishonest. They would not actually reach out and take someone else's money and place it in their pockets. Nevertheless, most people are involved in petty acts of thievery in their business practices by unfairly profiting from others' losses, and they reason that "business is different!"

Many theft-related negative *mitzvot* are stated in the Torah: "Do not steal," "Do not rob," "Do not extort," "Do not lie," "Do not be untruthful with your comrade," "One should not deceive his fellow," and "Do not falsify your neighbor's borders." These sorts of possible thievery cover many daily practices in the business world. And in each and every one there are many prohibitions, for not just the obvious, flagrant violations of extortion or thievery, for example, are forbidden. Things that lead to them are included in the prohibition as well.

Our sages pointed out (*Sanhedrin* 81a) that it is written (Ezekiel 18:6), "He did not make his neighbor's wife impure." That infers, they tell us, that "he did not enter into his friend's line of work." We find (*Baba Metzia* 60a) that Rabbi Yehudah forbad shopkeepers from handing out roasted treats and nuts to children which they used to accustom them to come to their store. The only reason the sages finally allowed it was because the competition could do the same if they wanted to. They also said that (*Baba Batra* 88b) "thievery against people is worse than thievery against the One above." We find (*Berachot* 16a) that they excused those working alongside their employers from taking the time to recite the blessings after meals, and only required them to interrupt their work to say the first paragraph of the *Shema Yisrael.* How much more so, then, does this notion of not taking what is not yours hold true for mundane things!

Workers have to occupy themselves with their assigned tasks exclusively, and if they do not they are considered thieves. Abba Chilkiah would not even return a greeting tended by certain scholars so as not to waste time at his job (*Taanit* 23b). Our father Jacob expressed it best when he explained to Laban (Genesis 31:38–40): ". . . I never took a ram from your flocks as food. I never brought you an animal that had been severed, but rather, I took the blame myself. . . . By day I was consumed by heat, and in the night by frost, when sleep was stolen from my eyes." What can someone who serves his own needs and busies himself with his own affairs when he is on the job say, therefore, other than the truth: that he has done what he wanted to, to his own benefit.

---

2. As Luzzatto points out later in this chapter, thievery and promiscuity (as well as the desire for forbidden foods) are "prohibitions . . . in the realm of coveting what is not your own." That is to say, aside from the harm and tragedy that can come from thievery and promiscuity themselves, the Torah is also concerned with how they indicate a profound and deeply felt dissatisfaction with their perpetrator's own lot in life. Such a dissatisfaction with one's material and familial well-being is woesome and runs counter to the great happiness and acceptance the Torah means to foster.

The principle of the matter is that one who is hired to do something sells his part of the day, as our sages pointed out when they said (*Baba Metzia* 56b), "Being hired is selling yourself for the day." And whatever you take for yourself[3] is taken in thievery, and you are not forgiven by God unless the employer himself forgives you, as "Yom Kippur does not forgive for sins one commits against another unless that person himself forgives," as our sages said (*Yoma* 85b).

Even if you were to do a *mitzvah* when you were supposed to be doing your job it would not be accredited to you as a righteous act, but rather a sin—because a sin is not a *mitzvah*. As the Torah says (Isaiah 61:8), "(God) hates thievery in a burnt offering." In a similar vein our sages said (*Baba Kamma* 94a), "One who steals a measure of wheat, then grinds it, bakes it and pronounces a blessing over it is not blessing God but blaspheming against God, as it is written (Psalms 10:3), 'The thief who blesses blasphemes.'" It is said in such a case, "Woe to the one who makes his defender a prosecutor." In the Jerusalem Talmud (*Sukkah* 3:3) our sages speak about a stolen *lulav*. It is decided there as well that stealing time is as much an act of thievery as is stealing objects. Just as when one steals an object and performs a *mitzvah* with it he turns his best defense into a case against him, when he steals time he does the same.

The Holy One (blessed be He) cares only for honesty. As it is said (Psalms 31:24), "God protects the honest"; (Isaiah 26:2) "Open up, gates, so that a righteous, an honest nation may enter"; (Psalms 101:6) "My eyes are towards the honest of the land, to those who will sit with Me"; and (Jeremiah 5:3) "Are not Your eyes directed towards honesty?"

Job said (Job 31:7), "If my steps have turned out of the way, or my heart has gone after my eyes, or if anything has cleaved to my hands, then let me sow and another eat." Notice how perfect this image is. It equates unintentional thievery with things sticking to the hand: that is, though the person may not willfully set out to take some particular thing, it nonetheless "sticks" to him and comes to be in his possession. In our case as well, though someone may truly not want to steal, he can nevertheless find it very difficult to be completely free of it.

In truth, all this comes about because the eyes have the heart arrive at rationalizations for what it finds attractive and wants instead of the heart being in control of the eyes, so that you are not attracted to others' possessions.[4] Job said that he had not acted so, that his heart was not drawn after his eyes—that was why nothing "stuck to his palms."

---

3. That is, whether it is time or property (cf. statement from the Jerusalem Talmud, *Sukkah* 3:3, in the following paragraph).

4. The eye takes things in in wonder and love. It latches onto a thing's essential loveliness and allure and wants for nothing else—at the moment. The heart craves essential loveliness and allure just as strongly but, though blind and dependent upon the eye, it is sensitive to the danger of stupefaction brought on by certain quite lovely and alluring things, so it often rejects the eye's yearnings. But it so loves the eye it can be talked out of its inclinations toward wisdom and discrimination. The point is to have the eye take in and record, and then have the heart decide.

Let us consider deceit.

It is so easy to fool yourself and stumble in this. You might think it is only right for example to make a product you are selling to a customer as attractive as possible so you could profit from your work, and to speak cunningly and enticingly to him so that he would want it. After all, have not our sages themselves pointed out that (*Pesachim* 50b) "It is an enthusiastic salesman who will sell, as it is written (Proverbs 10:4), 'The hand of the diligent will grow wealthy'"?

But if you do not fully reflect upon or are not conscious of your deeds, you might pick a thorn when you mean to get wheat—that is, you might inadvertently sin and stumble in matters of deceit. We have already been warned by the Torah (Leviticus 25:17) to "let no man deceive his fellow," to which our sages have added (*Chullin* 94a) that it is forbidden to fool a non-Jew as well.

The Prophet says (Zephaniah 3:13), "The remnant of Israel will not do iniquity, will not speak falsely, and no trickery will be found in their mouths." Our sages warned us (*Baba Metzia* 60a) not to paint over old wares to make them like new, and to "not mix together different bunches of fruit—even new fruit with other new fruit; even high priced with low so as to sell the higher priced for less," for (Deuteronomy 25:16) "whoever does this is guilty of iniquity" and is called five things (*Sifra* 19:35): wrong, hateful, abominable, unbearable, and reprehensible. Our sages added that (*Baba Kamma* 119a) "one who steals even a minute amount from his neighbor is likened to one who has taken his life from him," indicating the severity of even a minor act of thievery. They also said (*Taanit* 7b) "the only reason rain is withheld from the world is because of acts of thievery"; and (*Vayikra Rabbah* 33:3) "what testifies against you first out of a load of your transgressions?—thievery"; and (*Sanhedrin* 108a) "The judgment against the generation of the flood was what it was because of their thievery."

You may be saying, "How can I not try to point out the value of my product to my customers?" You should know that there is a difference between pointing out the true value, worth, or beauty of a product—which is a perfectly honest and honorable action—and covering over the product's imperfections, which is deceitful, and therefore forbidden. This is a major principle in honest business practice.

Needless to say this refers as well to the matter of honest weights and measures. The Torah clearly states that (Deuteronomy 25:16), "All who do these things are an abomination to God." Our sages said (*Baba Batra* 88b), "The punishment for dishonesty in weights and measures is more severe than that for promiscuity." And they have demanded (*Baba Batra* 71a) that the wholesaler clean his scales once in thirty days so that he might not unwittingly cheat his customers and have to be punished. All the more so is this true in the case of the great sin of loaning money on interest, which is likened to denying the existence of the God of Israel, God forbid.

Our sages said about the verse which reads (Ezekiel 18:13), "He has given out money on interest, and has accepted increase; shall he then live? He shall not live!" that it means to say that such a person will not arise at the time of the resurrection of the dead (*Shemot Rabbah* 31:6). Both he and his dust are abhorrent and abominable in the eyes of God. I see no need to expand on this; the dread of it already rests upon the hearts of all Jews.

The point is that the stumbling blocks on the path to them are as numerous as the yearnings for possessions.[5] Great and profound self-reflection is required to actually free yourself of it.

You should know that if you do free yourself of it, you have reached a very great level. Many have attained various of the many levels of righteousness and have not been able to abhor unjust gain. Tsopher the Namasite referred to this when he said to Job (Job 11:14), "If there is iniquity in your hand, put it far away: do not allow wickedness to dwell in your tents. Then you shall surely remove yourself from blemish, you will be steadfast, and you will not fear anything."

Up to now I have spoken about the particulars of just one of the *mitzvot*. I could certainly analyze the rest of the *mitzvot* the same way, but I will only do so for those which people are most likely to have their failings in.

Let us speak now about promiscuity, which is second only to thievery in the degree to which people transgress against it, as our sages indicated when they said (*Baba Batra* 165a), "Most people commit sins of theft, and some commit sins of promiscuity. . . ." No small amount of effort is required if you want to be thoroughly innocent of this transgression, because not only is the act itself forbidden, but actions related to it are forbidden as well.

The Torah clearly says (Leviticus 18:6), "Do not come close to uncovering nakedness." Our sages said (*Shemot Rabbah* 16b), "The Holy One (blessed be He) warned, 'Do not say that since it is forbidden to have illicit relations with this woman you will just hold onto her and you will not be committing a sin; or you will just hug her or kiss her, and you will not have committed a sin.' The Holy One (blessed be He) said, 'Just as if you had vowed to be a *Nazir*, disallowing wine for yourself, and it then became forbidden for you by the Torah to eat grapes and raisins and to drink grape juice, as well as all other products of the grapevine—so too may you not even *touch* a woman who is not your wife. And whoever does brings an early death upon himself. . . .'"

How profound this statement is when it compares the prohibition of illicit sexual relationships to the *Nazir*. For even though the main thing forbidden to the *Nazir* is the drinking of wine, the Torah itself explicitly forbids him all things connected with it. This principle was handed down to the sages to teach them how to build "protective hedges" that insure the keeping of the Torah. They learned from the *Nazir* to forbid all things equivalent to the main prohibition. The Torah taught this principle through the *mitzvah* of the *Nazir* to have the sages apply it to the other *mitzvot* and

---

5. Each yearning for an unneeded possession is an instance of being drawn from the dream of getting closer to God, and a flirtation, as well as another sign of essential dissatisfaction (see n. 2 above). Each instant of it is fraught with possible danger and strewn with stumbling blocks along the way.

to show that this is the will of God. And it did this by stating the prohibition to us outright along with its offshoots so that they would know how to infer further prohibitions from stated ones.[6]

In this case, the tradition forbids illicit intimacy and all other such things however they may be found—tactilely, through sight, speech, and hearing, or in thought. I will now bring you words of proof for all of these with statements of the sages.

Tactilely involves light physical contact or hugging, and so forth. We have already explained this above, and we do not have to say anything further.

In terms of seeing—our sages said (*Berachot* 61a), "It is written (Proverbs 11:21), 'Those who join hands for wicked ends shall not go unpunished'—that is to say, all shopkeepers who go out of their way to dispense change to women customers to stare at them shall not go unpunished in the judgments of *Gehinom.*"

---

6. It says in the Torah (Numbers 6:2–4): "When a man or a woman will clearly utter the vow of a *Nazir* to consecrate themselves to God, they must abstain from wine and wine-brandy and they shall drink no juices of the grape or eat any grapes or raisins. All the days of their being a *Nazir* they may not eat anything of the grapevine, the pressed grape or the grape-stone."

The fundamental thing to be avoided is wine, but the Torah itself forbids all things connected in any way with wine to insure that the *Nazir* will not inadvertently come to drink wine. Such a process of insurance is called a "protective fence" around the originally prohibited act. This system of insurance was passed on to the sages, and they used it liberally and wisely to guarantee the avoidance of transgression.

It has often been said that the sages went too far and out of the bounds of reasonableness when they put up so many "protective fences" around fundamental prohibitions. But it must be understood that nothing was more precious to the sages than the keeping of the Torah and whatever would protect it would be desirable although sometimes obtrusive.

Our age recognizes that what is valuable has to be safeguarded. That certainly seems reasonable. Does it have to be said that if you own valuable jewelry you should not leave it unprotected? Of course not. Everyone would at least put it in a protective case. In fact, most would be sure that the case would be locked—though that would call for putting yourself out by having to have the key on hand or getting it from its place. Others would go so far as to have the case placed in a strongbox itself, perhaps in a bank. And they would be perfectly willing to pay for that privilege and inconvenience themselves so much as to have to come to the bank, get to the vault, pass by the armed security officer, show their identification, search for their special key, work at the lock on the vault containing the jewelry box, then search for that box's key until they would finally come to take out their jewelry—and would not in the least consider the process to be either cumbersome or demanding, but would rather think it wise and even pro forma. "After all," they would reason, "my jewelry is worth that much to me, and I wouldn't want to lose it. The whole process is a small price to pay for peace of mind."

And would we laugh at them and call them unreasonable? Would we snicker and assume their jewelry could be perfectly safe at home, on the table? Of course not. The laws of the Torah were that precious and beloved by the sages, and they often went out of their way to protect them.

They asked (*Shabbat* 64a) why the Jews of a particular generation especially needed forgiveness, and answered that it was because their eyes strayed licentiously. Rav Sheshet asked (*Berachot* 24a) why the Torah discusses underclothing along with outerwear when it says (Numbers 31:50): "We have therefore brought an offering for God—what every man has gotten of jewels of gold, chains and bracelets, rings, earrings as well as girdles . . ." and answered that it was to teach you that whoever stares at even the little finger of a woman is likened to one who stares at her private parts.

The sages said further (*Avodah Zarah* 20a), "It is written (Deuteronomy 23:10), 'And you shall guard yourself from any evil'—this means to say that a man should not stare at an attractive woman, even if she is unmarried; nor at a married woman even if she is ugly."[7]

In terms of speech with a woman—we find it explicitly stated (*Avot* 1:5) "whoever overinvolves himself in small talk with his wife brings bad upon himself."[8]

---

7. The operative terms in this injunction are "stare" or "stray licentiously." What Luzzatto is pointing to here is that each of the five senses is capable of holiness and great physical communion with the Divine. Were it not for our sight, for example, we could not notice the great wonders and patterns God has us enjoy in His world; were it not for our hearing we would never sense the grand and lovely tumult of it all, and so on for all of our senses.

But, like all things connected with the world, our senses are capable of gross error and avoidance of the holy. The same sense that can acknowledge the presence of God in the world of matter can nullify that presence by overlooking or misreading it, and the Torah is only too well aware of that.

There is nothing inherently wrong with citing the beauty of another person. In fact, according to the *Halachah* you should see for yourself whether the person you might want to marry is attractive enough for your tastes. And wedding guests are encouraged to notice the bride's beauty at her wedding, to compliment her to the groom. We are to notice beauty in all aspects of the world and bless God for it.

But when you *stare* or have your eyes *stray licentiously*—that is to say, when you finish noticing God-given beauty and cross over the line to fantasizing about it—you will assuredly bring yourself to thoughts unbecoming a person of God, and will no longer notice the Source of that beauty so much as "ingest" the object itself.

8. The operative terms in this injunction are "overinvolvement" and "small talk." Needless to say (or perhaps not!) this is not saying that man and wife should not speak or be intimate. In fact it indicates the fact that the sages recommend the power of speech to arouse and move to action.

What it is saying is that man and wife should not waste each other's precious time in this world by chatting about things of no consequence and in this way overlooking each other's true self. Talk between husband and wife or others is healthy and vital, and to be encouraged. "Small talk," however, is often—but not always—avoidance and pettiness. Sometimes it can be healthy as well, and the verbal equivalent of a good dessert, that is, it adds a certain flavor and can be relaxing and intimate in a positive sense, and can restore your "batteries" for your Divine service. Too much small talk, however, is never good and always tends toward escapism and bringing bad upon yourself.

And in terms of the sense of hearing our sages said (*Berachot* 24a), "A woman's singing voice is considered nakedness."[9]

Our sages screeched like cranes about the promiscuous use of lips and ears, that is, speaking or listening to profanity. In the Jerusalem Talmud (*Terumot* 1:4) they observed that it is written (Deuteronomy 23:15), "Your campsites shall be holy so that God will see no unclean thing (*ervat davar*) amongst you and turn away from you." This, they say, refers to unclean speech (*ervat dibur*), profanity. They stated that (*Shabbat* 33a) "Troubles reappear and death (God forbid) comes to the young men of Israel because of the sin of profanity"; that (*Shabbat* 33a), "All who speak profanely deepen *Gehinom* for themselves"; that (*Shabbat* 33a), "Everybody knows why a bride gets married,[10] but anyone who utters profanity enunciating it can turn around even a judgment of seventy good years to bad"; and that (*Chagigah* 5b), "Even the small talk that goes on between a husband and his wife is related back at the time of judgment." They said about listening to this evil that (*Shabbat* 33a) "even the one who hears and remains silent (suffers), as it is written (Proverbs 22:14), 'The mouth of a prostitute is a deep pit; he who incurs God's indignation will fall therein.'"

So we see that all of our senses need to be innocent of licentiousness and matters associated with it.

If someone comes to confound you saying that when the Torah speaks against profanity it is only doing so to frighten and draw a person away from an actual sin, and that the prohibition is for the more "hot-blooded" type of person who might be brought to desire by his speech, but that someone who uses it as a joke does not have to worry about it—you should tell that person that what they are doing is speaking for the *yetzer hara*. The sages quoted a verse from the Torah that explicitly says other than what that person is saying. It says (Isaiah 9:16), "Therefore God shall have no joy in their young men, neither shall He have mercy on their fatherless or widowed: for everyone is a flatterer and a talebearer, and every mouth speaks obscenity." Notice that the passage says nothing about idol worshipping, outright licentiousness, or murder, but only flattery, talebearing, and obscenity. All of these are speech-related sins, and as a result of them a decree was made in Heaven that "God shall have no joy in their young men, neither shall He have mercy on their fatherless or widowed."

---

9. The idea that a woman should not sing to men other than her husband is often misunderstood or rejected, and calls for explanation.

It must be understood that a warning against something recognizes that thing's power and allure, whereas a lack of warning does not take its being seriously. A singing voice is the very tone and rhythm of the self expressed. Sensitive enough to it, a person could read the singer's heart and realize his or her being through their voice. The Torah teaches that that is especially so in the case of a *woman*'s voice, and that it is all a very intimate and sensual matter which should only be experienced by the woman's husband. It takes measures to prohibit others from that experience.

10. That is, everyone knows about the inherent sexuality of the situation.

The fact of the matter is that obscenity is truly the promiscuity of the power of speech, as our sages observed. It was forbidden because it, like other things like it, is within the category of licentiousness. And while these things do not carry with them the punishment of the soul being cut off from eternity, they are forbidden in their own right (aside from the reason that they cause the essential prohibition to come about, as we saw in the example of the *Nazir* above).

In terms of thought—we have already mentioned in the beginning of our *beraita* when the Torah says (Deuteronomy 23:10), "And you shall guard yourself from any evil," it means "a man should not think lewd thoughts in the daytime . . ." (*Avodah Zarah* 20b). Our sages said (*Yoma* 29a), "Thoughts of sin are worse than sins themselves," and based it upon the statement which reads (Proverbs 15:26), "Evil thoughts are an abomination to God."[11]

We have spoken thus far about the two most serious prohibitions people are likely to stumble in the details of, both because there are so many of them, and also because the heart is so often inclined in the direction of these desires.

The third category of prohibitions we will be addressing in the realm of coveting—after thievery and promiscuity—is forbidden food.[12] This includes foods that are inherently forbidden, those that are forbidden because they are accidently combined with forbidden food, mixtures of meat and dairy, forbidden fats, blood, meals cooked by non-Jews, utensils owned by non-Jews, and sacramental versus ordinary wines.

---

11. Essentially, we are souls encased. The casing, our bodies and personalities, obviously enjoys the benefit of exercise and challenge. The soul enjoys the same benefit, but not as obviously, and completely differently. The soul exercises and is challenged through the mind. In fact, the mind (not the brain, which is an organ and as physical as the rest of them) *is* the soul, but the aspect of it that is the least subtle and most manifest and the one that can evidence itself most clearly.

When you reflect or ruminate, that essential part of yourself which is your soul as your mind exercises and challenges itself—and evidences itself as well. That is, the essential self comes out through the mind and stands open to the world. At that moment it is no longer encased, but is free—and vulnerable.

So when you think un-Godly thoughts—thoughts that run counter to your true self's being—you seriously affect your unencased and raw soul. You certainly affect it when you *act* un-Godly, and seriously so as well, but not as starkly, because it is less vulnerable then.

So the central idea is that you can actually do more harm to your soul by thinking bad thoughts when you affect the core than you can by acting out on them.

12. What underlies this statement is the notion that one of the reasons Jews are forbidden to have certain foods is because they are simply not "our foods," and we are in general not to covet things that are not ours, as the last of the Ten Commandments tells us.

The tradition does not have to say why those things are not our foods (it doesn't much matter in the long run) any more than it says why Adam and Eve were not to eat from the Tree of Knowledge of Good and Evil. The fact remains that we are not to eat those particular foods, and we are not to covet others for their permission to eat them any more than we are to covet them for what God has given them as their portion in other areas of human experience.

Great care and determination are required to stay innocent in these matters, because the heart is easily drawn to good food, and there is often monetary loss in the accidental mixing of forbidden and permitted foods. As is known and taught in the books of the rabbis, the laws in these matters are numerous, and all who are lenient in their observance of them where the rabbis advise to be stringent are destroying their souls. The *Sifra* (*Shemini*) quotes Leviticus 11:43, where it is written: "Do not make yourselves unclean with them, that you should not be defiled by them," and explains, "If you will make yourselves unclean with them, in the end you will be defiled by them."

What they mean to say is forbidden foods actually cause spiritually unclean elements to enter into your heart and spirit, and the Holiness of God is removed and drawn away from you.[13] Our sages also said (*Yoma* 39a), "'And you will be defiled (*nitmaytem*) by them' should be understood as 'and you will be stupefied (*nitamtem*) by them'"—the sin will stupefy your mind: the true knowledge and sense of understanding God gives to His holy ones (cf. Proverbs 2:6, "For God will give wisdom") will be withheld from you. You will instead remain animal-like and of-the-earth, stuck in the coarseness of this world. This is more so for forbidden foods than for other prohibited things because they enter into your body and become your very flesh.

In order to let you know that not only the inherently forbidden animals and reptiles are defiling, but also those animals that are usually permitted but become forbidden for one reason or another, our sages quote the statement (Leviticus 11:47), ". . . to distinguish between the impure and the pure," and they explain that (*Sifra*, Leviticus 11:47) "it is not necessary for the Torah to spell out the need to distinguish between a donkey (which is forbidden) and a cow (which is permitted), so why does the Torah differentiate between the impure and the pure? So as to teach you that you must distinguish between what is pure and impure to you—between the animal whose windpipe is fully severed (making it permissible) and the one whose windpipe is only partially severed (making it forbidden). And what is the difference between 'partially' and 'fully' severed?—a hairsbreadth." And they use the phrase, "and what is the difference between 'partially'. . ." to teach you how wondrous the power of the *mitzvot* are—that a hairsbreadth makes the difference between impure and pure.

A thinking person would consider forbidden foods poisoned or mixed with poison. If you were sure or even suspected that some food was poisoned, would you eat it? Certainly not. You would be considered a fool if you did. That is how it should be with forbidden foods, which as we have explained are poisons to the heart and soul. What thinking person would be casual about forbidden foods when there is reason to be suspicious? It is asked (Proverbs 23:2), "Would you place a knife to your throat if you had any sense at all?"

---

13. The body can only take in a finite amount of matter (material or otherwise). This comes to say that you can choose to allow God's holiness to enter and fill you, or you can allow the unclean to. But the more you allow holiness to enter, the less room there is for the unclean, and vice versa.

Let us speak now about those sins that often come about in human interaction, such as verbal abuse, embarrassing or deceiving others, talebearing, hate, revenge, oaths, lies, and desecration of the Divine Name. Who can honestly say, "Oh, I'm innocent of that; I'm blameless as far as that's concerned"? The offshoots of those traits are very great and very subtle, and caution in them requires great effort.

In general, verbal abuse refers to speaking to someone in private in an abusive manner and shaming him. Or, in a more serious vein, shaming someone in public, or doing something which would cause someone shame. This is what our sages were referring to (*Baba Metzia* 58b) when they warned us that if someone you know has repented of his ways, "Do not say to him, 'Remember how you used to be. . . ,'" or if someone you know is ill, do not say as Job's friends said to him (Job 4:7): "Just try to remember—have the innocent ever perished; or, wherever were there upright who were cut off?" If donkey-drivers were to ask you for grain, they told us, do not say to them, "Go to so-and-so—he sells grain," knowing that he never sold grain in his life.

The sages said that (*Baba Metzia* 58b) "verbal abuse is worse than monetary abuse." How much more is this true if it is done in public! It explicitly says (*Avot* 3:11) "One who shamefaces his friend in public has no place in the World to Come." Rabbi Chisda said (*Baba Metzia* 59a), "All gates of prayer are closed except those reserved for the verbally abused." Rabbi Elazar said (*Baba Metzia* 59a) "The Holy One (blessed be He) demands retribution from all through his messengers but the verbally abused." And it has been said (*Baba Metzia* 59a) that there are three sins before which Heaven's curtains can never be shut, and one of them is verbal abuse.

Even in regard to abusive language for the sake of a *mitzvah*, while the Torah says (Leviticus 19:17) "You must admonish your neighbor," our sages warn (*Arachin* 16b), "You might think that this would allow you to cause him to blush. But the Torah continues with, 'And do not bear a sin because of him.'" From all of these sayings you can see how far the warnings against this trait go and how great is the punishment for it.

In regard to deceiving someone by giving him bad advice, we learn (*Torat Kohanim*) that "When the Torah says (Leviticus 19:14), 'Do not place a stumbling block before the blind' it refers to placing a figurative 'stumbling block' before someone 'blind' to anything. Should someone ask you if a particular woman would be permitted to marry a *Kohen*, do not tell him that she would be when she would not. And should someone come to you for advice, do not give him advice that is not right for him. . . . Do not advise someone to sell his property so that he might, for example, buy a donkey, and then go behind his back and buy the property yourself. And should you reason that, after all, you are still giving him good advice—in your heart you know the truth. As the verse concludes, 'And you must fear your Lord.'" The point is, whether you are going to benefit by the outcome or not, it is your duty to pass on the clear and unadulterated truth to whoever might come to you for advice.

But just see how deeply the Torah penetrates into the recesses of a deceitful person's mind. We are not concerned here with the words of an idiot, whose advice is clearly and obviously bad, but rather with the words of a schemer. By all appearances the advice is only in the interests of the person to whom it is directed, but in fact it is to his disadvantage and to the advantage of the schemer. Therefore it says, "And should you reason that, after all, you are still giving him good advice—in your heart you know the truth. . . ."

How many people stumble in this matter every day because they are drawn to and follow the strong urge for profit. The Torah enunciated the severe punishment for this trait when it said (Deuteronomy 27:18), "Cursed is he who misdirects the blind upon the path."

The honest man's duty when someone comes to him for advice is to offer the advice that he would give himself, and for no other reason than for the good of the person asking for it, not for any ulterior motive, no matter how likely or unlikely it may be. If by giving out such advice you might harm yourself, you should point that out. If pointing it out will be useless, simply do not give the advice.

But in any case, do not give advice that will be to the detriment of its receiver. But if *his* intentions are for bad, it is certainly a *mitzvah* to deceive him. As it is said (Psalms 18:27), "With the perverted, you act perversely." The incident of Chushai the Arkite (cf. 2 Samuel 15:32 ff.) is the paradigm of such a thing.

The seriousness of talebearing and slander as well as the great variety of situations in which it can be found is so well known that our sages noted that, as we already mentioned (*Baba Batra* 165a), "Most people commit sins of theft, some commit acts of promiscuity, but all succumb to some small measure of slander." They ask (*Arachin* 15a), "What are examples of small measures of slander?" and answer "a person's suggesting, for example, that a fireplace can only be found in so-and-so's house," or (*Arachin* 16a) "pointing out someone's good traits before his enemies," and so forth.[14] Even though these appear to be light matters, far removed from talebearing, they do bear traces of it.

The point is that the *yetzer hara* follows many paths, and anything that might be said whether to that person's face or not that may result in damage or embarrassment to him is within the parameters of that trait that is detestable and an abomination to God—slander. It is said (*Arachin* 15b), "Whoever spreads slander is likened to one who denies God" and (Psalms 101:5) "I will cut down whoever slanders his neighbor in secret."

The traits of hate and revenge are also very difficult to escape from, given man's scheming heart. We are very sensitive to insult, suffering very much because of it; and revenge, the best solution for it, is as sweet as honey. You would have to be

---

14. Saying "a fireplace can only be found in so-and-so's house" could intimate that only so-and-so would buy such a frivolous thing when others are perfectly satisfied with stoves and other, simpler heaters.

"Pointing out someone's good traits before his enemies" may have his enemies grumph and tell of his bad traits. You would then be guilty of spreading the gossip they contributed.

extraordinarily courageous and strong to have it within you to abandon what is innate to you, bypass this inclination and not hate someone who has aroused hate in you, and to not arise against him in revenge, or bear a grudge against him, but instead to forget it all, and wipe it away from your heart as if it never happened. Such an act would be easy for the ministering angels, who do not suffer from such attributes. But for (Job 4:19) "those who dwell in houses of clay, and are founded in dust" it is not. Yet, according to the decrees of the King, that is exactly what we must do. The Torah is explicit and clear about that, requiring no interpretation (Leviticus 19:17–18): "Do not hate your brother in your heart" and (Leviticus 19:18) "Do not take revenge or bear a grudge against one of your people."[15]

The elements of revenge and bearing a grudge are well known. Revenge involves refraining from doing good for whoever would not do good to you, or who has already done you harm. Bearing a grudge involves reminding a person of the harm he has done to you when you were about to do him a favor.

The *yetzer hara* waxes and infuriates the heart and wants to leave behind the memory or some trace of the incident that caused you pain. (And if it cannot retain a great deal of the memory, it will settle for a small amount). It might say to you: "If you would like to give him what he wasn't willing to give you when you needed it, at least don't give it to him cordially"; or "If you won't go so far as to do harm to him, at least don't do him any great favor or help him in any great way"; or "If you do care to help him out a lot, at least don't do it to his face"; or "You shouldn't befriend him again—it's enough that you have forgiven him and no longer hate him"; or "If you want be his friend again, at least don't be as close to him as you had been before."

Such is the way of the *yetzer hara* in its resolve to fool you in these things. The Torah has established a general, all-encompassing principle: (Leviticus 19:18) "And you will love your neighbor as yourself"—that is to say, "as yourself," without any differentiation; "as yourself," without any distinctions, contrivances or tricks—literally, "as yourself."[16]

---

15. If, as we have said, the mind is the central aspect of the self, it follows that *mitzvot* that concern it should also be central and should be the most difficult to manage. That explains the difficulty of (Leviticus 19:17) "Do not hate your brother in your heart," and (Leviticus 19:18) "Do not take revenge or bear a grudge against one of your people." Because they touch at the self they are faced with immediate uneasiness and resistance.

So why then does Torah ask such difficult things of us? To let us know that we are indeed capable of it. God created our "scheming hearts," knows them very well, and is telling us that we can "bypass this inclination."

The way to do it, Luzzatto tells us, is to "forget it all, and wipe it away from your heart as if it never happened." That can only be done by realizing the temporal nature of this world's circumstances and remembering the spirit that fills us all despite ourselves.

16. We said earlier on that the concept of the *yetzer hara* was highly misunderstood. The phrase is translated as the "evil inclination" and is usually taken to represent all that is bad and corrupt in the world. In non-Jewish circles it is represented as "Lucifer" and taken to

In regard to oaths said in vain, even though everybody except perhaps the ignorant is careful not to mention the name of God in vain, and especially not to vow in vain, there are some particulars of vain oaths which it is best to remain innocent of and which you have to watch out for, though they may not be the most serious. Our sages said (*Shavuot* 31a), "Rabbi Elazar said that 'yes' and 'no' are oaths. But Rava said that is only so if you have said 'yes, yes,' or 'no, no.'" They also said (*Baba Metzia* 49a), "It is written (Leviticus 19:36), 'An honest measure (*hinn*) . . . ,' that is to say that your 'no' should be honest as well as your 'yes' (*henn*)."

Lying is another malady that is widespread. But there are various degrees of lying.

---

task for all that is wrong and all that somehow moves man to evil. As such it is seen as a force external to ourselves and beyond our influence.

In fact it is nothing outside of ourselves—it is our humanity. As the tradition tells us, neither animals nor angels have a *yetzer hara*, only people—living people, in fact, because the dead do not have it either. The tradition also tells that children are all *yetzer hara* and do not get a *yetzer tov* (a so-called "good inclination") until they are twelve and thirteen years old.

So we see that God implanted the *yetzer hara* in us to be a quite natural and intrinsic part of ourselves, and it is that part of us we are most comfortable with because we are so used to it.

The tradition also intimates that it is often a very beneficial part of us and not to be denied. It reminds us that if it were not for the *yetzer hara* (as the sex urge, in this case) we would not get married; if it were not for it (as the need for comfort and material security) we would not build homes for ourselves; and were it not for it (as the need to compete and "make our mark on the world") we would not have careers.

As we said earlier on, the *yetzer hara* should be understood to be nothing other than "the urge to remain attached to the earth and things mundane." We have been taught all along in *The Path of the Just* that such an association (while oftentimes necessary) is fraught with possible danger and spiritual disappointment. But now we are being told something else— that it most exposes us to danger when it has to do with our relations with other people.

Our relations with others reflect our relations with ourself. The things we are bothered by in others, for example, are the very things we are troubled by in ourselves; and what we can see of the nobility of others is what we can see of our own. So when you cheat, steal from, deceive, lie to, hate, bear a grudge, or speak against another person you blemish your being and stand accused of being blind to your own soul and the soul of others.

The *yetzer hara* (in charge of such things) blossoms when you overlook the soul. Such an aversion *allows* it to remain attached to the earth and things mundane, breathes life into it once again, and lends it further credibility. When you deny your own being by denying the majesty and largeness of others you *become yetzer hara*—*merely* human, that is, capable of being less than an animal, certainly less than an angel, and as immature and as yet incomplete as a child.

So when we are told that the verse "And you will love your neighbor as yourself" implies loving him or her without any "differentiation, distinctions, contrivances, or tricks," literally, "as yourself," we come to understand that we are talking about no longer overlooking the soul in others as well as in ourselves (not making differentiations or distinctions), and of no longer fooling ourselves about who we are and what the stuff we are made of is (no longer falling for the contrivances or tricks of the *yetzer hara*).

There are people for whom lying is actually a profession. They go about concocting utter lies, either for laughs, or to be considered wise or knowledgeable. It is said about them (Proverbs 12:22), "Lying lips are an abomination to God" and (Isaiah 59:3), "Your lips have spoken lies; your tongue mutters wickedness." Our sages ordained (*Sotah* 42a) that there are four categories of people who will not be received by the Divine Presence, and one of them is the liars.

And there are others who, while like them in kind, are not quite as guilty as they. They are the ones who lie by telling stories and giving false reports. They are not "professional" storytellers who concoct whole tales or incidents that have never or could never happen. But when they come to relate something, they add on whatever occurs to them. This happens so regularly that it becomes second nature to them, and it is impossible to believe anything they say. Our sages said (*Sanhedrin* 89b), "Such is the punishment of the liar: people will not listen to him even when he speaks the truth." This bad trait has been so imbedded in them that it is not possible for anything honest to come from their lips. This is what troubled the prophet Jeremiah so when he said (Jeremiah 9:4), "They have taught their tongues to speak lies, and weary themselves in committing iniquity."

There is another category of liars whose malady is less serious than the former. They are not quite accustomed to lying, but they would not think of separating themselves from it, and if the opportunity for a lie would come up, they would take advantage of it. Many times they would do this for the sake of a joke, or for some other reason, with no particular malice intended. But as Solomon let us know, this is all against God's will and runs counter to His kindness. As he has said (Proverbs 13:5), "The righteous hate false things," which is exactly what the Torah warned us about when it said (Exodus 23:7), "Withdraw from a false thing." You might notice that this quote does not say "guard yourself from falsity," but rather, "withdraw from a false thing." This is so to warn us of how far we must withdraw from false things. It is said (Zephaniah 3:13), "The remnant of Israel will not do iniquity, will not speak falsely, and no trickery will be found in their mouths."

Our sages said (*Shabbat* 55a), "Truth is God's seal." And if God has chosen truth as His seal, its opposite must certainly be abominable to Him. The Holy One (blessed be He) has already warned us severely about truth. It is said (Zachariah 8:16), "Let man speak truth to his neighbor"; (Isaiah 16:5) "He has established His throne upon loving-kindness and will sit upon it in truth"; (Isaiah 63:8) "For He has said, 'Surely they are My people, children that will not lie'" (pointing out the fact that one is dependent upon the other); and (Zachariah 8:3) "Jerusalem shall be called the city of truth" (signifying its importance).

Our sages said (*Makkot* 24a), "It is written (Psalms 16:2), '. . . And he speaks truth in his heart.' This is in reference to those like Rav Safra." (According to Rashi's commentary Rav Safra had something for sale once. When a customer came to him and asked him to sell the object for a certain amount, Rav Safra did not respond, because he was reciting the *Shema Yisrael* at the time. The customer believed that

Rav Safra did not respond to his offer because he did not think it was good enough, so he made a better offer. When Rav Safra finished the *Shema* he told the customer that he could have the object for the price the man originally offered. "That was the price I had in mind to sell it for in the first place," he said.) This comes to teach us how far the obligation for truth goes. The sages have already forbidden a scholar from "altering the truth" in all but three extenuating circumstances (*Baba Metzia* 23b).

Truth is one of the very foundations upon which the world stands (*Avot* 1:18). As this is so, when you speak falsely it is as if you are nudging at the world's foundation. Conversely, when you are careful about truth you are likened to someone who maintains the world's foundation. The sages revealed (*Sanhedrin* 97a) that the angel of death does not hold sway in a place where truth is cared for. They tell the story of a peaceful town where, because a certain sage's wife adulterated the truth (albeit for a good reason), the angel of death was let loose. As soon as she was removed, the town returned to its original peaceful state. We need not delve further into the matter, as the implications of it are obvious.

The ramifications of the desecration of God's name are great and numerous as well. You must be very compassionate toward the standing of your Creator in the eyes of others by considering and reflecting upon all of your actions, and making sure that none of them (God forbid) lead to the desecration of God's name.

As we learned (*Avot* 4:4), "In matters of desecration of the Divine name—both purposeful and accidental incidents of it are one and the same"; and (*Yoma* 86a) "What is an example of the desecration of the Divine name? Rav said, 'For example, if I were to buy meat and not pay for it on the spot.' And Rabbi Yochanan said, 'For example, if I were to go a small distance without reciting words of Torah or without my *tefillin* on.'" The point is that each person, according to his standing, and according to how he is perceived by his generation, must recognize the fact that he can do nothing that would not be fitting for a person such as himself to do. He must be extremely careful and exacting in his Divine service in proportion to the greatness and value of his wisdom. If he is not, the name of God is desecrated through him (God forbid).[17]

The honor and glory of Torah comes about when the ones who study it very much perfect and ennoble their characters as well. Those amongst them who are lacking in this cause shame to be cast upon the study of Torah itself. That is (God forbid) a desecration of God's name. He has given us His Holy Torah and commanded us to occupy ourselves in it, and to reach perfection through it.

Observance of *Shabbat* and the Holy Days is also important because there are many laws involved. It is said (*Berachot* 12a), "There are many *Halachot* to *Shabbat*." And the rabbinic ordinances are central. The sages said (*Chagigah* 16b), "Never

17. If what we said in the previous note is at all correct it certainly applies all the more so to our relationship to God. When a Torah-person desecrates God's name by acting in a way unbefitting a representative of Him, he overlooks God's Self and grandeur, and he overlooks that part of the Creator of the Universe God nestled within him.

allow the rabbinic ordinances to appear light in your eyes: *smichah* is one, and the greats of the generation argued over it."[18] The many particulars, sections, and sub-sections of the laws are enunciated in the books of law, and they are equal in terms of our responsibility to them and the amount of caution required to carry them out.

What is most difficult for many to observe is refraining from doing and speaking about business. The prohibition against this is clearly stated by the prophet when he says (Isaiah 58:13–14): "If, because of the *Shabbat*, you will restrain your foot from pursuing your business on My holy day, and call the *Shabbat* a delight, the holy day of the Lord honorable; and you shall honor it, not doing your own ways, nor pursuing your own business, nor speaking of vain matters . . . ."

The principle is that all that is forbidden to be done on the *Shabbat* cannot be attempted or spoken of on the *Shabbat* either. The sages have also forbidden us from analyzing our holdings, or from seeing what might be needed for the next day, or to go to the borders to be ready to go off on business immediately after *Shabbat*, and they forbad us from saying on the *Shabbat*, "I'll do such-and-such tomorrow," or "I'll buy such-and-such tomorrow," and so forth.[19]

Up to now I have addressed those *mitzvot* which I perceive to be most people's downfalls. From those we can extrapolate to all the other prohibitions, as there is no forbidden act that does not have its divisions and subdivisions, both serious and light. Whoever wants to be innocent must be innocent and purified of them all. As our sages said (*Shir HaShirim Rabbah* 6:12), "It is written (Song of Songs 6:6), 'Your teeth are like a flock of sheep,' that is, just as sheep are modest, so too was Israel modest and righteous in the war against the Midianites. Rav Hunah says in the name of Rav Aicha that that was evidenced by the fact that not one of them put their head *tefillin* on before they put on their arm *tefillin*. Had one of them done so, Moses would not have praised them, and they would not have left the battlefield in peace." And as it says in the Jerusalem Talmud, "One who speaks between *yishtabach* and *yotzer* commits a sin and must leave the battlefield because of it."[20]

This shows you just how exacting and truly innocent you have to be in your actions. And your character has to be just as innocent. However, innocence of char-

---

18. *Smichah* is the act of pressing one's body weight down upon an animal's forehead just before it is slaughtered and offered on the Altar. The first rift among the greats of the early generations of the sages centered upon the permissibility of *smichah* on the holy days.

19. That is to say, we are to appreciate the ample opportunity to withdraw from the workaday world and should not substitute longing for participation. There are times when God wants us to build and rework, and times when He wants us to loiter and restore. But you cannot do the latter as long as you are longing to build and ruminating about building and reworking.

20. The morning prayer service is comprised of several major divisions. *Yishtabach* is the last paragraph of one major division and *yotzer* is the beginning of another. While we are permitted to speak at certain portions of the service, we are not allowed to at others. One might reason that since *yotzer* starts a new division we should be allowed to talk between it and *yishtabach*, but we are not, and one who does transgresses.

acter is more difficult to achieve than innocence of actions, as your nature is more manifest in your character than in your actions. Temperament and disposition either greatly cooperate with or summarily oppose the development of character. And anytime you struggle to do something beyond your nature you are involved in a great battle, which our sages referred to when they said (*Avot* 4:1), "Who is a great warrior? One who conquers his *yetzer hara*."

There are many character traits—as many of them as there are deeds in the realm of human possibility, as they come from deeds. To this point we have stressed the *mitzvot* that especially needed innocence (because they were the ones people are likely to stumble in). We will now delve deeply into the common and primary problematic personality traits, which are: arrogance, anger, jealousy, and desire. Their harm is universally recognized and does not have to be substantiated. They are intrinsically harmful, harmful in consequence, and are outside the realm of the intellect and wisdom. Each can lead you on to grave sins in its own way.

The Torah is explicit in its warnings against arrogance saying (Deuteronomy 8:14), "And you will come to make your hearts haughty and you will forget God your Lord. . . ." Our sages spoke about anger, saying (*Shabbat* 105b), "Angry people should be seen as idol-worshipers." And it is clearly said about jealousy and desire (*Avot* 4:21), "Jealousy, desire, and glory remove a man from the world." The profoundest thing that can be said is to flee from them and their offshoots for they are each (Jeremiah 2:21) "a degenerate plant of a strange vine." We will now begin to speak of them one at a time.

Arrogance entails consciously or unconsciously thinking yourself worthy of praise, for various and many reasons. For example a person might think himself very intelligent, or handsome, venerable, great, or wise. The principle is if one attributes to himself any of the good things of the world he is in immediate danger of falling into the trap of arrogance. After a person implants in his mind the notion that he is important or praiseworthy, not just one but many and various things may result—and while some of them would have been intended for the same end, they may actually be diametrically opposed to each other.

It may be that a self-centered person will think himself unique, impressive, and worthy of praise and would think it only proper that he conduct himself uniquely, impressively, and respectfully in the way he walks, sits, stands, speaks, and so forth. So he would only walk at a leisurely, studied pace, and would not sit without leaning. He would arise slowly and deliberately like a serpent, and would not speak to just anybody, but only with the eminent—and even when he would speak with them he would only speak in short, pithy, seerlike phrases. And in all the rest of his deeds—his movements or actions; his eating, drinking, and dressing—he would conduct himself in a heavy-handed manner, as if his flesh were lead, and his bones were stone or sand.

Another egotist would think that since he is so praiseworthy and of such high quality, he should be the very instigator of all things in the world, that everyone should tremble before him, and it is only fitting that no one dare speak to him or ask anything of him. And should they be so presumptuous as to do so he would verbally crush and confound them in all impudence, enraged all along.

There is another sort of egotist who believes that he is already so great and important that glory can never depart from him anyway, so he really does not need any more of it. And to prove that point he acts modest to draw attention to his character and to exhibit great humility and endless modesty, while his heart is actually exalted within him and he says to himself: "I am so great and important that I no longer need respect. I can renounce it. I already have a lot of it to begin with."

Another egotist can be found who wants to make a great impression with his greatness and to be recognized as being unique. It is not enough for him that everyone praises him for the greatness he believes he exhibits. He would like everyone to further praise him as being the most humble person there is. This type of person is arrogant in his modesty, and wants to honor himself with the very thing he makes himself out to have transcended. This type of arrogant person places himself below people actually much lower than himself and vulgar people, thinking that he might prove utmost humility this way. He does not want to assume any titles of greatness, and refuses all honors, while all along in his heart he says, "There's no sage or modest person like myself in the entire country."[21]

Even though these kinds of egocentrics appear to be modest, they do not lack for clues to the contrary. Unbeknownst to them, their arrogance will peek through like flames between pieces of potters' clay. Our sages drew a parallel to the situation when they said (*Bamidbar Rabbah* 18:13) that such a person is like a house full of straw that has a lot of holes in it. Everyone discovers the fact that there has been straw in it all along when it starts to fall out. That is just like our situation. Such a person cannot hide his nature forever. His misguided thoughts will become manifest in his actions, and it will become known that he was dishonestly modest and dishonestly humble.

There is another sort of egotist whose pride is buried deep within him and is never made manifest. He believes that he is already a great sage who knows the way

---

21. The term used for this bad trait is *gaavah*. We have purposefully translated it as arrogance rather than pride, because pride is oftentimes an important and healthy trait to have while arrogance is not. Pride is satisfaction with something difficult well done. It involves a recognition of your own worth and accomplishments, and encourages you to go on with more difficult things. Arrogance, on the other hand, is a shallow turning around of a deeply felt sense of inadequacy, and is a shortlived push to keep going before you are "found out." It is rooted in delusion and fantasy and disallows for perfection.

But it must not be forgotten that pride can also lead to complacency, as when you overlook what you still have to accomplish, despite your own best efforts. A healthy attitude would involve recognizing your accomplishments, realizing your self-worth and your abilities to take on other challenges—without self-congratulation. The egotist recognizes the reprehensibility of the trait and often tries to cover it up by feigning modesty. So he is guilty then of both arrogance and deception.

of all things, and that no one else quite shares his sagacity. He does not pay attention
to anyone else's opinion and reasons that if the matter is difficult for him it could not
possibly be easy for anyone else. And he holds that whatever his mind conceives of is
so straightforward and obvious that he need not even listen to people with other
opinions, be they earlier or contemporary scholars. He has no doubts whatsoever about
his opinions.

All these things hold sages back and stupefy their minds, and abrogate the hearts
of the very wisest. Even novice scholars whose eyes have just started to open often already think they are great sages. The Torah says about all of these (Proverbs 16:5), "The
haughty are an abomination to God." One who wants to acquire the trait of innocence
must free himself from all of this and come to realize that arrogance is literally blind-
ness as it causes you to overlook your imperfections and to not notice what you lack.

If you were able to see and to realize the truth you would certainly flee and
escape from these harmful, damaging things. With the help of Heaven we will continue to speak about this when we come to the trait of modesty, which was placed at
the end of Rabbi Pinchas's *beraita* because it is so difficult to obtain.

Let us discuss anger now. There is the furious type of person, about whom it is
said (*Shabbat* 105b), "One who is angry is likened to one offering to idols." He is the
type of person who gets angry at everything done against his will. He is so filled with
fury that he grows heartless, and his sensibilities dull. This sort of person would
destroy the world if he could. He is irrational and as utterly unreasonable as a wild
beast. It is said of him (Job 18:4), "You (who) tear yourself in your anger: Shall the
earth be forsaken for you?" It is very easy to commit all sorts of transgressions once
rage has brought you to this state, as there is nothing but your anger to control you,
and you must go where it leads you.

There is a different type of angry individual—one who is not as easily brought
to fury if something or another is not done exactly as he would like it. But when he
gets angry, he gets *very* angry. He is referred to as (*Avot* 5:11) "difficult to anger, but
difficult to appease." This too is certainly bad, for many damaging, ruinous things
may come out of this anger which cannot be undone.

There is a degree of anger less serious than this which is exemplified by someone who does not easily anger. When such a person gets angry, he just gets a little
angry. He does not lose his wits, but he does seethe in his anger. This sort of person
does less damage than those mentioned above, but he has certainly not reached the
trait of innocence. He has not yet even acquired caution. For as long as anger leaves
something of an impression in a person he is still said to be an angry person.

And there is a level than is even lighter than this. It belongs to the person who
finds it hard to get angry. Should such a person get angry, his anger would be short-lived
and not the destructive nor annihilating type. How long would this person's anger last?—
a moment and no longer. The very moment anger would start to appear in him his sensibilities would take over to control it. Our sages referred to this sort of person as (*Avot*
5:11) "difficult to anger, and easy to appease." This is certainly a good trait.

Human nature is easily incited to anger. A person would be praiseworthy if he could take control of himself so that it would not flair up in him and take him over,[22] and even a slight anger would not stay for any period of time, but would pass quickly. Our sages said (*Chullin* 89a), "It is written (Job 26:7): 'He hangs the earth upon nothing (*b'lee-mah*).' That comes to teach us that the world is only maintained through the merits of one who restrains (*bo-lame*) his mouth when arguing." That is, when the urge to express anger was aroused in him, he gained control of himself, and did not express it.

Hillel the Elder exemplified this. He was not fastidious about anything, and was never even provoked to anger. He was utterly innocent of anger.

Our sages even warned us against getting angry for reasons of a *mitzvah*, and warned a teacher not to get angry with a student or a parent with a child. They did not say that one is not to reprimand, because oftentimes you must. But you must reprimand without anger and for the express purpose of setting the child upon the right path, and what appears to be anger should only be on the surface and not felt (*Shabbat* 105b).[23] As Solomon said (Ecclesiastes 7:9), "Be not hasty in your spirit to be angry, for anger rests in the bosom of fools"; and it says in Job (5:2), "For anger kills the foolish man. . . ." Our sages said (*Eruvin* 65b): "A man's character comes out in three things: his drinking glass, his pocket, and his anger."

Jealousy is another instance of foolishness and temporary loss of sensibility. The jealous person gains nothing, and does nothing against the person he is jealous with, but he causes damage to himself. And as the verse we quoted above from Job goes on to say (Job 5:2), ". . . Envy slays the simpleton."

There are those whose foolishness in these things goes so far that they will get depressed, worried, and bothered by the fact that an acquaintance becomes successful at something, and their own successes will give them no pleasure. This is what the wise man was referring to when he said (Proverbs 14:30), "Jealousy is the very rotting of the bones."

There are others who would not be quite so bothered or wounded, but they would experience some pain, or at least a certain chilling of the spirit when they would see someone other than someone close and dear to them enjoying some advantage. And they would experience this more if it would happen to someone with whom they do not share an affinity, and even more so if it would happen to a stranger. They

---

22. This seems to be the danger in anger: the fact that it can flair up *and take you over*. As Luzzatto said some paragraphs back, the worst sort of anger is the kind that causes someone to be "so filled with fury that he grows heartless, and his sensibilities dull . . . [until he becomes so] irrational and as utterly unreasonable as a wild beast . . . [that it becomes] very easy [for him] to commit all sorts of transgressions. . . , as there is nothing but [the] anger to control [him], and [he] must go where it leads [him]."

23. That means to say that you often must reprimand, but should not come to do it out of anger, but rather out of the moral and pedagogical *need* to reprimand in the course of your instruction. Where a teacher may err is when he or she takes what a student does personally and wants to take revenge on that pupil or whoever the student represents to the teacher.

might have it within them to offer some encouraging words or acknowledgment of the fact, but in their hearts they would be hesitant.

This is very common. Even though this sort of person cannot be said to be jealous he cannot be said to be innocent of it either, especially when it comes to a competitor's success—as our sages said (*Bereishit Rabbah* 19:2), "One craftsman is always hated by another"—and especially when that competitor's success is greater than his own.

But you must know and come to realize that (*Yoma* 38b), "You cannot even approach within a hairsbreadth of something that is reserved for another," and that absolutely everything is from God, and emanates from His wondrous counsel and unfathomable wisdom. There is no reason to be bothered by your neighbor's good fortune.[24]

This is what Isaiah required for Israel's destined good fortune to be complete. He taught that God will precede this good fortune with the cessation of this disgraceful trait: no one will suffer over anyone else's success, and the successful will not have to be secretive for fear of jealousy. He said (Isaiah 11:13), "The envy of *Efraim* shall also depart, and the adversaries of *Judah* shall not vex *Efraim*." This is the sort of peace and tranquility that the ministering angels enjoy. They are happy in their service, and set in their places, and not one of them is ever jealous of another. They all know the truth and rejoice over the good they enjoy, and they are happy with their lot.

Related to jealousy is coveting and desire, which burden your heart till the day you die. As our sages said (*Kohelet Rabbah* 1:13), "You will not have obtained half of your desires by the time you die." Desire can be subdivided into two categories, both of which are bad and cause a lot of misfortune: the desire for possessions, and the desire for respect.

Coveting of possessions confines you to the constraints of this world, makes you prey to the entanglements of toil and labor—as the verse says (Ecclesiastes 5:9), "Someone who loves silver will never have enough silver"—and it distracts you from your Divine service. How many prayers are lost and how many *mitzvot* forgotten—not to mention Torah study waylaid—because of overconcern with and struggling for wealth? Our sages said (*Eruvin* 55a), "It says in the Torah (Deuteronomy 30:13), 'It (the Torah) is not across the seas,' and it means to say that it is not to be found with those who cross the seas for business concerns." They also said (*Avot* 2:5), "Not all who increase in business become wise," for such a person exposes himself to many dangers and saps his strength with worry even after he has already earned a lot. And

---

24. To be jealous and "bothered by your neighbor's good fortune" is to worry that God is only capable of doing so much, that your neighbor has somehow gotten your rightful share, and there is nothing left over for you now. That is an absurd and immature perception of the powers-of-supply available to the Infinite. The person of full faith realizes there is nothing that God cannot do, and that all He does is done for a good reason and for our ultimate (though perhaps not readily obvious) benefit.

so we learn (*Avot* 2:7), "If you increase in wealth you increase in worry." Such a person often transgresses *mitzvot* as well as the dictates of common sense.[25]

More serious than this is the coveting of respect. It is possible for a person to subdue his *yetzer hara* for possessions and other such pleasures. But the need for respect is more compelling because it is impossible for you to endure being lower than your friends.

Many have slipped and been lost in this matter. Jeroboam ben Nevat, for example, was driven away from his place in the World to Come because of his thirst for respect. As our sages said (*Sanhedrin* 102a), "The Holy One (blessed be He) took hold of Jeroboam by his coat and said to him, 'Repent, and you, I and King David will stroll in the Garden of Eden.' Jeroboam said to God, 'Who will lead?' God said, 'David will,' to which Jeroboam replied, 'If that's the case, I don't care to.'"

What was it that caused Korach and his cohorts to be destroyed? The pursuit of respect. As the Torah explicitly states (Numbers 16:10), "Would you also seek the priesthood?" Our sages told us (*Bamidbar Rabbah* 18:2) that this happened because Korach saw Elitzaphan ben Uziel come to be prince, when he wanted to be prince instead. According to our sages (*Zohar* IV 13:3) this is what caused the spies to speak out against the land of Israel, bringing death to them and their generation. It was a result of their fear of diminishing their glory upon entering into the land of Israel where others, not they, were to be princes of the people.

What was it that instigated Saul to ambush David if not the need for respect? As it is written (1 Samuel 18:7–9), "And the women answered one another as they danced and said, 'Saul has slain his thousands, and David his ten thousands!' And Saul was very angry and the saying displeased him. He said, 'They give David ten thousands, and me thousands—and what else can he have now but the kingdom?' And Saul viewed David with suspicion from that day onward."

And what was it that had Joab kill Amasa? The drive for respect—because David said to Amasa (2 Samuel 19:14), "Will you not be my general in Joab's place for all times?"

The point is that the quest for respect tugs at your heart more than any lust or longing in the world. Without it, you would be satisfied eating whatever you could, you would dress just to cover your nakedness, you would live in a house that would merely protect you from the elements, livelihood would come easily to you, and you would not struggle to become wealthy. But just so as to not see yourself as lowly or lesser than your friend you take this thick yoke upon yourself, and there is no end to all of your efforts. That is why our sages said (*Avot* 4:21), "Jealousy, desire, and the

---

25. To covet is to believe that the having of that thing will at last bring you something else you do not yet have and which you very much want. It is usually felt that the object coveted will make you happy, respected, content, wise, and so forth. So you should consider what it is you ultimately want to have that you are hoping to procure through that object, consider whether you really want it, and go after it if you do. The person who covets an object and does not realize what it acts as an agent for in his own mind can never be satisfied and will never rest. He will often come to sin and avoidance of his self in his hopeless and absurd search for something other than what he is searching for.

quest for respect expunge a man from the world." They warned us (*Avot* 6:5), "Do not ask for greatness, and do not covet respect."

How many people starve or denigrate themselves by taking charity just not to have to work at something that is not prestigious enough in their eyes because they are afraid to diminish their honor? Is there anything more idiotic than this? They would prefer idleness—which carries melancholy, lewdness, thievery, and all sorts of transgressions along with it—to lowering their status and detracting from the respect they see as coming to them. However, our sages, who have always instructed and directed us in the ways of truth, suggest (*Avot* 1:10) "Love work and detest power"; as well as (*Pesachim* 113a), "(Just) strip carcasses in the marketplace (but) do not say, 'I'm a great man; I'm a priest!'"; and (*Baba Batra* 110a) "A man should always do work that is foreign to him rather than have to depend on other people."

The point of the matter is that the desire for glory is one of man's greatest stumbling blocks. It is impossible for him to be a faithful servant to his Creator as long as he is attached to his own self-respect, because this foolishness will necessitate his giving less honor to God. This is what King David was referring to when he said (2 Samuel 6:22), "I will become yet more insignificant than this, and be lowly in my own eyes."

The only true glory is knowledge of Torah. As our sages said (*Avot* 6:3), "There is no glory other than Torah, as it is written (Proverbs 3:35), '(Torah) sages will inherit glory.'" Other kinds of glory are false, self-perceived kinds that are worthless and in vain. The innocent should free himself and thoroughly purify himself from it. Only then will he succeed.[26]

To this point I have generalized about many of the particulars of innocence. I have thus presented a basic principle for all the other *mitzvot* and commendable character traits. "The wise man will hear and will increase learning; and the man of understanding shall obtain devices" (Proverbs 1:5).

I cannot deny that there is something of a struggle necessary to go through to obtain this kind of innocence. Nonetheless, I must say that it is not as difficult as it appears to be. In fact, the thought of it is more difficult than the act. When you have it in mind and firmly set it in your heart to be one of those people who has this good trait then, with just a little practice, it will come to you with much more ease than you might have imagined. Experience can attest to the truth of this.[27]

---

26. In other words, we expend so much of our energies on the pursuit of the unnecessary, and foolishly work ourselves into a frantic, maniacal spin over things that will themselves not make us happy, and all for respect, which emanates from nothing else but the study of the Torah, which we come to avoid in our drives for false glory.

27. The advice offered seems to be that you must have a picture of such a person in your mind and ask yourself when you are likely to go off the path if he or she would do such a thing. There are two ways to do that: find one in life (that is, find a holy person who lives by these tenets and use him as a role model) or form a sense in your mind of how you would be if you were to become such a person, and slowly evolve into that.

12

The Means of
Acquiring Innocence

The best way to acquire innocence is to constantly study the teachings of our sages in matters of *Halachah* and *musar*. After the obligations of innocence and its requirements will have become clear to you, and you will have already obtained the states of caution and enthusiasm (by being involved in the things that help you obtain them and keeping away from the things that keep them away from you) there is nothing that can keep you back from obtaining innocence other than the lack of knowledge of the minutiae of the *mitzvot* so that you could be cautious and thorough in them all.

Therefore you must know the *Halachot*—the ramifications of the *mitzvot* and the extent of them—thoroughly. Also, you must constantly study the books that explain the particulars of these things so that you can refresh your memory. Forgetfulness is common in such technical matters as these, and by reviewing them you will certainly be encouraged to do them.

This is true of matters of your personality as well. You must study the moral teachings of both the earlier and later teachers. Many times, even after a person will have established in his heart that he wants to be exacting in matters of innocence, it is still possible that he can be guilty of some minor transgression simply because he never got to understand it. No one is born a sage, and it is impossible to know everything.

When you study the material you will be shocked to see what you do not know, and you will have an opportunity to reflect upon what you had not originally understood. And because your heart will be attuned to such things you will continue to observe everything from all angles and will even discover for yourself, from the source of truth, things not mentioned in the books themselves.

The deterrents to this trait are all the deterrents to the trait of caution.[1] In

---

1. They include: overconcern for things of the world, levity, and keeping bad company. See the fifth chapter for a full discussion of those deterrents.

addition to that must be added the aforementioned lack of expertise in the laws and moral principles. As our sages remarked (*Avot* 2:5), "An illiterate person cannot be saintly." That is so because someone who does not know cannot possibly do. They also said that (*Kiddushin* 40b) "scholarship is only great when it brings you to action."[2]

---

2. Luzzatto is careful to include this last quote in order to ensure the fact that we realize *why* we are to study these things: that is, to be active with their guidance. One who does not study these works—an "illiterate person"—can never be holy because he will never come to know what God requires of him. But one who only *studies* works of *musar* and does not act on them can never be holy either, because scholarship only brings you to greatness when it "brings you to action."

Summation of Part IV

Chapter 10

1. You enjoy innocence when you are free of all bad traits and sins, when you long for nothing material, and when you are your own master.

2. This only comes about after thorough caution and the process of being cleansed of all manifest sins, then further preparations for the desire and love for God, and for Divine service. That will lead to separation from mundane desires and an attachment to whole-spiritedness. Only such a person is fit to see the Countenance of God.

3. Coming to this is very difficult, as it requires the meticulous extrication of those subtle transgressions that are often covered over and overlooked. But our natures are weak, our hearts are easily swayed, and we allow ourselves things that are detrimental to us, so one who has reached this state has reached a very high level.

Chapter 11

4. There are as many means to innocence as there are negative *mitzvot*. Yet, they can be broken down into those that are related to *action*, and those that are related to *character*.

5. There are several transgressions that are related to action, but there are two that human nature is especially drawn to: thievery and promiscuity (and their offshoots), and we will start out by speaking of them.

6. While most people are not out-and-out thieves, they are nonetheless guilty of minor acts of thievery and extortion in their business dealings. The Torah is straightforward about the details of thievery and extortion and takes

great pains to ensure it does not occur. The sages went so far as to lessen the religious obligations of workers to make sure that they would not be guilty of stealing time from their employers to do them.

7. Thievery comes about when your heart is affected by your eyes rather than the reverse; that is to say, when you are attracted to others' possessions.

8. Deceit (an offshoot of thievery) is warned of in the Torah. As it is written (Leviticus 25:17): "Let no man deceive his fellow." Its prohibition applies to dishonesty in weights and measures, and to loaning money on interest.

9. As to promiscuity, not only is adultery itself forbidden, but other acts of intimacy with people other than your spouse are just as forbidden. Also forbidden is casual physical contact, voyeurism, enticement, profanity, and fantasy.

10. The third category of action-related prohibitions to be considered is the one concerning forbidden foods. Great care is required to remain free from error in this matter, because the heart is drawn to good food, and monetary loss is often involved. Forbidden foods cause spiritually unclean elements to enter into the systems of those who ingest them, and do not allow God's holiness to enter. They should be considered poison.

11. The fourth category of action-related prohibitions to be considered is those that have to do with interpersonal relations. They involve: verbally abusing (publicly or privately shaming) someone; embarrassing or deceiving others (by purposefully giving bad advice); talebearing and slandering (by saying something that may result in damage or embarrassment to someone); hating and taking revenge (refraining from doing good for whoever would not do good to you, or who has already done you harm), taking oaths in vain (even small and seemingly insignificant ones), lying (which is done for various reasons, such as to appear wise or knowledgeable, for a joke, etc.) and desecrating the name of God (brought about when those who practice Torah act in an unbecoming manner).

12. And the fifth category of action-related prohibitions to be considered are those related to the keeping of the *Shabbat* and the Holy Days. Our considerations of these center around the prohibition against doing business and thinking about business on those days. It must be remembered that whatever is forbidden to be done on the *Shabbat* or the Holy Days cannot be thought of or spoken about then either.

13. There are many, many transgressions that are related to your character, and innocence in character is harder to achieve than innocence in actions as you are approaching something far deeper and more stubborn. We

will discuss four such transgressions which are clearly problematic: arrogance, anger, jealousy, and desire.

14. Arrogance entails thinking yourself worthy of praise for one reason or another and attributing any of the good things of the world to yourself. It causes some people to act haughty and regal. It causes others to act abrasive and impudent. It has others act with great "modesty" because they think that that is the only way so great a person as themselves should act. It has others of that ilk wanting nothing more than to be recognized and praised for their "modesty," while they refuse all honors. Others are so arrogant as to believe that they alone are "in the know," and they will never take anyone else's advice ("for, after all," they reason, "if I could not figure it out, who could?")

15. There are various forms of anger. In ascending order: there is the kind that has you fume at anything done against your will. There is the kind that, while not easily ignited, is voracious when it is brought out. There is the kind that is low-key but tends to seethe beneath the surface. And there is a quiet and short-lived sort of anger which is eradicated as soon as it surfaces. The fostering of the latter is praiseworthy.

16. Jealousy evidences temporary insanity. It does nothing but harm for its instigator and absolutely nothing for the person it is intended for. Some get so worried and anxious over another's success that they would see nothing of their own accomplishments. And some suffer a certain chilling feeling when others succeed. The only way to overcome jealousy is to realize that all is from God and that we each get exactly what is coming to us.

17. Coveting and desiring are related to jealousy and are heavy burdens upon the heart because, despite it all (*Kohelet Rabbah* 1:34): "You will not have obtained half of your desires by the time you die." Desiring can be divided into two categories: the desire for possessions, and the desire for respect. Someone who desires possessions exposes himself to danger and saps his strength with worry. The desire for respect is more fundamental and compelling than any other longing in the world and it is one of man's greatest stumbling blocks. With it, it is impossible to be a true servant of God. True respect only comes about in fact through knowledge of Torah. All other kinds are false and worthless. The innocent should utterly rid himself of the quest for them.

18. While innocence is certainly difficult to achieve, it is not as difficult as you might think. What is called for to achieve it is setting the image of the kind of person who lives that way firmly in your mind. With practice it will come, and more easily than you would have imagined.

Chapter 12

19. The best way to acquire innocence is to constantly study and review the sayings of the sages so that you become acquainted with the minutiae of the *mitzvot* and the requirements for character development. This should not be a detached and academic study, but rather one that brings you to action as (*Kiddushin* 40b), "Scholarship is only great when it brings you to action."

V

ABSTINENCE

Introduction to Part V

The fifth part comprises three chapters (13–15) and concerns itself with the trait of "abstinence." The chapters are entitled "An Explanation of the Trait of Abstinence" (chap. 13), "The Subdivisions of Abstinence" (chap. 14), and "The Means of Acquiring Abstinence" (chap. 15).

This part starts a new aspect of the book. As Luzzatto writes in chapter 13, "whereas all that we have discussed thus far is what you would need to become righteous, from here on we will discuss what you would need to become pious." A leap is made into a more sophisticated and self-affecting mode of change that is not for everyone. As he writes there, "most people cannot be pious, and it would be sufficient for them to be righteous. Those lone individuals among the people who desire to merit closeness to God, and to make meritorious those others who are dependent upon them by *their* merit, have to live by the laws of the saintly— these abstentions—which those others cannot live by."

Subjects discussed in this section aside from abstinence itself include: the difference between Torah and Rabbinic prohibitions; self-denial; the allure of food, drink, promiscuity, and other such pleasures; the difference between most people and the potentially pious; a healthy versus an unhealthy attitude towards the attractions of the world (chap. 13); stringency in *Halachah*, isolation and seclusion (chap. 14); and seduction, short-term gains as opposed to long-term losses, association with the wealthy and powerful, the slow progression into a second nature (chap.15).

Abstention is defined therein as the "withdrawal from and avoidance of something; that is, disallowing for yourself something the Torah permits so that you do not come in contact with something it forbids." It implies temperance, self-denial, forbearance, and (to a degree) asceticism, but does not imply indifference, evasiveness, repression, or escapism.

13

An Explanation
of the Trait of Abstinence

Abstinence is the beginning of piety.[1] And whereas all that we have discussed thus far is what you would need to become righteous, from here on we will discuss what you

---

1. The *beraita* of Rabbi Pinchas ben Yair upon which *The Path of the Just* is based has set up and been following a pattern up to now. It begins with a trait that would devolve around undoing something, which is then followed by another trait that would devolve around doing something righteous and Godly in the place of what had been expunged.

In the first part of this book that pattern was exemplified by the traits of caution and enthusiasm. Caution involved undoing your harmful traits and replacing them with holiness enthusiastically—in other words, not just passively or matter-of-factly undoing what you had done incorrectly in the past, but with vigor and newfound purpose. That pattern seemed to continue with the introduction of innocence, which involved a deeper and fuller undoing of your harmful traits.

We would then have expected the next trait to center on moving further along in a positive vein, and assuming more of an active *taking on* of Godliness. But instead we find that the trait after innocence, abstinence, is not that, but rather a deeper yet and more clearly demanding *doing without*, as the literal sense of the word would clearly indicate. And it is followed by purity, which demands an even *higher* undoing.

Then the pattern is reintroduced with a discussion of the trait of saintliness, or piety. Piety is founded upon gloriously selfless and bold acts of giving and loving, and upon deeply sensing the Godly. It is a thorough replacing of something nudgingly though very subtly undesirable with something unarguably Divine. Piety is followed by humility, which involves yet more replacing of what had been (in this case, one's own tastes, drives, and proclivities) with something else (the tastes, drives, and proclivities of others).

So it turns out that by this point the pattern has changed from one "undoing" (caution), which becomes elevated to a "replacing" (enthusiasm), to several "undoings" (innocence, abstinence, and purity), which become elevated into several "replacings" (piety and humil-

would need to become pious.[2,3] Abstinence is to piety what caution is to enthusiasm: the former is in the category of (Psalms 34:15) "depart from evil," and the latter is in the category of "do good" (ibid.).

---

ity). Then the original pattern of one negative to be transformed into a positive returns with the introduction of the last two traits, fear of sin and holiness.

So when Luzzatto says here that "abstinence is the beginning of piety" he means to indicate that whereas it follows innocence and as such would be expected to contrast with it, it will not, but will rather veer toward the next "replacing trait," which is piety, as soon as this undoing mode is finished, with the introduction of the trait of purity.

2. Let us try to understand the difference between righteousness and piety. To do that, we will have to understand something about our souls.

The tradition speaks of five levels of the soul: *nefesh, ruach, neshamah, chayah*, and *yechidah*. But while they all translate as "soul" or "spirit," and they are different from each other in function, they are in fact five different names of the same radical element in the self that assumes five different flavors and inclinations, which constantly blend into, course through, and adhere to each other.

The *nefesh*, related to the Hebrew word for the act of exhaling (*nefishah*), is that part of the soul that is closest to the body. And just as the breath connects the inner self with the outer world (by keeping us alive), the *nefesh* connects body with soul, as we shall soon see. It is identified with the blood, and as such represents the coursing and flowing relationship of the soul to the body—the element of the body that keeps it alive, but just so. As such, it is synonymous with animality and rank physicality. It carries precious little apparent spiritual weight, but it too is derived from God.

As the *nefesh* is so close to the body as to be a veritable part of it, we can see that the body can be said to be a part of the soul as well, albeit the "lowest" part (but since all parts of the soul "blend into, course through and adhere to each other," whatever is connected to the "lowest" part of it is connected to the "highest" part as well, so the body is a part of the Divine soul, the *yechidah*, as much as it is a part of the *nefesh*).

The next part of the soul, the *ruach*, from the Hebrew word for "wind," is the volatile, mercurial, and freely blowing part of the soul, and as such is related to the emotions. We see from this that our emotional lives are "higher" than our physical being, but lower than many other parts of our selves. Like the wind, the *ruach* is invisible in itself but obvious in its results: you could never point to the wind but you could certainly point to the air it forces along in its power, the dust it may unsettle, the havoc it may wreak, and the changes (constructive or destructive) it may bring about.

The *neshamah* comes next. It is the "center," or middle level of the soul, and is therefore the most common term for the soul. It is related to the Hebrew word for the act of inhaling, *nesheemah*. But as exhaling has the inner self interact with the outer world, inhaling has the outer world enter into the inner self, which then has to process and come to terms with it. That is why the *neshamah* is related to the mind (not necessarily the brain, which is a particular organ of the body, but the mind, or what would be referred to today as consciousness, which can be located, that is to say focused, anywhere in or out of the body).

The part of the soul yet higher than the *neshamah* is the one referred to as the *chayah*, which comes from the Hebrew word for beast. That seems to be an anomaly—why would

The general principle behind abstinence was expressed by our sages when they said (*Yevamot* 20a), "Sanctify yourself through what is permitted to you." This is the very meaning of the word "abstinence": withdrawal from and avoidance of something;

---

the second from the highest level of the soul be referred to as a *beast*? But it is easily explained by taking into consideration the fact that the soul's five parts can be divided into two major subdivisions: the "upper" (the *chayah* and *yechidah*), and the "lower" (the *nefesh, ruach*, and *neshamah*). In that case, the *chayah*, while very sublime and lofty a level of the soul, is nonetheless "bestial" in comparison to the level above it, the Divine *yechidah*. It is to the "upper" part of the soul what the body is to the soul itself: related and attached, but invisibly so, and apparently separate and more primitive. The *chayah* can be likened to or represented by nothing we can explicate in the world of relativity, and is just translated as "spirit."

And the last, highest form of the soul is the *yechidah*. The term comes from the Hebrew word for "together," *yachad*, and indicates that it is that part of the soul that is "together with God." While the other parts of the soul are increasingly metaphysical, the *yechidah* is inexplicably metaspiritual. It is the very shadow and echo of God, if one may say as much.

What you have here is a delineation of the full self: body, psyche, and soul. But, as we have been saying, all of it is vital and electric, so one part is part of another, which is part of yet another, and so on up and down the line, and all of it constantly blends, courses, and adheres within the whole of it, so that no one part can be isolated from another, though we do isolate each "part" for easier analysis. And while the body is part of the soul, as we have said (both the "highest" and the "lowest" parts), that cannot be determined in the course of human action or being because we live in the world of space, time, and duality.

The majority of our conscious and functioning being, therefore, is invested in the "lower" part of the self: our rank animality, emotionality, and consciousness. The "higher" part of our selves is rarely communicated with and, apparently, only occasionally comes to interact with the "lower" part of us. And of the two "parts" of the "higher part" of us, the "highest part," the *yechidah*, it would appear, never deigns to commune with the rest of it. But in fact, that is not at all true. That can be explained thusly:

We can each be seen as being a person with one hundred percent of a self. Usually, a full sixty percent of the self is active and interactive. That is the "lower" part of the soul. Some people are eighty percent active and interactive, making use of their *chayah*'s potential. And some rare and special individuals actually make use of their full selves, and consciously involve their *yechidah* in the natural process of it all.

But no one can be said to be sixty percent or even eighty percent of a full person—much less twenty or forty percent of one. Every single person is one hundred percent of a person and no less. But not every single person *irradiates* that full one hundred percent of self. That is to say, while everyone *has* the full makeup of the soul, not everyone *uses* it or has come to find it in himself. So while we are each one hundred percent a person (composed of body, psyche, consciousness, spirit, and soul) most of us oblige ourselves with the full and conscious use of some forty to sixty percent of our beings, and leave the rest of it to run its course without our conscious direction.

To attempt to make full and intentional use of the self is to cross over a wide and dark chasm that is fraught with mysteries and threats. Not everyone is so bold as to dare the great leap. But those who do are referred to as the "holy," the *kadosh*—the ones who have tran-

that is, disallowing for yourself something the Torah permits so that you do not come in contact with something it forbids. The point is, you should withdraw from anything that is likely to cause you to come to do bad, even though it is not bad itself or currently causing bad.[4]

You will note that there are three levels of avoidances: those things actually forbidden by the Torah; the "fences," that is, the ordinances and preventive measures enacted by our sages for all of Israel; and the "safeguards," those optional prohibitions taken on as personal protective walls by anyone who wants to practice abstinence, which include those things that were never forbidden to other Jews but which these individuals forbid themselves to have for the express purpose of greatly avoiding bad.

Perhaps you will say, "What right have we to continue adding on prohibitions? The sages themselves asked (*Nedarim* 9:1), 'Hasn't the Torah forbidden enough things for you—would you forbid even more?'" Perhaps you will say, "What our sages saw fit in their wisdom to prohibit and to use as a safeguard should be such, and what they saw fit to allow should be allowed and not prohibited. So why are you coming up with decrees they didn't see fit to make?" Or, "There's no end to this! It would

---

scended their beings and evolved to the point referred to at the end of *The Path of the Just* (chapter 26).

Those souls that do not quite make the grandest leap, but who nonetheless irradiate the mighty *chayah*, are referred to as the "pious," the *chasidim*. And whereas in relation to the holy they are "bestial," in relation to the order of persons below themselves, the righteous, they are quite sublime and metaphysically evolved, as we know only too well from our own experiences.

To this point in the book Luzzatto has brought us to the use of sixty percent of our beings. From here on in he carries us along in the great leap into piety, which must necessarily be preceded by abstinence and purity, and then on to holiness.

3. Certain terms must be clearly defined here as they are often misconstrued. A *tzaddik* is a righteous Jew, and a *chasid* is a saintly Jew. Because of the chasidic movement, *tzaddikim* are taken to be "higher in rank" than *chasidim*, but that is not the case in the classical definitions of the words as they are used here and elsewhere, such as in the Talmud. Whereas in the vernacular a *tzaddik* "outranks" a *chasid*, in *musar* the roles are reversed—not politically, in terms of power and control, but in terms of spiritual rank.

It must also be borne in mind that you must *evolve* into a *chasid* after having been a *tzaddik*, but that will become clearer in the further development of the theme of piety. To attempt do be a *chasid* too soon, before one is prepared to do it, may be dangerous and counterproductive.

4. That is to say, the devout Jew is not to abstain from the pleasures of this world for no reason at all—as Luzzatto points out later on in the chapter, the Talmud warns that (*Kiddushin* 4:12) "'You will have to give a reckoning and account before God for each permitted and available thing your eyes saw to eat that you did not eat (for no good reason)"! He is only to abstain so that he does not inadvertently "come in contact with something (the Torah) forbids" or something "that is likely to cause (him) to come to do bad."

come out that a person would have to suffer desolation and deprivation, and derive no pleasure from this world at all! Have our sages not said (*Kiddushin* 4:12), 'You will have to give a reckoning and account before God for each permitted and available thing your eyes saw to eat that you did not eat, which they connected to the verse (Ecclesiastes 2:10), 'I withheld nothing they ever asked for from my eyes.'"

The only answer to that would be that abstinence is certainly necessary. In fact, our sages (*Sifra*) exhorted us about it by saying that when the Torah says "You are to be holy" (Leviticus 19:2) it means to say "You are to be abstainers." They also said (*Taanit* 11a), "If the Nazirite is called holy, we may extrapolate from there that one who fasts is all the more so to be called holy"; and "It is written (Proverbs 13:25), 'The righteous person eats to satisfy his soul.' This refers to Chizkiyahu the King of Judah who had just two bundles of vegetables and a measure of meat placed before him every day, while the Jews would laugh and say, 'This is a king?!'" (*Pesichta*); and they said (*Ketubot* 104a) about Rabbi Judah the Prince that when he was dying he lifted his ten fingers and said, 'It is known and revealed before You (God) that I have not derived even a pinky-finger's worth of benefit from this world'"; and (*Yalkut* 830) "Until a man prays that words of Torah fill his belly he should pray that food and drink not enter it." All of these statements clearly indicate the need for and the obligation to practice abstinence. We must nonetheless respond to those teachings that say otherwise.

The point is that there are many fundamental differences in the matter: there are abstentions we are *commanded* to follow, and there are abstentions we are *warned* about so as not to come to stumble. It was this category that King Solomon was referring to when he said (Ecclesiastes 7:16), "Do not be overrighteous."

We will now discuss the good type of abstinence.

After we have come to see that all that happens to us in this world is a test[5] (as we have said and proven beyond the shadow of a doubt already), and after man's overall weakness has become self-evident to us as well as how natural it is for him to lean toward the bad, it becomes clear that you should do all that you can to escape from these things so that you will be well-protected from the bad that comes in their aftermath.

There is in fact no earthly pleasure that does not have some sin following in its train.[6] Let us take food and drink as an example. After you will have removed all forbidden aspects of it, eating certainly becomes a permitted thing. However, a full stom-

---

5. . . . of our morals and of our abilities to choose between the ephemeral delights of the world and the eternal ones (see chap. 1).

6. The person who is reflective and God-fearing cannot help but come to the conclusion by this point that everything is indeed a test of our abilities to reckon the true worth of things and to act upon that reckoning.

Would a recovered alcoholic ever doubt that the only logical way to avoid what, clearly, must be avoided—liquor—is to not even come close to it if at all possible? He would know that if he would get too close to liquor he would either slip or, if not, he would have to withstand a great internal battle that is hardly desirable. This is the realization all substance abusers have to come to, as has been proven.

ach carries with it the removal of the yoke of the Kingdom of Heaven,[7] and wine-drinking leads to licentiousness and all sorts of immorality.

How more so is this true when you are accustomed to filling yourself with food and drink. And if you will not be able to do so once, you will be pained and very aware of the lack. You will eventually be forced to subject yourself to the clutches of the drive for livelihood and possessions so that your table could be set the way you would like it to be, which will lead you to wrong doings and thievery, which will themselves lead you to vain oaths and all sorts of transgressions that naturally follow these. Ultimately you will remove yourself from Divine service, Torah, and prayer. You could have been free of all that if you had not drawn yourself toward those pleasures in the first place.

In this vein our sages taught us about the rebellious son that "the Torah was projecting forward to his ultimate intentions" (*Sanhedrin* 72a).[8] So too in regard to licentiousness our sages said (*Sotah* 2a), "Whoever sees a promiscuous wife in her disgrace should become a *Nazir* and abstain from wine."[9] You should note that this is a wonderful device to save yourself from your *yetzer hara*. When you are in the midst of a transgression it is hard for you to conquer your *yetzer hara* and stop; therefore you should stay farther away from the transgression from the first so it will be difficult for your *yetzer hara* to draw towards it.[10]

Sexual relations with your spouse is certainly thoroughly permissible. Yet the

---

The incorrect and merely material use of things of this world is a form of substance abuse as well, though it is not recognized as such. If you are trying to recover from such a problem you will have to adopt the stance of a recovered alcoholic who admits his problem, is willing to suffer the laughter and jeers of others who do not understand and goad him on to have "just one drink," when he himself knows only too well that he would do best to avoid any and all alcohol.

When Luzzatto says, "there is . . . no earthly pleasure that does not have some sin following in its train" that is not to be taken to be the statement of someone with a life-denying and morose view of the world. What it means to say is that, as everyone with a substance-abuse problem surely knows, when you have slipped and gotten caught once again in the traps of your dilemma, real and concrete bad will result. A person who has recovered from such a problem cannot deny the inevitability of such an outcome and would immediately refer to it as "bad." He would not claim that alcoholism is "evil," only that it can lead to "evil" or, if he were inclined to call it such, "sin."

7. That is, when you are full, you tend to forget how you depend upon God for your well-being, and you tend to imagine that you will be as satisfied and well-cared for all the time, which of course is not necessarily the case unless God wills that.

8. . . . when it punished him so severely for what appeared to be a relatively insignificant act (cf. Deuteronomy 21:18–21).

9. That is, since drinking wine often leads to licentiousness, when you see a licentious person, such as a promiscuous wife (a *sotah*), you should voluntarily take your seeing of her upon yourself as a warning to avoid the things that could bring you to such a way of life.

10. Someone who knows his own problems recognizes his weaknesses and does not obstinately forge ahead where danger may be imminent just to test his will-power.

sages once ordained that a man was to immerse himself in a *mikveh* after having relations so that Torah scholars "would not act like roosters" with their wives, even though the act is perfectly acceptable between them. They enacted such a law because the sex drive is so ingrained in people that they can be driven to sexual prohibitions. As our sages said (*Sanhedrin* 107a), "A man has a certain small organ which is only satiated when famished and is famished when satiated." Even when it was fitting and proper for him to have sexual relations Rabbi Eliezer said (*Nedarim* 20b) that he would uncover a handsbreadth and cover up two, and he would be like one coerced by a demon so that he would derive no pleasure even as he was involved in it.

The Torah never warned us against beauty or stylishness associated with clothing or jewelry other than to tell us that we are not to wear the combination of any materials which cannot be worn together, and that we must put *tzitzit* on the ends of our garments. Otherwise, all is permitted. But as everyone realizes, the wearing of fine embroidered clothing and accessories is bound to encourage arrogance and licentiousness—in addition to jealousy, lust, and extortion, which follow in the wake of the acquisition of things that are difficult to come by. As our sages said (*Bereishit Rabbah* 22:6), "As soon as the *yetzer hara* sees someone genteelly balancing on his heels, fussing with his clothing, or curling his hair it says, 'This one's mine!'"

Even though pleasure trips and small talk are certainly not things forbidden by Torah law, a lot of neglect of Torah study comes as a result of them, as well as much slander, deceit, and levity. As it is said (Proverbs 10:19), "There can be no avoiding transgression with a lot of conversation."

The point is that since everything in this world is potentially gravely dangerous,[11] how can you not praise someone who wants to escape from or avoid all that?

This is considered to be good abstinence, taking nothing from this world in all your usages of it other than what you absolutely need by your nature. It is what was so praiseworthy about Rabbi Judah when he said that he would not even take as much as a pinky-finger's worth of enjoyment from this world. And he was a leader of the Jewish nation whose table was like a king's table because of his high stature. As our sages said about the verse (Genesis 25:23), "There are two nations in your womb"— "This stands for Rabbi Judah and Antonious who always had lettuce, cucumbers, and radishes on their tables—whatever the season (*Avodah Zarah* 11a)." This was the case with Chizkiyahu, King of Judah, as well.

This statement (as do all the others we have quoted) comes to teach us that you are to abstain from all earthly delights so that you will not fall into their traps.[12]

Should you ask, "If it is true that abstinence is such a necessary and important thing, then why didn't our sages institute more protective fences as they so often did?" The only clear and forthright response to this would be that our sages only instituted the sorts of protective fences the majority of the Jews could abide by (*Baba Kamma*

---

11. . . . to our spiritual well-being . . .
12. See note 10 above.

79b). Most people cannot be pious, and it would be sufficient for them to be righteous. Those lone individuals among our people who desire to merit closeness to God, and to make meritorious those others who are dependent upon them by *their* merit, have to live by the laws of the saintly—these abstentions—which those others cannot live by.[13]

This is the way God chose it to be. While it is impossible for a whole nation to be of one spiritual type, and there are all sorts of degrees in people, based upon their comprehension, there will at least be found some special individuals who could completely prepare themselves, and by means of this make meritorious the unprepared for the love of God and the indwelling of His Presence. In the same vein, the sages said about the four species used in the *lulav* on *Sukkot* (*Vayikra Rabbah* 30:11), "These will come to atone for those." And we find (*Terumot* 8:4) that Elijah the prophet communicated to Rabbi Yehoshua Ben Levi in regard to the incident of Ulah Bar Koshev, in answer to the question, "Is it not a *mishnah*?": "Yes, but is it then a *mishnah* for the saintly?"

---

13. This paragraph should be well noted. It states clearly that not everyone is made of the stuff required to cross over that deep and threatening chasm we spoke of in note 2 above. As such, most people should not assume the habits of those few and rare individuals who *are* of that type. To even suppose that you should do so when you are not ready to is to be like the parent who reasoned that her baby should not settle for formula and soft cereals when he could eat some good, nutritious foods like meats, vegetables, and breads.

There are times and lives when the "formula and soft cereals" of Divine service are required, and others when the "meats, vegetables, and breads" of Divine service are required. A serious and all-encompassing mistake is made when the person who is on a relatively immature spiritual level tries to force spiritually mature-level food down his throat with the assumption that it is fuller and healthier. He will inevitably find that his system will reject it and vomit it up. And it is as much a mistake for the mature servant of God to "settle" for nutrition that will never fully satisfy him simply because it is easier to swallow and digest.

We tend to either prematurely rush along our spiritual development or stultify it. It is incumbent upon us to be realistic about our standing day by day and act accordingly. In Luzzatto's words, "it would be sufficient for (us) to be righteous"—if that is our lot. But if we are in fact one of those "lone individuals amongst the people who desire to merit closeness to God"—and only we ourselves can know that, and only through honest self-examination—we should "live by the laws of the saintly—these abstentions—which those others cannot live by."

As Luzzatto puts it at the end of this chapter, "You should abstain from whatever is not necessary for your station in this world, but you are to be referred to as a sinner when you abstain from something you need." That means to say, you should know what you personally need to maintain "your (spiritual) station in this world" and allow yourself it, for it alone will help you along in your progress, and you must abstain from whatever you do not need, *including abstention*, if it will damage you. Contrarily, "you are to be referred to as a sinner when you abstain from something you need," which may include higher spiritual practices, such as abstention.

But the bad forms of abstinence are those absurd ones used by certain gentiles who are not satisfied with not taking from the world what is not necessary, but withhold from themselves even what is necessary. They afflict their bodies in all sorts of weird ways. God does not at all desire that. In fact our sages said (*Taanit* 22b), "it is forbidden for one to torture himself." They said regarding charity (end of *Pe'ah*), "Whoever needs charity and does not take it is like a murderer." They also said (*Taanit* 22b) it is written (Genesis 2:7), ". . . A living soul"—that is to say, "I have placed a soul within you (God said)—keep it alive" (*Taanit* 22b). And they have said (*Taanit* 11a), "One who fasts (when he is incapable for one reason or another of doing so) is called a sinner." Hillel used to quote Proverbs 11:17 and say, "One who is generous to his own soul is called saintly." Before breakfast he would wash his hands and face in honor of his Maker, arguing that all the more so should he do so seeing as how the statues for kings were washed every morning (*Vayikra Rabbah* 34:3).

Here you have the true underlying principle: you should abstain from whatever is not necessary for your station in this world, but you are to be referred to as a sinner when you abstain from something you need (for whatever reason). This is a principle you can depend upon.

The specifics of this general principle, however, cannot all be enunciated, but should be considered on an individual basis, and each person is to be praised according to his own understanding. As it is impossible to garner all the instances as they are infinite in number, and no one mind can contain them all, you should only handle one case at a time.

14

The Subdivisions of Abstinence

There are three primary subdivisions of abstinence: pleasure-based, *Halachah*-based, and personal habit-based abstinence.[1]

What we discussed in the previous chapter (which involved taking nothing from the world other than what, for your nature, is absolutely necessary) refers to pleasure-based abstinence. It includes food-related, sexual, ornamental, recreational, and conversational pleasures and the like. The only time acting on these drives is irrelevant to abstention is when it involves a *mitzvah*.[2]

Halachah-based abstinence involves being stringent in the *mitzvot* at all times—to the point of siding with the minority opinion in arguments of the law where that opinion is not the accepted one (as long as following that opinion does not provide a leniency). It also involves being stringent in "gray" areas where you might legitimately be lenient.

Our sages already illustrated this notion for us (*Chullin* 37b) by explaining Ezekiel's statement (Ezekiel 4:14), "My soul has not become impure," as meaning that he never ate from an animal the ritual purity of which a sage ever had to decide, and he never ate the meat from an animal that had to be slaughtered hurriedly so that it would not soon die from natural causes. Even though these would certainly have been permitted according to the law, he was stringent on himself.

As we said above, you cannot derive what would be permitted to the abstinent by what is permitted to others. The abstinent has to stay away from the repulsive, the nearly repulsive, and even the vaguely repulsive. As Mar Ukva said (*Chullin* 105a),

---

1. These three major subdivisions of abstinence cover the whole of man: his physicality (pleasure), sociability (personal habit), and his spirituality (*Halachah*).

2. Which is to say, the abstinent, like any other Jew, must refrain from doing something forbidden by the Torah. He may take it upon himself to refrain from doing certain other things that others may do, which do not go against the *Halachah*, but the abstinent *may not* refrain from doing those things when it is a *mitzvah* to do them.

"In this matter I am like vinegar to wine compared to my father. Had my father eaten meat just now, he would not eat cheese until tomorrow this time. But where I will not eat cheese at this meal, I *would* eat it at the next one."[3] In fact, the *Halachah* was not as Mar Ukva's father practiced it, for if it were, Mar Ukva himself would certainly not have gone against it. It is just that Mar Ukva's father was stringent in his abstinence. Mar Ukva referred to himself as "vinegar in relation to wine," because he was not himself as abstinent as his father.

And personal habit-based abstinence refers to secluding and detaching yourself from the company of others, and directing your heart towards Divine service instead, and reflecting upon that, as you should. But such a practice is only good as long as you do not go to an extreme. As our sages instructed (*Ketubot* 17a), "Your mind should always be concerned with other people"; and (*Makkot* 10a) "It is written (Jeremiah 50:36), 'A sword shall be upon the liars and they will become fools'— which means to say that a sword shall be upon those who hate certain sages who sit in isolation to learn the Torah.'"

You should join in with good people[4] for the amount of time you need to study or to earn a living, then go in seclusion to attach yourself to your God and come to comprehend the good path and the true form of service to God. Included in this is lessening your speech and avoiding small talk, not looking beyond your own environs, and all other such restrictions which you should accustom yourself in until they become second nature to you.

Though I have presented these three divisions in an abbreviated form to you, you cannot help but see that they include within them very many human actions. I have already pointed out that it is impossible to illustrate all of the instances where these principles can be applied. Only careful thought and consideration can determine those.

---

3. . . . six hours later. Meals were fewer in number but heftier in those days, and were separated by at least six hours. One might eat a morning meal at eleven and not eat again until five that afternoon, and be finished with formal meals for the day. An additional meal, the "third meal," was added on the *Shabbat*. This is the derivation of the predominant custom of not eating dairy for six hours after having eaten a meat meal (though there are other authentic customs to not wait as long)—in order to eat the two sorts of food, which may not be eaten together, at two utterly separate meals and to be certain that all remnants of meat have disappeared. And it is the derivation of our custom of eating a "third meal" on the *Shabbat*.

4. That is the criterion by which such a person (as well as we) should choose his company: their goodness—not their influence, attractiveness, power, or wealth.

The Means
of Acquiring Abstinence

The best way to acquire abstinence is to realize the crassness of the pleasures of the world and their inherent inferiority, as well as the great bad that can so easily result from them.

What inclines us towards these pleasures so much that we require a lot of strength and ingenuity to escape from them is their seductive powers. The eyes are seduced by things that seem to be good and tempting. Seduction is in fact what caused the first sin to be committed. As the Torah attests (Genesis 3:6), "The woman saw that the tree was good to eat and that it was pleasing to the eyes. . . . She took from its fruit and ate from it."

When it becomes clear to you how utterly false, unreal, and ephemeral these pleasures are and how real and imminent the bad that will come from them is, you will certainly be disgusted by them and have no desire for them at all. So this is all you have to learn to do: come to recognize the vacuity and inanity of these pleasures to the point where you are disgusted by them and you will not find it difficult to get rid of the desires for them.

As an example, the most concrete and palpable of pleasures is the desire for food. Is there anything shorter-lived than this pleasure, which only lasts the length of your gullet, from where your food goes to your stomach and is completely forgotten? You could be just as full eating stuffed swan as you would eating coarse bread. You just have to visualize the many diseases you could expose yourself to by your diet, or the feeling of heaviness or dull-mindedness that could come over you after eating to realize the truth of what we are saying. Certainly, no one would want anything to do with something whose disadvantages are real and whose apparent benefits are a sham. It is true of all the other pleasures of the world as well: if you would just reflect upon them you would see that even the apparent good in them is only short-lived, while the bad that can come from them is serious and long-lasting.[1] It does not make sense for an intelligent person to endanger himself for the minute benefits that might accrue to him through them. Is not that obvious?

When you accustom and convince yourself in the truth of what we have pointed out, you will slowly, surely, and willingly free yourself from the entrapment of all the foolishness that is brought about by the darkness of the material world. You will no longer be seduced by its so-called pleasures, but you will be disgusted by them and come to realize that you should only take from the world what you absolutely must, as we have said.

Just as reflection upon all this can bring you to abstinence, confusion in it and closeness with people of power and control who run after glory and add to the general emptiness can destroy it. It is impossible to be around riches and elegance and not desire or long for them. Even if your *yetzer hara* will not get the better of you, you would still find yourself in the midst of a great battle and be in danger. Solomon referred to this when he said (Ecclesiastes 7:2), "It is better to go to a house of mourning than to a tavern."

The best thing to do is practice seclusion, because by removing worldly matters from your eyes you remove the lust for them from your heart. King David praised solitude by saying (Psalms 55:7–8), "If I could be given the wings of a dove I would just fly away and dwell somewhere else. I would go far away; I would lodge in the desert." We find that the prophets Elijah and Elisha set aside places in the mountains to be alone in, and the early sages and saints followed in their footsteps. They all found solitude to be the most propitious means of acquiring wholeness and abstinence, and of not being swayed by the emptiness of empty company.[2]

---

1. What he means to say is that the pleasure to be found in such things is *apparent* pleasure at best, not real and thorough pleasure. And that as ephemeral as it is, is also short-lived. But the damage that can come from the act thought to produce pleasure is real, serious, and long-lived.

2. Often, when we ruminate, we come to dream about things we do not really want but which we have been told we do. Do not think that that only happens to fools, the gullible, and the very young. It happens to the best of us, as our age knows only too well. Few are the people today who are not given their dreams by television, newspaper, theater, and sports. The person of rare originality is the one who craves the different and foreign thing or life in our days.

But there are times when, somewhere in the dark and the rain, we take hold of ourselves and hear ourselves out again for the first time in a long while. Those are the times when we breath deeply and emit self, when we envision our true beings expanded. We find then that we have had dreams all along that have been tucked into the back of our beings that are still alive, albeit flattened and crumpled, that are waiting for us. The best of those dreams (not to be confused with our fantasies which are things of fluff and external influence) involve lives of simplicity, direction, and goal. In fact, the greater the dream, the greater the simplicity, and the more dynamic the direction and goal.

What you have to be careful about when acquiring abstinence is to not leap to the opposite extreme in one fell swoop, as this will certainly not be to your advantage. Instead, you should come to it slowly, settling into and upon one aspect of it today and another tomorrow until you accustom yourself to it so thoroughly it becomes second nature to you.

Those times are rare enough, even for the best of us. And they never happen when we are with company—unless the company is that of dear and beloved people whom we trust and from whom we would like nothing more than to hear out their selves put clearly as well. Those moments never happen in instances of concentration upon materiality, rather in instances of concentration upon love, nobility, and Godliness.

We all know that, and it cannot be denied. But we tend to avoid such moments of private or shared reverie. We seem to be frightened by them, so we veer toward the other moments, which focus upon the stark and material, and we spend lives overlooking ourselves. Luzzatto is saying that we cannot. Such an overlooking is fraught with emptiness and sham. It encourages soul-damage (God forbid) and it is too well satisfied with small accomplishments of the spirit and little essences.

The person who has avoided such failure long enough becomes sad when he meets it again. He would sense the same sickening wretchedness someone who used to smoke cigarettes would when he would come near a smoker. He would know that he would want nothing more than to call out, but that that would be too much for polite company to stand. So to avoid a scene he would leave. Is there anything else he could do? Could we help but sympathize with him?

So we are asked to act that way right off—leave the party because it will inevitably sicken us; avoid the battle which is sometimes won and other times not, but which is always scarring. Life is very short—we know only too well—and its meaning is elsewhere. Avoid waste and move on, we are being advised.

Summation of Part V

Chapter 13

1. From here on we discuss how to become pious, whereas to this point we discussed how to become righteous.

2. The essence of abstinence is doing without the permitted so as to never come to the forbidden. We have already indicated how human beings are naturally drawn toward the physical rather than to the spiritual, and that everything that happens to us is a challenge to respond to that dilemma. It only stands to reason that you must take measures to be sure that you will not get caught up in the draw toward the material and suffer its inevitable consequences, and those measures involve abstinence. But there are beneficial abstinences and there are harmful ones. We will start off by analyzing the beneficial ones.

3. There is nothing wrong with eating and drinking what is permitted to you, for example. But habitually overeating or -drinking those same things causes you to set up structures by which you can maintain such a style of life, which in turn disrupts your relationship with God.

4. And there is certainly nothing wrong with sexual relations between husband and wife. But because sexuality is so ingrained in us it is easy to come to licentiousness, and we must take measures to be sure not to.

5. There are other acts or things that are not inherently harmful but which can nonetheless lead to spiritually harming consequences, and they include: dressing stylishly (which may lead to arrogance, licentiousness, jealousy, envy, and extortion), taking pleasure trips, and holding idle conversations (which may lead to neglect of Torah study, slander, deceit, and levity), and so forth.

6. As to the harmful forms of abstinence, they involve refusing to partake of the *necessary* and healthy benefits from this world, such as bodily well-being and the like.

Chapter 14

7. All in all there are three types of abstinence: pleasure-based (discussed in numbers 3–5 above), halachic-based, and personal-behavior-based abstinence. Halachic-based abstinence involves being particularly stringent and punctilious in the law, and following the more difficult and less-often-followed opinion in such things.

8. Personal behavior-based abstinence involves absenting yourself from human company and concentrating upon your relationship with God. But you must be sure not to go to the extreme in this and make a recluse of yourself. You should be with people (good ones) as much as you have to in order to study Torah or make a living, but no more, and while you are with them you should speak minimally and righteously, and mind your own affairs.

Chapter 15

9. The eyes are often seduced by things that seem to be good or beneficial, so it is difficult to abstain. But the best way to do so is to come to realize the ephemeral and low relative worth of those things, and the harm that can come as a result of them.

10. You can easily do that with the desire for food, for example. To free yourself of its enticements you only have to think about what it goes through once it is inside of you, or about the stuffed or dull-witted sensation it brings, or you can realize how short-lived the delight it brings to you is. The best overall advice is to live a life of solitude, because when you keep away from things, their temptations and allures stay away from you.

11. But you must realize that you cannot come to abstinence immediately. You have to move toward it step by step, day by day until it becomes second nature to you.

VI

PURITY

Introduction to Part VI

The sixth part concerns itself with the trait of "purity." It is very short and comprises just two chapters (16 and 17), entitled, "An Explanation of the Trait of Purity" (chap. 16) and "The Means of Acquiring Purity" (chap. 17).

The matters aside from the subject at hand discussed within these small chapters include: following the dictates of wisdom rather than the *yetzer hara*, altruism, unequivocal reward for all of our efforts, the criterion by which those who serve God are ranked, the place of the heart in the service of God (chap. 16); and the true nature of the supposed pleasures of the world, proper preparation for doing *mitzvot* by establishing presence of mind (chap. 17).

As Luzzatto says at the very beginning of chapter 16, "purity is the reparation of your emotions and thoughts." As such, it devolves around the inner and unconscious workings of your motivations and drives. It speaks of the central place of the heart in service to God, of the interaction of heart and mind, and of coming to focus heart and mind together for the full worship of God.

Purity, the Hebrew word for which is *taharah*, does not have the connotation of simplicity, delicacy, coldness, frigidity, or celibacy as it often does in English. It denotes a state of being absolved of all sin and of all ritual impurity. It connotes the clearness of the sky after the rainy season (*Berachot* 59a), and (in the case of its cognate, *tiharah*) noontime (*Yoma* 59a). As such it refers to a clearing away of impediments and a new beginning.

16

*An Explanation
of the Trait of Purity*

Purity entails the reparation of your emotions and thoughts.[1] It is what David referred to when he said (Psalms 51:12), "God has created a pure heart within me."[2] Its essence

---

1. The phrase literally reads, "purity is the reparation of your *heart* and thoughts," but we have translated "heart" as "emotions" because that is how it is used later on in context, and also because the two are used simultaneously in common parlance. But the word "heart" is purposefully used for the emotions. That can be explained thusly: in essence, there are three centers of the physical being and each is symbolized and controlled by three crucial and single organs (as opposed to the other, for the most part, nonessential and doubled organs).

Those physical centers are: (1) rank physicality, represented and controlled by the organ of procreation, (2) emotionality, represented and controlled by the heart, and (3) mentality, represented and controlled by the brain (your "thoughts"). (See chap. 13, n. 2, for a discussion of these centers and their rectifications as to how they relate to the various levels of the soul.)

The organ of procreation sits at the center of the lower third of the physical self and is the symbol for and controlling force behind rank physicality because it requires neither conviction nor analyses (though it may use them), just drive to do its job.

The heart sits at the center of the middle third of the physical self and is the symbol for and controlling force behind emotionality because it requires both drive and instinct, as well as the will to live (a vital and central emotion) to do its job.

And your "thoughts" (the brain) sit at the center of the topmost third of the physical self and are the symbol for and controlling force behind mentality because they require both drive and instinct, the will to live, and conscious and unconscious mental effort to do their job.

Each third is a universe unto itself, or so it would appear, though each does in fact influence the other. And each has to be rectified in its own right.

So far (with the exception of innocence) we have concentrated upon the rectification of the lower universe, that of rank physicality and the drive toward it, hence the concentra-

is that you not allow your *yetzer hara* to interfere with your actions, and that you act only through wisdom and reverence, not through sin and desire.[3]

This even refers to the physical and material acts you might involve yourself in after you will have habituated yourself in abstinence and taken nothing but what you must from the world. Even then you will need to purify your emotions and thoughts so that even that small bit of pleasure you might take from the world will not be taken with the intent of enjoying pleasure or fulfilling a desire, but rather with the intention of doing it for the good that will come from it in terms of wisdom and Divine service.[4] As it was said of Rabbi Eliezer, (*Nedarim* 20b) "he would expose a handsbreadth and cover over two handsbreadths during intercourse, and he would be like one coerced by a demon"—he would derive no pleasure from the act at all, and would only do it for the *mitzvah* and the Divine service inherent to

---

tion upon sexuality and the like. Now we begin the rectification of the other two universes: emotionality and mentality. This part focuses upon the rectification of the emotions for the most part, and somewhat upon rectification of thoughts, even though it says, "purity is the reparation of your emotions *and thoughts.*" In fact, the rectification of thoughts comes later. Luzzatto is wont to tell us to do something before it is actually called for (cf. note 1 of chap. 10: he tells us in chap. 10 that we are to be "utterly free from all bad traits and sins" when we do not come to that level of self-discipline until *this* chapter, as will be discussed below), and he does that to warn us that it is coming our way and we should ready ourselves for it.

2. That is, "God has created pure *emotions* within me."

3. We said before that the *yetzer hara* is "nothing other than the urge to remain attached to the earth and things mundane." Such an urge can obviously be all encompassing, partly so, or not at all, depending upon your spiritual stature. Someone who has evolved to the point where he is working toward purity is partly influenced by his *yetzer hara*, that is, he is *somewhat* attached to the earth and mundane desires and objects. As such, a part of him irrationally overlooks the Presence of God even yet and has him act unwisely and irreverently. Even if such a person hardly acts so (as we would expect of a person who has obtained all that preceded this trait), he is still said to act that way, and is still said to be controlled by sin and mundane desire, albeit to a minute degree.

But to be pure is to no longer allow yourself to be swayed by the *yetzer hara*. It is to be so in control of your being that you only follow the counsel of wisdom and God-reverence. It is a life of doing only what is right and what should be done for the sake of general excellence, and of fulfilling the needs of the soul alone.

It follows then that the more influenced a person is by his *yetzer hara*, the more he falls under the sway of sin and desire, and the less likely is he to be driven by the dictates of wisdom and reverence.

4. This means to say that even physical acts must be so subtly dealt with, and so widely opened to correction that the very thoughts and slight, nudging inclinations that accompany them must be changed at their source, which is your mind. You must so sensitize your being that it can hear the small and low reverberations of your thoughts and come to change them.

it. King Solomon would say (Proverbs 3:6), "Know Him in all of your ways and He will right your paths."[5]

But you should know, that just as purity of thoughts pertains to bodily actions, which are inherently close to the *yetzer hara* (and should be avoided so they will not become his own) it also pertains to righteous deeds, which are close to God, are not connected to the *yetzer hara*, and which you should not avoid. This is the whole matter of doing *mitzvot* "for an ulterior motive" mentioned many times by our sages.

But, as has been explained, there are many varieties of *mitzvot* done in the mode of "for ulterior motives." The lowest level of them is when you do something not for the sake of service to God, but only to deceive people and to propagate honor or wealth for yourself. It is what the sages were referring to when they said (*Berachot* 1:7), "It would have been better for him to have been turned around in his afterbirth (and suffocated)," and what the prophet was referring to when he said (Isaiah 64:5), "We've all become sullied and our righteousness has become like rags."

But there is another sort of doing of *mitzvot* for ulterior motives. It involves doing something good for the sake of the reward. It is regarding this that it is said (*Pesachim* 50b), "A person should always be involved in Torah and *mitzvot* for ulterior motives so that he might eventually, thusly, come to do them altruistically." However, if you have not yet reached the level of doing the *mitzvot* altruistically after having done them for ulterior motives you are still far from whole.

What requires even more reflection and effort are the subtle admixtures of the prohibited within the permitted. You may start out to do a *mitzvah* utterly altruistically, simply because it is something our Father in Heaven has decreed, and yet may not hesitate mixing in some other motivation: either the fact that people would compliment you for it, or that you would get some other reward for it. Sometimes, even if you do not intend to be complimented for having done the *mitzvah*, you might be pleased with the praise nonetheless and become more exacting in it. This was the case with Rabbi Chaninah Ben Tradyon's daughter (*Avodah Zarah* 18a) who would walk daintily, and who would take even more care in her walk when she would hear people say, "How prettily that young girl walks!" Her additional effort was a direct result of the power of the compliments given to her.[6]

---

5. This can be understood in two different ways: either that you are to know God, that is, come to realize at all times the fact that God exists and act accordingly, and He Himself will "right your paths."

Or it can be understood to mean that you must so clearly hear your thoughts and inclinations, and so train your mental "ear" to pick up the small "voices" humming at all times in your mind that you thus excavate down to the outer rim of your *yechidah*, and come to "know God" (who is attached to the *yechidah*) through this very fine and wide knowledge of your self, at which point God will "right your paths."

6. In other words, there are three levels of doing *mitzvot* less than altruistically: for utterly selfish reasons, "to deceive people and to propagate honor or wealth for yourself" (and it is assumed that the person who has progressed to this point would not fit into this category,

And even though this prohibited aspect is nullified by the minute part it plays in the big picture, it nonetheless makes the act somewhat impure by its inclusion.[7] Just as a sacrifice is not acceptable on the altar unless it is of the finest flour that has been sifted through thirteen sieves (*Menachot* 76b) and smelted of all dross, so too is it impossible to raise yourself upon the altar of His Will and be amongst the whole and choice servants of God without the choicest of actions—those purified of all sorts of dross.

But I am not saying that everything less than this is completely rejected. God does not deprive anyone of his due reward, and He rewards all according to their

---

as it is the lowest level); for external gain, "for reward" (one who has progressed so far may yet experience traces of this); and altruistically, but not without a willingness to enjoy the benefit after the fact (which must be expunged at this point).

People of low spiritual stature would certainly be capable of doing something ostensibly good for a less than grand and noble end. How many people have donated large sums of money just so that their names may be immortalized on the walls and doorways of institutions? And the Torah encourages us all to do good deeds for the sake of the spiritual reward that will inevitably come from them when it says, "A person should always be involved in Torah and *mitzvot* for ulterior motives so that he might eventually, thusly, come to do them altruistically." It recognizes how we are often driven, allows for that, and encourages us on in that pursuit because by the very nature of the matter we will be using to gain rewards (which is the fulfillment of the *mitzvot*) we will come to altruism.

But the rare and special person who is heading toward piety and holiness must go further yet and veer toward altruism from this point on. And it is expected that the *mitzvot* he will have done by now for some slight and fine less-than-altruistic reason will have raised him to the state *approaching* clear altruism, because when you (Proverbs 3:6, cited above [p. 136]) "Know Him in all of your ways . . . *He* (through his *mitzvot*) will right your paths."

7. As we indicated in the first note above, it is just now that we are being asked to be "utterly free from *all* bad traits and sins," as it is put in the beginning of chapter 10. All the shadows and rubbings of sin and bad in us are to be removed by this point. Whereas before we could not have been said to be "sinful," we nonetheless carried along with us all sorts of untoward motivations as we actively pursued good and fled from evil. It is only from this point onward, if we are successful, that we can be said to be "pure" and "*utterly* free from all bad traits and sins."

8. This must be taken to heart by all. Often in a rush of longing to be holy and cling to God we turn our eyes upward and set ourselves to the task, then turn our eyes downward to see where we stand, and grow depressed. "I should think of holiness and piety!" we say. "Who am I? God only knows what I am capable of doing for the ruination of my soul!" A bitter self-contempt overtakes us and we brood.

That can only lead to two things: growth, or despondency and a giving up. But we must not let it lead to despondency. We must remember that in His great mercy, God "does not deprive anyone of his due reward, and He rewards all according to their deeds." And whereas we may certainly have been capable of great error and illusion in the past we are as capable of great rectification and clear-sightedness in the future, and whatever we will have done toward that rectification and clear-sightedness remains with us at all times, while our errors and illusions can be undone through *teshuvah*.

deeds.[8] What I am addressing is the sort of perfect service that befits those who truly love God and who would not refer to any service as perfect unless it were utterly pure and had no other motive attached to it than being for the sake of God.[9] And the farther an act is from this level, the more imperfect it is. King David referred to this when he said (Psalms 73:25), "Whom have I in heaven (but You), and when I have You, I desire nothing on this earth," and when he said (Psalms 119:140), "Your word is thoroughly refined, and Your servant loves it."

In fact, true service to God has to be smelted even more finely than gold or silver. As it is said about Torah (Psalms 12:7), "The sayings of God are pure sayings—silver smelted in the crucible of earth, refined seven times over." And if you would want to truly serve God you could not be satisfied with less than that—you would not be pleased with silver tainted with dross and alloys, that is, Divine service mixed in with impure motives—you could only be satisfied with the pure and refined. Only then would you be referred to as one who does a *mitzvah* "as it is supposed to be done," about whom it is said (*Shabbat* 63a), "whoever does a *mitzvah* as it is supposed to be done is never given bad news." Our sages said (*Nedarim* 62a), "Do things for the sake of their Maker, but speak of them in their own name," which is the choice of those wholehearted in their service to God.

One who does not cling to God with true love will find this process of refining Divine service a great burden. He would say, "Who could withstand this? We are only human. It's impossible for us to reach this level of refinement and purity!"[10] But those who love God and want to do His will will be happy to show faithfulness in their love for Him by intensifying their refinement and purification of it. King David summed it up when he said (Psalm 119:140), ". . . and Your servant loves it."

This is in fact the criterion by which those who serve God are differentiated from each other, for those who especially know how to purify their emotions are closer and dearer to God. Such was the case with the first ones to reach this level, who fought and triumphed in this: the Patriarchs and the other Shepherds who purified their emotions before God. This was what David warned his son Solomon about when he said (1 Chronicles 28:9), "God searches the hearts of all, and understands the inclinations of thoughts."

---

9. True love of God is discussed somewhat in chapter 18, but especially so in chapter 19.

10. A person with such an attitude would not grow despondent over his failures, as we indicated in note 8 above. He would grow *cynical*, and would not be propelled by the aforementioned "rush of longing to be holy and cling to God," but rather by a deep-seated reticence toward progress and growth. Such a person is convinced he is limited and makes sure to be so.

A natural outcome of such cynicism is a dark and constant state of falling short. And that leads to embitterment and anger, which has its victim hate himself and avoid all exposure to the Divine. And whereas the person in note 8 can be rectified by growing in his love for God and coming to realize how God loves him as well, the cynic can never come to that and can never escape the mire into which he has placed himself.

Our sages said in this vein (*Sanhedrin* 106b), "God desires the heart," because God does not want only our actions to be involved in *mitzvot*. His main concern is that your heart be pure and set on performing your true duty. The heart is the king and commander of the rest of the body. If it does not bring itself to serve God, the service of the rest of the organs is for naught, for they will only go where the spirit of the heart will take them as the Torah tells us when it says (Proverbs 23:26), "Give your heart to Me, My son."[11]

---

11. Because the heart is that organ in command of the centermost of the three universes spoken of in the first note above, it is empowered with the ability to control the rest. That means to tell us that our emotions can affect our thoughts as well as our drives, and that we must not underestimate them. If you feel a certain way, and that feeling courses through the whole of your physical being (through the power of the heart), you will be affected to the core and react accordingly.

17

The Means of Acquiring Purity

It is easy for the person who has already tried for and obtained the various traits discussed up to now to obtain this one. When you consider and reflect upon the petty nature of the pleasures of the world and their supposed benefits, as I have said already, you will come to despise them and consider them to be nothing but the outcome of the bad and defective nature of the dark and coarse state of things.[1] And

---

1. That is to say, you will *only* come to despise the supposed delights of the world and "consider them to be nothing" when you will have come to realize that they are "nothing but the outcome of the bad and defective nature of the dark and coarse state of things."

We seem to live in an odd and rumbling sort of age. So many of the mysteries of the workings of the full self and of the world at large are revealed to us now. So much sits right before our eyes and so much else is fecund with possibility. Yet so very many people are opposed to the Torah's cogent explanations of it all and are virile in their abandonment of it. Irony of ironies: a vast cornucopia of information and revelation, a broad and ancient tradition of explanation and statement, and a dogged unwillingness to listen. Out of that tension comes production, as all tension leads to one sort of production or another, but it is a coarse and often lethal sort of production. But that has been the case all along: every age has produced its disease and has done its fair share of avoidance of God.

The person who enjoys purity comes to realize all that. He knows that the grand electricity of the age, as smudged and sooted as it is, is the same grand electricity of every age translated into the current age's media. To him there is no time without its elemental profundity. But there is also no time that has not failed woefully and deeply, and only because it has forgotten the Grand Design, which is the Torah, and overlooked its Maker.

As such, the person enjoying purity cannot accept the things of the world for what they are. To him they are tragic and piteous in their delusion. The people who accept them as the idols of the age are tragic and piteous in the eyes of the person of purity as well. From where he stands, all is indeed "nothing." But not because it is inherently so, because it is not.

when the very real defects and bad aspects of them become self-evident to you it will certainly become easy to separate yourself from them and remove them from your heart. And the more deeply and constantly you come to recognize the pettiness of materiality and its delights, the easier it will be for you to purify your thoughts and emotions so that they will no longer be inclined toward the side of the *yetzer hara*, and you will only be involved in worldly deeds if you absolutely have to.

However, just as purification of thought is divided into two parts (the first being in terms of physical actions and the second in terms of Divine service) so too is the sort of reflection needed to acquire it divided into two parts. The way to purify your thoughts in relation to bodily actions is to constantly take notice of the pettiness of the world and its delights, as I have said. The way to purify your thoughts in relation to acts of service to God is to increase your reflection upon the fallaciousness of honor and train yourself to flee from it. Then you will be cleansed of all desire for the praise and compliments people will pay you when you serve God, and you will be focused on Him, who alone is our praise, our good and our wholeness, as it is written (Deuteronomy 10:21), "He is your praise, and He is your God."[2]

Among the acts that direct a person towards this trait is proper preparation for Torah and *mitzvot*. You should not suddenly and immediately rush into doing a *mitzvah* before having had time to reflect upon what you are about to do.[3] Rather, you should ready yourself for it and compose yourself until you are properly focused, then consider what you are about to do and before Whom you are about to do it. As soon as you enter into this process of reflection you will find it easy to rid yourself of all external motivations and to set the proper and desirable intentions in your thoughts instead.[4]

The early pious ones would wait a whole hour before they would actually begin praying (*Berachot* 30b) so that they could direct their hearts to God. They certainly would not waste the hour. What they would do is ready themselves by focusing their attention upon the prayers they were to pray and they would eliminate any untoward thoughts. Then they would fill themselves with the necessary reverence and

---

Such a person recognizes God in them. But they have *come to be* "nothing but the outcome of the bad and defective nature of the dark and coarse state of things" in his eyes because he has enjoyed association with the truth, and can no longer endure the husk without its fruit.

2. Can the person who has come this far fail to recognize that all that he does is done through the power, hence the permission of God? Can he for a moment take credit for his good works any more than for an avalanche? To such a person, honor is a failure to recognize the Source and to give credit to the vehicle which is himself.

3. Can anyone overlook the fact that when you are about to do a *mitzvah* you are manhandling the very means to perfection of yourself and your world? No, no more than the scientist cannot help but handle with reverence and love the slide on which he has found the very thing he has sought for decades.

4. Luzzatto is alluding to the establishment of presence of mind, which only comes about with silence, calm, focus, and studied contemplation.

love, about which it is said (Job 11:13), "If you have readied your heart, and spread your palms out to Him."

The detriments to this trait are the lack of reflection upon the foolishness and pettiness of worldly pleasures, running after honor, and insufficient preparation for Divine service. The first two seduce your thought and draw it toward extraneous motives like an adulterous woman who sleeps with men other than her husband. Untoward thoughts have already been referred to as "licentiousness of the heart" in the Torah, which says (Numbers 15:39), "And you may not go after the inclinations of your heart or your eyes which you licentiously follow." The heart is easily distracted from the wholesome path it should be following and is attracted to ephemeral and false fantasies. Insufficient preparation brings on the natural foolishness that comes from the element of physicality yet unremoved that leaves a foul stench behind in your Divine service.[5]

We will now go on to explain the trait of piety.

---

5. That is to say, if you have not yet removed your being from what you are about to do, and do not recognize the full Presence of God in your actions, you can neither be said to be pure or anything but ever so slightly foolish.

Summation of Part VI

Chapter 16

1. You enjoy purity when you rectify both your emotions and thoughts, when you disallow the *yetzer hara* to interfere with your actions, and when you act with wisdom and reverence, rather than through the influence of sin and desire.

2. You will need to purify yourself even after mastering abstention. You do that by being sure that the pleasure you derive from something permitted you will not be derived for its own sake or for the sake of fulfilling a desire, but rather for the sake of wisdom that will come of it or the fact that it will make your Divine service more successful.

3. There is a level of purity that must be attained in the doing of righteous deeds as well. The ultimate degree of this involves doing them altruistically, and not for any ulterior motive, such as for recognition or reward. To do otherwise is to sully an otherwise pure act, and one who truly loves God would not settle for that.

4. The heart is the commander of all the organs in the body, and where it goes, they go. So the more you purify your heart, the closer and dearer you are to God. As the Talmud says (*Sanhedrin* 106b), "God desires the heart." And as it is written (Proverbs 23:26), "Give your heart to Me, My son."

Chapter 17

5. The way to obtain purity in your deeds is to consider the petty nature of the pleasures of the world, to despise them, and to recognize them as being

the outcome of the dark and coarse state of the world. That way you will come to involve yourself in those pleasures only if you are forced to.

6. And the way to obtain purity in your Divine service is to reflect upon the false nature of personal honor and to flee from it.

7. What also helps in the fostering of the trait of purity is the preparation for Torah study or *mitzvot*. This involves composing yourself, then realizing what you are about to do and before Whom you are about to do it. With such an attitude you will find it easy to rid yourself of all stray motivations and to address the subject at hand.

8. What prevents successful purity is a lack of reflection upon the absurdity of earthly delights and the pursuit of honor, as well as insufficient preparation for Torah study or *mitzvot*.

VII

PIETY

Introduction to Part VII

The seventh part comprises four chapters (18–21) and concerns itself with the trait of "piety." The chapters are entitled "An Explanation of the Trait of Piety" (chap. 18), "The Subdivisions of Piety" (chap. 19), "The Evaluating Needed for Piety" (chap. 20), and "The Means of Acquiring Piety" (chap. 21).

The matters discussed in this part aside from its subject include: false versus true piety, extending yourself for the love of God (chap. 18); fastidiousness in *mitzvot*, easing people's burdens, satisfying others' needs, living a long life, benevolence, compassion and grace for all—human and animal, being judged measure for measure, submission to God's will, reverence for God's grandeur, give-and-take in prayer, honoring *mitzvot*, creativity in Divine service, honoring Torah and Torah scholars, love of God under all circumstances, happiness with your lot, attachment to and obsession with God, grieving for the exile and the destruction of the Holy Temple, working for the well-being of the generation (chap. 19); weighing and balancing the outcomes of your actions, not acting on first impressions, setting aside piety when necessary (chap. 20); reflecting upon God's great goodness, collecting your thoughts, reciting and coming to understand Psalms, preoccupation and worry, trust in God, and knowing that we need not work for our food and shelter (chap. 21).

It is written in chapter 19 that, "The very word piety (*chasidut*) is based upon kindness (*chesed*)." As such, piety is related to holiness, charity, graciousness, goodness, dedication, devoutness, fervor, sacrosanctity, and virtue. It does not carry the connotations of sanctimoniousness, formalism, puritanism, fundamentalism, sectarianism, sacerdotalism, or missionaryism.

18

*An Explanation
of the Trait of Piety*

Piety actually requires a lot of explanation.[1] There are many people doing a lot of
things in the name of piety which are in fact only pale and irreparably formless, shape-

---

1. Much of this section harkens back to Luzzatto's introduction.

When he says in this chapter, for example, that "there are many people doing a lot of
things in the name of piety which are in fact only pale and irreparably formless, shapeless
shadows of the real thing" such as "the incessant recital of petitions and confessions, accompanied by weeping, exaggerated prostrations and all sorts of odd flagellations people could
kill themselves doing, such as immersion in ice and snow and the like," we are immediately
reminded of his statement in the introduction that "it has come to appear to most that piety
is dependent merely upon the recitation of many Psalms and long, convoluted confessions;
upon difficult fasts; and upon ablutions in ice and snow."

And when he says here that people who have made themselves out to be pious "have
. . . gone the way they deduced they should, without having weighed and considered all the
factors on the scales of wisdom," we recall his earlier statement that "if one would reflect upon
the matter he would find that true piety is not dependent upon those things the fools who
make themselves out to be pious think it is, but rather upon true wholeness and profound
wisdom."

In fact, a major aspect of the introduction, the discussion of the verse (Deuteronomy
10:12–13), "And now, Israel—what does God your Lord require of you if not to revere God
your Lord; to go in all of His ways, to love Him and to serve God your Lord with full heart
and soul, and to keep all of God's commandments and statutes . . . ," which seems to be so
central and significant when it is mentioned there, is only just *now* analyzed, in this part. And
that is especially odd because it is said there to include the "preferred subdivisions of the perfection of Divine service," that is, the gist of the matter.

He goes so far there as to define these "preferred subdivisions" and to do the same in
this chapter and in chapter 19. In the introduction he says that the "reverence" mentioned in

less shadows of the real thing. And that comes as a result of improper understanding and analysis on the part of the people who act this way. They have not bothered to delve deeply, with clarity and determination, into the way of God. Instead, they have assumed a false piety, and have simply gone the way they deduced they should, without having weighed and considered all the factors on the scales of wisdom.

---

the verse refers to "reverence for His exaltedness—that you be in a state of reverence before Him comparable to what you would experience being before a great and awesome king: that you be abashed before His greatness, and that, as a result of His greatness, you be aware of every move you make before Him—especially when speaking to Him in prayer or Torah study." And he defines it in this section as "reverence for God's grandeur," adding that "while you are praying or performing a *mitzvah* you are to consider the fact that you are praying and standing before the King of kings."

The "walking in His ways" alluded to in the verse he says there "includes all manner of character correction and reparation." He says in chapter 18 that "piety . . . is founded upon great wisdom and the ultimate rectification of actions."

The "love" of the verse is defined in the introduction as "a type of love of God . . . set in your heart that would lead you to do what satisfies Him as energetically as you would do the same for your mother or father." And he says in chapter 19 that love of God should be "the kind of love a son has for his father."

"Fullness of heart" as he understands it in the introduction means "your service to God should be done with the purest of intentions" while in chapter 19 he says that "the motivation in serving God found among the truly pious . . . is that His glory grow and spread."

And finally, he defines "Keeping all of God's commandments" there as "keeping all of the Divine commandments in their fullness and with all of their conditions" and in chapter 19 as "keeping . . . the *mitzvot* with all their minutiae as carefully as humanly possible."

So we see that piety seems to be the entire focus of the book and that all that has brought us to here has been in preparation for this moment for which he has been anxiously waiting. This is even hinted at by the fact that Luzzatto seems to hurry us through the section that immediately precedes this one (purity) and almost gives a sigh of relief at its very end with his odd and unnecessary statement, "we will now go on to (finally?) explain the trait of piety." Apparently he feels that all that follows this trait is meant for the exceedingly special, the utmost gifted, the specially blessed individuals. And while he would not leave it out, he would not be so unrealistic as to imagine that many people could hope for it.

If that is the case, why is this book entitled *The Path of the Just* rather than *The Path of the Pious*? Who are "the Just" anyway? Where do they come in, and why is that trait never mentioned?

To respond to that we have to know that the Hebrew word for "the Just," *yesharim* (sing., *yeshar*) literally means "the straight," that is to say, those headed in the right direction, those taking the most direct path, those following the dictates of wisdom and not swerving from it. It means to say that the *yeshar* do not start out pious, or even cautious, enthusiastic, innocent, and so forth. They simply start out *yeshar*, that is, well-intended and focused, and will more likely turn out to be pious by virtue of the fact that they are "headed in the right direction" and "well-intended" from the start. Indeed, this attitude has to be maintained in order to follow through on all of the ensuing levels.

These sorts of people have left a foul impression of pious acts in the eyes of both the lesser- and the well-educated, who have come to associate piety with fool-ishness and absurdity, and have come to believe that piety is dependent upon the incessant recital of petitions and confessions, accompanied by weeping, exaggerated prostrations, and all sorts of odd flagellations people could kill themselves doing, such as immersion in ice and snow and the like.[2] They do not realize that while some of these practices *are* required of the penitent and others of them are required of abstinents, piety itself is nonetheless not based upon any of this (though the best of such acts may often accompany piety).

But piety is a profound thing in its own right. It is founded upon great wisdom and the ultimate rectification of actions. Such a course of action would be fitting for the wise-of-heart to follow. Only a wise person could obtain it, in fact. As our sages have put it (*Avot* 2:5). "An unlearned person can never become pious."[3]

That teaches us an invaluable lesson—perhaps the most essential one in the book: that to change you have to be willing to change from the start, and that if you are willing to change, you certainly will, because you will be willing to make the effort to change.

But something else is being said here as well that cannot be overlooked. Dear reader: only a *yeshar* would read a book such as this. A fool or an evildoer never would. Understand that and take it to heart. There will be times in this part when you will be tempted to try on the subject at hand right away, when you may succeed at it for a while, then slip, and lose heart. Do not fall into that trap. Realize that while much of what you are about to read in this part can be lived up to by anybody, irregardless of his or her present spiritual standing (who, for example, cannot be or is not occasionally benevolent, compassionate, kind, or reveren-tial?), it cannot be lived up to *at all times* until you will have evolved to the point of being pious! Please do not forget that. You can have your moments of great piety—and all *yesharim* do—but you cannot expect to live up to that at all times until you will have obtained all that has preceded this. To believe otherwise is to leave yourself open to despair and to fall from the lofty perspective of following the dictates of wisdom.

Onward.

2. There is a notion we all have of piety that is unshakable and does not have to be described. It is not, as some might think, the picture of a puppet, liar, or fool, but rather one of a giant of a being, full of love, mission, and vision. And though we can all conceive of it, and we believe in our hearts it exists, few of us see it in the world and fewer yet have met such a person.

Granted, few people in our age have even seen people of false and superficial piety, as piety is a lost art in our age, and there are few great ones and few bad ones. But we have clung tenaciously to a dream of its existence. So when you see a bad "artisan" of piety in our days you are overwhelmed by the memory of your hidden dream of it, and you are reviled by its rarity. And that reaction is sad and tragic, in that it threatens the dreamer and it withholds the attainment that much longer.

The only solution: intelligent, directed, and authentic piety in others and in ourselves.

3. That is to say, one could never know what God requires of him if he were not open to the knowledge of God and could not fathom the ways of His world. Could one so foolish

We will now explain the matter in sequence. The root of piety is illustrated by the statement of our sages which reads (*Berachot* 17a), "The man who toils in Torah and brings satisfaction to his Creator is fortunate."[4] The point is that the *mitzvot* that have been given to Israel, and the extent of their obligations are well known. One who truly loves God would not set out to do just what all of Israel is obliged to do. He would act as a loving son would to his father by doing more than his father would ask for. He would do all he possibly could even if his father had only unobtrusively hinted at a desire for something. And if his father asked for that thing just once, and demurely at that, that would be enough for such a son to perceive the extent of his father's unstated true desires. He would deduce that such-and-such—something beyond what he was told—would bring satisfaction to his father, and he would not have to wait for an explicit and reiterated request to do it.

We see this sort of thing happen all the time between friends, lovers, husbands and wives, fathers and sons. Where there is a strong bond of love between people, you would never find one of them saying, "I haven't been asked to do more than this, and it's all right to do just what I've been asked." Instead, that person would surmise what the other person really wants, based upon what he said, and would try to do all that he could to bring satisfaction to the loved one.

One who truly loves God will have just this sort of reaction to Him, because that sort of person is a lover as well. The commandments that are so well-known to

---

as to be self-centered and to care for nothing but his own needs, never sensing his place in the great rush and blossom, ever come to realize the Divine? Could one steeped in smallness and inconsequence, who overlooks the grand, and is bored with genius and license, ever hear God's opera?

4. Rules of human conduct, from our perspective, seem to be very complex. There are so many millions of things to consider and act upon in the course of life, we think. In fact, there are not quite that many things to do—perhaps there are a dozen or two—but the applications of them are infinite in number.

For example, all that is required of a businessperson is that he be honest and make a substantial enough profit; he is not asked to be aesthetic, dramatic, or quiet. All that would be required of a statesman is that he see to it that the government operates fairly under an agreed-upon system of laws that are enforced, and that it maintains required services. The *means* the businessperson and the statesman use to do those things are infinite in number, and each is capable of being subdivided infinitely in its own right, yet the principles behind them are always few and easily definable.

So all that is required of a pious person—someone serving his Creator in such a capacity—is that he "toil in Torah and bring satisfaction to his Creator." How he manages to do that is the problem, and Luzzatto enunciates some of those means in this part. But the rock-bottom requirements are just those two: toiling in Torah and bringing satisfaction to God.

The requirements for living correctly are actually elegantly simple. We tend to forget that and to fog them over with all sorts of complexities, confusing the means for the ends, and we actually have no one else to blame for that but ourselves.

all of Israel would merely be indicators to him of God's actual wishes. He would not say, "It's enough I do what is said" or "I can get away only with what is asked of me." On the contrary, what he would say is, "Since I've already come to see where God's intentions lie, I can expand upon it all in the sorts of ways I would imagine He would want me to." This is the kind of person who would be referred to as one who satisfies his Creator.

So the essence of piety involves widening the possibilities of the *mitzvot* in as many ways as possible. You could say that piety is a form of abstention, and where abstention refers to the negative *mitzvot*, piety refers to the positive ones. But the two are actually one and the same thing: superseding the letter of the law as much as is necessary to bring satisfaction to God. That is the true definition of piety.[5]

We will now explain its primary subdivisions.

---

5. All in all, there are three aspects to the world. In Hebrew they are referred to as the *mashpiah*, the *hashpah*, and the *nishpah*—put simply: the "doer," the "doing," and the "done-to." For example, when I say, "John threw the ball," John is the "doer" (*mashpiah*), the ball is the "done-to" (*nishpah*), and the act of throwing is the "doing" (*hashpah*).

But in truth, *mashpiah*, *hashpah*, and *nishpah* translate more literally as "affecter," "affecting," and "affected." In this world, God is the great Affecter and we, every person and thing, are the affected. So we share that trait with everything, and as such, everything is "one" in that we are all affected by the same Affecter, but different by virtue of the type and degree of "affecting" we experience.

You can come to understand your brotherhood with anything there is by ruminating upon the Source you both are affected by, and you can come to understand the uniqueness of everything by coming to realize the radical difference in effect everything enjoys. So while I am at one with a flower, because we are both nourished and enlivened by the One God, I am separate from it in the *way* it and I are nourished and enlivened. So it is the "affecting" that defines things.

We can be affecters, too. And other people and/or things can be affecteds, thanks to us. That is an awesome right and responsibility and should not be taken lightly. And whereas God invariably affects things in the most equitable way, we do not just naturally do it that way, and we have to have rules to affect correctly. Those rules are called *mitzvot*. They are the means of fostering an end, that is, they are the *particular* "affectings" for desired effects. Just as when you want a plant to grow you must water it, and no matter how hard you try it will not grow if you paint it—to accomplish a desired end in the world you have to do the *mitzvah* significant to its accomplishment.

In fact, the essence of the Torah is the study and practice of the means of affecting (*hashpa'im*) so that one can come to understand in some small way the Affecter (the *Mashpiah*), who cannot be understood any way other than in how He interacts with us, the *nishpa'im*.

Other philosophical systems go wrong in that they either concentrate upon the oneness of everything, or the uniqueness of everything. So, for example, occultists concentrate upon the vision of unity, and scientists concentrate upon the vision of diversity. Both are limited in that they overlook or chose to ignore the Affecter, without Whom affecting is impossible. As such, they worship the means or the end rather than the Cause, whereas the Torah speaks to all three and worships the Cause.

Back to our subject at hand. It stands to reason that the more aligned one is with the affecting mechanism, the closer he is to the Affecter. Hence the more deeply and intensely one is involved in the *mitzvot*, the more at one with God is he. One who would want to be pious would just naturally veer toward "widening the possibilities of the *mitzvot* in as many ways possible," to use Luzzatto's phrase, so as to adhere onto the Affecter of them as deeply, intensely, and finely as he could.

But there are actually two sorts of effecting: referred to as "going" and "coming," or "exposing" and "concealing." Sometimes it is best for the affecter to "expose" himself, "go out," and act in full force; and other times it is best for the affecter to hold back, "come back," and "conceal" himself. That is, sometimes I must water my plant, and other times I must not if I do not want to drown it and thwart my purpose. Likewise in *mitzvot*, there are "exposing" *mitzvot*, and there are "concealing" *mitzvot*—positive and negative *mitzvot*, which correspond with the times to abstain and times to act.

So the person who would be pious must imitate that system and act according to the rules set out by the Affecter. That alone brings ultimate "satisfaction" to God.

Satisfaction is the realization of a correctly accomplished effecting. When God is "satisfied" it indicates that He has then become an Affected thanks to us, and we have become His affecters. That is His ultimate dream for us: that we be volatile and eternal affecters in imitation of Him.

19

The Subdivisions of Piety

The primary subdivisions of piety are actions themselves, the way they are done, and the motivations behind them.[1] The first subdivision can be divided into two parts as well: actions that are between a person and God, and those that are between one person and another.

The first aspect of the first subdivision—actions between a person and God—involves the keeping of the *mitzvot* with all their minutiae as carefully as humanly possible. This is what was referred to by our sages as keeping the "residues" of the *mitzvot*, about which they said (*Sukkah* 38a), "The residues of the *mitzvot* are what hold back retribution." For while the performance of the *mitzvah* itself is complete without these "residues" and one can fulfill his obligation without them, that is only true for the general populace. A pious person must supplement his fulfillment, not diminish it.

The second aspect—actions between one person and another—involves the great betterment you can bring about in the world by constantly improving people's lot rather than worsening it. And this can be accomplished in three ways: corporeally, monetarily, and psychologically.[2]

---

1. In other words, your spiritual standing is based upon *what* you do to interact with the world, *how* you do it, and *why*.

In actual practice, the order is reversed: you come to an understanding that you must do something for one reason or another, which is your "why"; you set out to do it by readying yourself and the mechanisms by which you will do it, and that is your "how"; then you do it. They are mentioned in reverse order here because the pattern of the book all along has been to go from one level to another, deeper one.

2. Improving a person's lot in life corporeally is comparable to interacting with the world on the "what" level mentioned above; doing so monetarily corresponds to interacting on the "how" level; and doing so psychologically corresponds to interacting on the "why" level.

Corporeally involves helping all people as much as possible and easing their burdens. This is what our sages were talking about when they referred to (*Avot* 6:6) "bearing a friend's yoke with him." And should any physical harm threaten to come to a person and you are able to defer or prevent it, you should try as much as you can to do so.

Monetarily involves helping a friend as much as you possibly can to avoid any loss. And all the more so does it mean preventing any potential or actual monetary loss that might come to individuals or groups of people through your own doing. In fact, when any loss just *might* come about, you should defer. As our sages said (*Avot* 2:12), "Your friend's money should be as dear to you as your own."

Psychologically involves providing your friend with all the contentment you can, whether in terms of respect for him or any other way.[3] It is a *mitzvah* in the realm of piety to do all you know will bring satisfaction to your friend. It goes without saying that you should not cause him any problems. This all falls under the category of acts of benevolence, which our sages praised so much and saw as such an obligation, and it includes striving for peace, which is the most essential factor for the betterment of human relations.

I will now bring you proof for all of this from the words of our sages, even though it is all obvious and requires no convincing evidence.

In the chapter of the Talmud entitled "The Residents of the City" our sages said (*Megillah* 27b), "Rabbi Zakai's students asked him to what he attributed his long life.[4] He told them that he had never urinated within seven feet of anyone praying, he had never given a friend a nickname, and he had never missed making *kiddush* on *Shabbat*. He said that he had had an old mother who had once sold the hat from her head so that he might have the means for *kiddush*."

Here you have an instance of piety in terms of being as fastidious in the *mitzvot* as possible. While he could have been excused from making *kiddush* over wine because he did not have any, and it was necessary for his mother to sell her hat so that

---

3. When Luzzatto spoke earlier on about the problems of maintaining the need for respect, he was taking our spiritual growth into consideration. But the need for respect is not to be used as an excuse for not honoring others, simply because it is our obligation as well as our privilege to honor another, whether or not he needs our honor (just as we are obliged to honor God).

4. We will now be discussing a number of great and pious men who enjoyed a great reward for their piety: long life. Luzzatto goes on to illustrate how their fastidiousness in *mitzvot* and their deep and wondrous compassion for others earned them that reward. The question may be raised: if that is what they did, and they were so great in it, why did they merit an extended stay in this world, which suggests that their true reward, their standing in the World to Come, was delayed?—as Luzzatto pointed out in the very first chapter, it is written (*Eruvin* 22a), "Today (was created) to do them (the *mitzvot*); tomorrow to receive the reward for them"!

The answer is that such a person would want to remain in this world because it is here that one accrues the merit to become even closer to God, which is the true reward.

he might have the money for the wine, this was all done in accordance with the practice of the pious. And, as to his respect for others, he would not give a friend a nickname (not even one that is not at all insulting; cf. *Tosafot*). As another example of such piety we find that Rav Hunah would be forced to tie a rubber strap around his waist because he had sold his belt to buy wine for *kiddush*.

We find further there that Rabbi Elazar Ben Shmuah's students asked him how he had lived such a long life. He replied, "I never made a shortcut through a synagogue in my entire life, and I never stepped over the heads of the holy nation." This is piety made manifest in respect for the synagogue and in respect for other people, in that he did not step over the area people sit in so he would not appear to be belittling them.

We also find that the students of Rabbi Freedah asked him the same question, and he responded that "No man ever came into the study hall earlier than I did, I never blessed in the presence of a Cohen, and I never ate from an animal that had not yet had its gift-offering portion removed from it."

Rabbi Nechuniah (*Megillah* 28a) was asked that question by his students and responded, "I have never been glorified by the shame of my friend, and I never went to bed cursing a friend."

It is pointed out there that Rav Hunah was once carrying an axe on his shoulders for them when Rav Channah Bar Chanilai came along and took it from him to ease his burden. Rav Hunah said to him, "If you're in the habit of carrying it that way, carry it. But if you are not, I don't want to be glorified by your disgrace." We see from this that even though the intonation of the phrase "being glorified by the shame of your friend" is consciously setting out to disgrace your friend so that you yourself will be glorified, nonetheless the pious feel that it is not right for them to get honor if the other person is somehow disgraced, even if that other person does not object.

Rabbi Zaira said in the same vein (Megillah 28a), "I have never in my life been tyrannical in my home; I never stepped in front of someone greater than me; I never thought of Torah in unclean alleyways; I never walked seven feet without Torah and *tefillin*; I neither napped nor fell asleep for the night in the study hall; I never rejoiced in my fellow's bad fortune; and I never called a friend by his surname." Here you have an example of pious ways in all of the aforementioned categories.

We find further (*Baba Kamma* 30a) that Rabbi Yehudah said, "Whoever wants to be pious should live according to what it says in Tractate *Berachot*," because it addresses matters that are between a person and God; ". . . whoever wants to be pious should live according to what it says in the Order of Damages," which addresses all interpersonal matters; and ". . . whoever wants to be pious should live according to what it says in *Pirke Avot*," for there are discussed matters from both categories.

One of the main elements of piety is benevolence. The very word piety (*chasidut*) is based upon kindness (*chesed*). Our sages said (*Avot* 1:2), "The world stands upon three things . . . ," one of which is benevolence. They also included it among those things that a person enjoys the fruits of in this world, while enjoying their principle in the World to Come (*Pe'ah* 1:1). Rabbi Simlai explained that (*Sotah* 14a) "the Torah begins and ends with benevolence." Rava added that (*Yevamot* 79a), "Whoever has these three traits is sure to be a descendant of Abraham: compassion, shyness, and benevolence."

Rabbi Elazar said that (*Sukkah* 49b) "benevolence is greater than charity. As it is written (Hosea 10:12), 'Plant for yourselves in charity, and reap in benevolence.'" And it is also said (*Sukkah* 49b), "Benevolence is greater than charity in three ways: while you may give charity with your money, you are benevolent with your whole body; you may give charity to the poor, but you can be benevolent to the poor or the rich; you may give charity to the living, but you can be benevolent to the living or the dead." Our sages said (*Shabbat* 151b), "It is written (Deuteronomy 13:18), 'He will offer you compassion and be compassionate to you'—that means to say that whoever is compassionate to his fellows enjoys compassion from Heaven." This is clear, because it is known that God recompenses measure for measure (*Sanhedrin* 90a).

One who is compassionate and gracious to others will enjoy God's compassion. God will absolve his transgressions in kindness. This absolution will be the judgment toward him in recompense for how he has acted, which is what our sages were referring to when they said (*Rosh Hashanah* 17a), "Whose transgression does God overlook? One who overlooks a transgression done against him." Divine retribution will come to one who does not want to transcend his own personal character traits, or who does not want to be benevolent. He will be judged according to the letter of the law because he acted that way.[5] And who is it that can withstand God's judgment of him according to the strict letter of the law? King David would pray (Psalms 143:2), "Do not bring your servant to judgment. No living thing can prove righteous before You." But one who acts kindly is reacted to kindly. And the more you act thusly, the more you receive. Kind David would laud his own share of this trait, and would even try to be kind to his enemies. He referred to this when he said (Psalms 35:13), "In their illness I donned sackcloth and deprived my spirit with fasting . . ." and (Psalms 7:5) "If I have recompensed those who did me wrong. . . ."

The point of the matter is that you should not cause suffering to any being—human or animal—and you should be compassionate and kind to all. Thus it says (Proverbs 12:10), "The righteous person knows the soul of his animals." In fact, there are some of the opinion that compassion for animals is biblical in origin (*Shabbat* 128b); if not, in the least, rabbinic.

---

5. One who refuses to "transcend his own personal character traits, or who does not want to be benevolent" cannot accept his own Divine root and soul. He assumes he or his means are limited. Doing that, he denies God's omnipotence, and God allows Himself to remain "limited" in relation to that person who limited himself. He refused entry to God, so God "acquiesces" to that wish, because that is His way.

In summary, compassion and the willingness to do good are traits imbedded in the heart of the pious. They are constantly driven to satisfying people's needs and to not causing any sorrow.

The second aspect of piety involves how actions are performed. This too can be divided into two aspects, which can themselves be further subdivided into many, many subsections. But the primary subsections would be reverence and love, the two pillars of true Divine service, without which there can be no content to the matter whatsoever.

Under the heading of reverence we find the subcategories of submission to God, humility upon coming to serve Him, and the honor accorded His *mitzvot*, Name, and Torah. And under the heading of love are the subcategories of happiness, attachment to Him, and obsession with Him. We will now explain them one by one.

The main aspect of reverence is reverence for God's grandeur. While you are praying or performing a *mitzvah* you are to consider the fact that you are praying and standing before the King of kings. This is what the Talmud was referring to when it said (*Berachot* 28b), "Know before Whom you are praying when you pray."

To obtain this sort of reverence you will have to consider and reflect upon three things: that you are quite literally standing before God and involved in a give-and-take with Him, even though you cannot see Him. While this may be too difficult to fathom because your senses can do nothing to help you in it, with just a little reflection and contemplation, however, most anyone will be able to realize that he is actually involved in a give-and-take with God, that he is imploring and pleading before God Himself, and that God is listening to and hearing him as a person would while carrying on a conversation with a friend.

After you will have set this in your mind, you should reflect upon God's grandeur—how He is so elevated and above all the blessings and praises of the world and all concepts of perfection you could possibly imagine. You must also reflect upon the low state of mankind, with its imperfections, brought on by corporeality and materiality (not to mention all our transgressions).

Taking all this into consideration, it would be impossible for your heart to not tremble or be moved when you speak to God, mention His name, or attempt to please Him.[6] This is what was referred to by (Psalms 2:11), "Serve God with reverence and

---

6. In other words, in order to come to reverence you must realize three things: (1) that when you pray to Him, you are actually involved in a dialogue with God, though you may not seem to be, (2) that God is above your praises, as well as all the notions of perfection you might have, and (3) that, due to your corporeality and your transgressions, you are highly imperfect.

But how will the realization of these three things bring you to a state where "it would be impossible for your heart to not tremble or be moved when you speak to God, mention His name, or attempt to fulfill His wishes"—an exceedingly strong reaction?

Apparently, that will occur when you consider that, despite the fact that God is above your praises and all the notions of His perfection you might have, and despite the fact that, due to your corporeality and your transgressions, you are highly imperfect, He is nonetheless

rejoice in trembling" as well as (Psalms 89:8), "(God is) a God dreaded in the great
council of the holy ones and held in reverence by all those round about Him" (referring to the angels who can more easily imagine His grandeur and have more reverence for Him than humans because they are closer to God than mortals can ever be).
David used to say (Psalms 5:8), "I will prostrate myself towards Your holy Courtyard
in reverence." It is written (Malachi 2:5), "because he was afraid of My name," as
well as (Ezra 9:6), "My God, I am abashed and embarrassed to lift my face, my God,
towards You."

However, this sort of reverence must be instigated in the heart before it can be
manifested in the limbs in the form of a bent head, a prostrated body, lowered eyes,
and hands folded like a lowly servant before a great master, referred to in the Talmud
with (*Shabbat* 10a), "Rava would fold his hands and pray, saying, 'I am like a servant
before his master.'"7

We have spoken thus far in terms of submission and humility. We will now
speak about the matter of honor. Our sages have already spoken of honoring *mitzvot*

"listening to and hearing (you) as a person would while carrying on a conversation with a
friend." And that would agree with the talmudic statement that points out that God evidences
His modesty wherever He evidences His greatness, that is, He is as approachable as He is
transcendent.

Yet we have to wonder—how do you foster so strong a reaction? According to Luzzatto
it is done through reflection and contemplation. That means to say that a serious and studied
consideration of how the Master of the Universe presents Himself in this world has to be
taken to heart. But we have trouble comprehending that. While we sense the vast rolling and
turning of heaven and earth, we can only stutter and gasp. It is beyond us how God can be
everywhere and engage everything.

Yet with reflection and contemplation we can come to realize that it is only in our
relativistic eyes that the vastness, might, and triumph of the sun, for instance, is any more
vast, mighty, or triumphant than the "lowly" act of eating kosher food rather than unkosher.
The truth of the matter is that God cares about and is as impressed with our tiny mastications
and the flow of our saliva as He is with galaxies, cosmos, and the spin of billions of stars,
because He is above relativism. To Him we are tiny, nearly inconsequential, and absurd, as
well as essential, central, and potent. He loves us with the love of attachment and union. In
His eyes we are not small: we are *mighty* small, as small as an atom, and as potential.

Realizing that, we can only stand stunned and weeping at the great Lover who is God,
and come to "tremble or be moved when [we] speak to God, mention His name, or attempt
to fulfill His wishes," because He is both transcendent and distant, intimate and present.

7. See chapter 7, where it is written that the person who finds that enthusiasm is not
an intrinsic part of his makeup should arouse that trait within himself, and that he can do
that thanks to the fact that the "external . . . arouses the internal." So when Luzzatto says here
that "this sort of reverence has to be instigated in the heart before it can be manifested in the
limbs . . . ," he is telling us that while enthusiasm, a self-contained emotion, can be aroused
externally until it becomes internalized, a trait like reverence, which focuses on a subject external to oneself, has to be instigated internally before it can be externalized.

and considering them precious. They said (*Shabbat* 133b), "It is written (Exodus 15:2), 'This is my God and I shall praise (or beautify) Him.' That means to say you should praise Him with *mitzvot*—by using beautiful *tzitzit, tefillin,* Torah scrolls, *lulav,* and so forth."

Our sages said (*Baba Kamma* 9:2), "For the sake of the beautification of a *mitzvah* you are allowed to increase what you will pay by one third. What you pay to that point is your expense; anything past that is paid for by God." They are clearly saying that it is not enough to simply perform a *mitzvah*; you should honor and glorify it.

There are those who would ease their burdens by reasoning that honor may be necessary for humans, who are seduced by such vanity, but not for God who does not care for such things because He is above them all and transcends them. Certainly, they would reason, if the *mitzvah* is done faithfully, that would be enough for Him.[8] But the truth of the matter is God is referred to as (Psalms 29:3) the "Lord of Honor." It is incumbent upon us to honor Him even though He does not require it, and though our honor is not of great importance or consequence to Him. And whoever diminishes in it when he is capable of increasing it is a sinner. This is what the prophet Malachi was protesting about in the name of God when he said (Malachi 1:8), "And if you offer the blind for sacrifice, is it not evil? And if you offer a lame or sick animal, is that not evil? Offer it now to your governor. Would he be pleased with you or would he show you favor? says the Lord of Hosts."

Our sages told us to act in just the opposite manner. They said (*Sukkah* 50a) that water that was left exposed and rendered unfit should not be put through a sieve to make it minimally usable. While you might offer it like that to a commoner, you certainly would not offer it to a nobleman. As the Torah puts it, "Offer it now to your governor. . . ." That is to say, though water that has been filtered can be used in an ordinary situation, it may not be used for sacred purposes, because that is not the honorable thing to do.

It is said further in the *Sifre* on the verse (Deuteronomy 12:11), "and (you shall offer) all your choice vows"; that means to say you are only to offer the best of what you have. We find in the case of Cain and Abel that Abel made an offering from the firstborn of his sheep along with their fat, and Cain only offered from the remnant of his fruits, as our sages said (*Bereishit Rabbah* 22:5). And what happened?—(Genesis 4:4) "God regarded Abel and his offering, but did not regard Cain or his offering." It is said as well (Malachi 1:14), "Cursed be the deceiver who has in his flock a male and yet vows and sacrifices to the Lord what is blemished, for I am a great king, says the Lord of Hosts."

---

8. It must be pointed out that only people who "would ease their burdens," lazy people, would say such a thing. A rational and zealous person, Luzzatto is intimating, would not. A lazy person often says many things that seem to be reasonable but prove to be rationalizations, as has been discussed above in chapter 6.

Our sages warned us in many ways about denigrating *mitzvot.* They said (*Shabbat* 14a), "Whoever grabs hold of an unadorned Torah scroll (which would indicate a contempt for the *mitzvah*) shall be buried unadorned."

The procession for the offering of the first fruits to the Temple was an example of beautifying *mitzvot.* We learn (*Bikkurim* 3:3) that "an ox would precede them with gold-covered horns and a crown of olive branches . . . ," and (*Bikkurim* 3:8) "the wealthy would bring their offerings in gold baskets, and the poor in wicker." We also learn there (3:10) that there are three categories of first fruit offerings: standard first fruits, special first fruits, and decorative first fruits. So we find it here explicitly stated, and we can extrapolate it to all other *mitzvot,* that adding on to a *mitzvah* so as to adorn it is the correct thing to do.

It is said (*Shabbat* 10a), "Rava would put on ornate shoes to pray, basing his actions upon the verse (Amos 4:12), 'Prepare yourselves to call upon your God, O Israel.'" Our sages said (*Bereishit Rabbah* 65:16), about the verse (Genesis 27:15), "And Rebecca gave the clothes of her elder son, Esau"—"Rabbi Shimon Ben Gamliel said: I serve my father . . . but when Esau would serve his father, he would do so in regal clothing." If someone were to act that way for flesh and blood, how much more so should he do so before the King of kings, the Holy One (Blessed be He). So, it is only fitting that when you stand before Him to pray, you should dress regally and when you sit before Him, you should sit as you would before a great king.

Included within this category is honoring the Sabbath and Holy Days. Whoever increases in the honor of them certainly gratifies the Creator, for He has commanded us to (Isaiah 58:13) "honor it." Since it is clear that honoring the Sabbath is a *mitzvah,* and there are many ways to honor it, we should do anything that would bring out the importance of the Sabbath. The early sages would each prepare for the Sabbath in their own way. (*Shabbat* 119a) "Rabbi Abbahu would sit on a stool of ivory and stoke the fire; Rav Safra would singe the head of a cow for the meal; Rava would salt carp; Rav Hunah would light a fire; Rav Papa would ready the wicks; Rav Chisda would shred beets; Rabbah and Rav Yoseph would chop wood; and Rav Nachman would carry things in and out on his shoulders, reasoning that if Rabbi Amai or Rabbi Assai would visit he would certainly carry things in and out on his shoulders."

The reasoning of Rav Nachman gives us pause to reflect upon the fact that he would consider what he would do in his own way to honor a person, and then do the same to honor the Sabbath. Regarding this it is said (*Berachot* 17a), "Let a man always be creative in his reverence," that is, let him reflect upon things, and arrive at new means of giving satisfaction to his Creator whichever way he can so that he might recognize God's exalted nature, and so that everything associated with Him will be honored as much as possible.

Since, in His great humility and goodness and despite our lowliness, God wants to honor us by passing on to us His holy words, let us at least honor those holy words with all of our might, and show Him how precious they are to us. This is true reverence—reverence of His exaltedness as we said. The honor that brings about the long-ing-love we will be writing about is dependent upon this sort of reverence, not the inessential fear of punishment from which these great traits do not come.

Let us return now to the matter of honoring the Sabbath. It is said (*Shabbat* 119a), "Rav Annan would dress in overalls, that is, he would dress in black clothing purposefully on Friday, so that it would be noticeable on the *Shabbat* that he was dressed in fine clothing." We see from this that preparation for the *Shabbat* is not all there is in honoring it: even contrasting it by withholding something during the week matters, because it accentuates the honoring of it, and is part of the *mitzvah*. In the same vein, our sages forbad the partaking of a full meal on Friday afternoon for the honor of the *Shabbat*, and the like (*Gittin* 38b).

Honoring the Torah and those who study it is another aspect of reverence. As it is said (*Avot* 4:6), "Whoever honors the Torah is honored by people." We find (*Sanhedrin* 102b), "Rabbi Yochanan says, What was it that merited Achab's twenty-two year reign over Israel?—his honoring the Torah, which is written with the twenty-two letters, as it is said (1 Kings 20:2–9), '(Ben Hadad) sent messengers into the city to Achab, king of Israel, and said to him, "Thus says Ben Hadad: your silver and your gold are mine; your wives also, and your children, even the best, are mine." And the king of Israel answered and said, "Indeed, my lord, O king: according to your saying. I am yours and all that I have." And the messengers came again and said, "Thus speaks Ben Hadad saying, 'Although I have sent for you saying you will surely give me your silver, your gold, your wives and your children, yet I will send my servants tomorrow about this time, and they will search your house . . . and take [your possessions]. . . .'"' Wherefore he said to the messengers, 'All that you sent for your servant [to do] I will do, but this thing I will not do. . . .' And what was so precious to him?—A Torah scroll."

It is said (*Berachot* 18a), "If you travel from place to place, you should not leave a Torah scroll in a bag and place it on your donkey, which you yourself then ride upon. You should rather place the bag on your lap. . . ." The sages further forbad us from sitting on a bed a Torah scroll is lying on (*Mo'ed Katan* 25a). They said (*Eruvin* 98a), "You are not to discard sacred writings—even *Halachot* and *Aggadot*." And they forbad us (*Megillah* 27a) from laying books of the Prophets and the Writings on top of the Pentateuch. These are things that the sages forbad all of the people of Israel. The pious are to learn from these examples and to add to each and every one of them to give honor to the Name of their God.

Also included within this category are the innocence and purity necessary for Torah study. You are not to be engaged in it or even give thought to it in untoward places or when your hands are unclean. Our sages expanded upon this and warned us about it in various places.

As to your attitude toward those who study Torah, the Torah itself says (Leviticus 19:32), "Rise up before a grey-haired person and honor the face of an elder." From this we can extrapolate all sorts of honoring fitting for the pious to be a part of. The sages said (*Ketubot* 103b), "It is written (Psalms 15:4), 'He will honor the reverential.'" This refers to Jehosephat, king of Judah. Whenever he would see a Torah scholar he would arise from his throne, hug and kiss him, and call out to him "My Rabbi, my Rabbi! My teacher, my teacher!" Rabbi Zaira, we are told, would seat himself at the doorway to the study hall when he would be fatigued from his own studies and engage in the *mitzvah* of rising before a Torah scholar (*Eruvin* 28a).

We have already seen how, in His infinite wisdom, God has revealed and enunciated these desires of His. One who would like to bring satisfaction to his Creator will do whatever he can to do what is righteous before Him.

Within this category we also find respect for synagogues and study halls. Not only must you not be frivolous within them, you must also show respect and reverence for them in your behavior, and do nothing within them you would not do in a king's palace.

Let us now speak about the matter of love of God. There are three aspects to it: happiness, attachment, and vengeance.[9] This love is an actual desiring and longing

---

9. Love is the emotional outcome of a high sensitivity toward something or someone. In the great rushing in of all sorts of information and impressions, we simply cannot manage to be sensitive to everything and everyone, which is actually for the good. If we allowed ourselves to truly be open and sensitive to all sorts of things, we would be overcharged and exhausted. So we tend to select and reject.

But there are times when someone's being aligns with a deep and central need of ours, and we are moved to love. It seems though that at first love does not manifest itself as an emotion, but rather as a series of quick elemental thoughts. When we meet the person we will come to love we are initially struck by a vague sense of the collaboration of need and person, and we become curious about him or her. "Who is that?" we wonder, as if the person were familiar. And we very quickly progress into a state of pleasant curiosity.

We then allow ourselves to become more receptive and try to process gestures and signals. If the moment is right, we find that a certain symbol we cherish is expressed downright openly by that person and we are struck. Needless to say, this all goes on in a very subtle and nearly blind way.

Then we start to become edgy and volatile because that person becomes necessary for our well-being, and we are drawn and have come to be vulnerable. At that point emotions well up, and "need" and "person" meld together into a great rushing fixation. Then, what to then might be described as the acting out of a self-centered need-fulfillment becomes a gracious and resonating love. Waves and waves of lighter-than-air yearnings issue from the heart and the lovers vow to each other.

Such a relatively drawn-out and primitive series of goings-on seems to happen in your relationship to God as well. But the difference is that in the case of love of God, the need that matches up with the Lover is far more fundamental and essential, and the Lover is far more compelling. Nonetheless the steps are the same as the ones Luzzatto speaks of: an initial happiness, which leads into attachment and eventual obsession. The object here is to allow that high sensitivity to God to blossom.

The love of God is a powerful and rushing emotion, like none other. For most of us there are moments of it—moments when we sense the welling up of the great inner waters

for closeness to God. It is pursuing God's Holiness as you would pursue something you strongly long for—to the point where even mentioning His name, speaking His praises, and occupying yourself in His *mitzvot* and Godliness is a pleasure and delight to you, the way someone who loves the bride of his youth, or his only child so strongly would be pleased to just speak about them. As the Torah says (Jeremiah 31:19), "As I speak of Him I yet remember Him."

One who truly loves his Creator would not abandon his worship of Him for any reason in the world other than an utterly compelling one. He would not need convincing or persuasion to serve Him—in fact, unless he is held back by a major deterrent, his heart would have him surge forward and would drive him towards this love. This is the lovely trait the early pious ones who were referred to as "the supremely holy" had. As King David put it (Psalms 42:2–3), "My soul yearns for You, God, like the hart yearns for the rivulets. My soul thirsts for God—the living God. When will I see God's face?" and (Psalms 84:3), "My soul longs for, pines for God's courtyards," as well as (Psalms 63:2) "My soul thirsts for You, my flesh hungers for You." This comes with the greatness of the yearning that is a yearning for God. As the prophet said (Isaiah 26:8), "The longing of the soul is for Your name and Your remembrance" and (Isaiah 26:9) "My soul has longed for You in the night. While the spirit is still within me I will seek You."

King David used the expression (Psalms 63:7), "When I think of you on my couch during the night-watches I meditate upon You," as an explanation of the delight and pleasure he experienced when he spoke about or praised the Creator. He said further (Psalms 119:47), "I delight in Your *mitzvot,* which I so love," and (Psalms 119:143) "Your ordinances are also my delight."

One thing is certain: the love of God should not be the sort that is dependent upon something. It should not be that you love God because He has done good for you, given you wealth, or made you successful. It must be the kind of love a son has for his father—a visceral love that just naturally overtakes you. The Torah refers to this when it says (Deuteronomy 32:6), "Is He not your father, your master?"

The true test of this love comes during troubles and sorrows. Our sages said (*Berachot* 54a), "It is written (Deuteronomy 6:5) 'And you will love God, the Lord, with all of your heart, and all of your soul'—even if He should take away your soul—'and all of your might'—with all of your possessions."

But in order for sorrows or woes not to deter you from this love, you would have to say one of two things to yourself. The first of these should be said by all, and the second should be said by the wise and fully understanding.[10] The first statement

---

and the charging out, and we come to be carried along in a wondrous glee and longing. Those are the times when the soul is unbound and all sorts of electric reactions go alternately on and off in a rapid, whipping type of way. But the pious and holy enjoy such a love all the time. They are enraptured and swept away at every turn, and they enjoy God's love back.

10. Curiously, Luzzatto never included the statement that was to be said only by the "wise and fully understanding."

is that (*Berachot* 60b) "Everything done by Heaven is for the good," which means to say that even our sorrows and woes are only for our ultimate good, though they may not seem to be. It can be compared to going to a doctor who sutures your flesh or an infected limb to make you healthy and prevent a mortal disease. Even though on the surface the act seems to be cruel, it is actually an act of great compassion for your ultimate good. The patient would not lessen his love of the doctor because of the procedure. In fact, he would love him even more. In the case of God's love for you as well, when you consider the fact that all that God does to you, physically or monetarily, is for your good, even though you may not understand how, you will not lessen your love for Him for any woes or sorrows, but will rather strengthen and enlarge upon it at all times.

Those of true understanding have no need for this sort of explanation, because they have no self-serving needs. Their prayers are for the express purpose of increasing the honor of God and bringing satisfaction to Him. Whenever deterrents that would require a lot of determination to overcome get in their way, they simply strengthen their hearts and become pleased with the opportunity to manifest the power of their faith. They are like the warrior famous for his strength who constantly chooses to fight difficult battles just to illustrate his might and abilities. This sort of behavior is common amongst lovers who become happy when anything that gives them the chance to show their great love comes their way.

We will now go on to explain the various aspects of love of God. As we have said, there are three of them: attachment, happiness, and vengeance.

Attachment involves clutching onto His name at all times with all your heart, so that you care about nothing else.[11] This was the object of Solomon's metaphor when he said (Proverbs 5:19), "A loving hind and a pleasant roe—let her breasts sat-

---

11. *Devekut*, attachment to God, is mentioned in passing in the introduction ("there are few . . . who would dedicate their research and study to the means of attaining wholeness in Divine service, on love of and reverence for God, [and] on the attachment to Him. . . ."), then it is not mentioned again until the fourteenth chapter ("join in with good people for the amount of time you need to study or to earn a living, then go in seclusion to attach yourself to your God"), and finally it is mentioned here, where all that is said of it is that it "involves clutching onto His name at all times with all your heart, so that you care about nothing else."

But the fullest treatment of it comes in the last chapter of the book, where the most exalted and sublime levels of attainment are discussed. See there, where Luzzatto goes on to associate attachment to God with: the existential state of the soul, the removal of self from physicality, constant practice, strong love and powerful reverence, the descent of a spirit on high, and solitary meditation.

In essence *devekut* involves the directing of a sure and steady alignment of heart, mind, and will toward God. The surer and steadier the alignment, the faster the adhesion. The popular notion of it is that of an inexplicable rush of smoke and light that sweeps its beaming, beatific object up and away in a chariot. Of course that disallows for the Torah's *requirement* of it. It says (Deuteronomy 30:20): "Love God your Lord, listen to His voice, and attach yourself to

isfy you at all times and be ever ravished with her love." Our sages said (*Eruvin* 54b), "It was said of Rabbi Elazar ben P'dat that he would sit and study Torah in the upper part of the marketplace of Tziporri while his cloak would be hung on the lower part of the marketplace."[12] Attaching yourself to God at all times is the ultimate degree of this trait. At the very least attach yourself to Him at the time of worship, if you truly love God.

It is said in the Jerusalem Talmud (*Berachot* 5:1), "Rabbi Chaninah ben Dosah was standing and praying, and if a lizard came by and bit him, he did not stop praying. . . . His students asked, 'Master—didn't you feel that!?' And he said, 'When my heart is concentrating on prayer, I don't feel anything come what may.'"

The Torah refers to attachment many times (Deuteronomy 30:20): "Love God your Lord, listen to His voice, and attach yourself to Him . . ."; (Deuteronomy 10:20) ". . . attach yourself to Him"; and (Deuteronomy 13:5) ". . . attach yourselves to Him." David said (Psalms 63:9), "My soul is attached to You." The point of all of these verses is the same—the attachment you have for your Creator should be the sort that will not allow you to separate or disassociate yourself from Him.

Our sages said (*Bereishit Rabbah* 80:7), "Rabbi Shimon ben Lakish said, 'The Holy One (blessed be He) expressed his love for Israel in three ways: by His attachment, longing, and desiring. . . .'" These categories—the aforementioned longing, attachment, satisfaction, and enjoyment—are in fact the central offshoots of love.

The second aspect is happiness, which is a big element of Divine service. This is what David was referring to when he said (Psalms 100:2), "Serve God with joy; approach Him with song"; and (Psalms 68:4) "The righteous will rejoice—they will exult before God and be joyously happy." Our sages said (*Shabbat* 30b), "The Divine Presence only dwells within a person that is happy doing a *mitzvah*."

About the verse "Serve God with joy," the *Midrash Shochar Tov* says, "Rabbi Abihu says that this indicates that your heart should be happy when you are praying, for you are praying to the incomparable God." This is truly the kind of happiness the heart should rejoice with—happiness for the fact that you are worthy to serve, and be engaged in the Torah and *mitzvot* of the Lord, who is like no other. This is the true, most valuable and eternal sort of wholeness you can obtain.[13]

Him. . . ."; (Deuteronomy 10:20) ". . . attach yourself to Him"; and (Deuteronomy 13:5) ". . . attach yourselves to Him." So while the popular notion of it, which may be the figurative, ultimate result of it, is not the actual *process*.

12. Perhaps one can say that while Rabbi Elazar ben P'dat would physically be sitting in the world ("while his 'cloak' [i.e., his body] would be hung on the 'lower part of the marketplace'"), his soul would be communing with God ("he would sit and study Torah in the 'upper part of the marketplace.'")

13. When we are happy it is because we seem finally to have arrived at a solution. Happiness is the ultimate successful resolution of an irritant. Unhappiness is the sore experience of that irritant coupled with the fear that it will never go away. Ironically, of course, the more biting the irritant, the greater the happiness in its resolution.

Solomon said it in this wise and parabolic way (Song of Songs 1:4): "Draw me out—we will run after you. The king has brought me to his chamber; we will be happy and rejoice in you." That is to say, the closer you merit to draw toward the chamber of the knowledge of God, the happier you will be and the more your heart will rejoice in intimacy with Him. As it says (Psalms 149:2), "Israel will rejoice with its Maker; the sons of Zion will regale their King."

David reached this level to a very high degree and said (Psalms 104:34), "May my ruminations be sweet to Him; I will be happy in God"; and (Psalms 43:4) "I will go to the sanctuary of God—to the God who is the very happiness in my rapture— and I will acknowledge God with the harp as *my* God"; and (Psalms 71:23) "My lips will rejoice when I sing to You as well as my soul, which You have redeemed." This means to say that happiness so overpowered him that his lips moved by themselves and were thrilled to be engaged in the praise of God. This was a result of the great incandescence of joy with which his soul was burning before God. That was why he finished with, ". . . my soul, which You have redeemed."

We find that God was furious with Israel when they lacked this in their worship. It is said (Deuteronomy 28:47), "Because you have not served God your Lord with joy and a good-natured heart. . . ."

When he saw that Israel had already attained this great trait because the people had been so generous in the building of the Holy Temple, David prayed that it would be fixed in the people and would never leave. He said (1 Chronicles 29:17–18), ". . . and now I have seen Your people here, offering to You joyously and freely. O God, Lord of Abraham, Isaac and Israel, our fathers—keep this forever in the inclinations of the hearts of Your people, and direct their hearts to You."

The third subdivision involves vengeance and refers to your being vengeful in regard to His Holy Name. It includes hating those who hate Him and trying to subjugate them as much as you can so that worship of Him can be carried out and His glory can be magnified. This is what David was referring to when he said (Psalms 139:21–22), "Do I not hate those who hate you, God, and contend against those who rise up against you? I hate them thoroughly." The prophet Elijah said (1 Kings 19:10), "I have avenged for the Lord of Hosts." And we have already seen what he

---

The greatest irritant is the perceived loss of God. When someone suffers from such an irritant he is sure there is no end to the thundering emptiness, and he is unhappy. (He may certainly have his moments of some real happiness, because he will have managed to successfully resolve other, more minor irritants, but he will never be, let us say, "centrally" happy.)

So when Luzzatto says that the best happiness is the one that comes with the realization "that you are worthy to serve, and be engaged in the Torah and *mitzvot* of the Lord" he means to say that full and true happiness only comes in the realization of God's ever-presence, and the active acknowledgment of it by following His dictates.

The pious are not ebullient or frothing in their happiness. Their happiness is unchecked, but slow-moving and thorough.

merited because of his vengeance for the sake of God. As it is said (Numbers 25:13), "Because he was vengeful for His God and brought atonement to Israel."[14]

Our sages underscored the notion by saying that one who has it within his power to rebuke and does not is in the same category as the transgressor himself (*Shabbat* 54b). It is written in the Midrash (*Eichah Rabbah* 1:6), "It is said, (Lamentations 1:6) 'Her leaders were like harts,'—just as harts hide their heads one under the other in the scorching heat, so did the leaders of Israel hide their heads one under the other when they saw transgressions being committed. The Holy One (blessed be He) said to them, 'The time will come when I will do the same for you!'"

The reason for this is obvious. One who loves his friend could never endure seeing him attacked or abused. He would certainly come to his aid. Likewise, one who truly loves God could never endure seeing His name being profaned, God forbid, or His commandments being overrun. Solomon was referring to this when he said (Proverbs 28:4), "Those who abandon Torah would praise the wicked, while those who keep it would rebuke them." Those who would praise the wicked for their wickedness instead of castigating them for their blemishes are abandoning Torah and allowing the name of God to be profaned, God forbid. But those who keep Torah and strengthen themselves to maintain it would certainly rebuke them, and would not hold themselves back or keep still.

God said to Job (Job 40:11–13), "Cast the rage of your wrath abroad. Behold everyone that is proud and abase him. Look upon everyone that is proud and bring him low, and tread upon the wicked in their place. Hide them in the dust together and bind their faces in the hiding places." This is the greatest love one who really loves his Creator could ever exhibit. As is written (Psalms 97:10), "Those who love God hate evil."[15]

To this point we have explained piety in terms of the actions themselves that are required for it. We will now discuss it in terms of the motives behind those actions.

We have already spoken about the notion of acting either altruistically or for an ulterior motive, and all the degrees in between also. The truth of the matter is that someone who serves God so that his soul could be purified before Him, that he might merit residing among the just and pious and (Psalms 27:4) "witness the pleasantness

---

14. The verse quoted from Numbers seems to have nothing to do with Elijah the prophet as it is speaking about Pinchas, who was himself obsessed with God. But when Luzzatto says that it refers to Elijah he is basing that upon the tradition which speaks of Elijah being Pinchas himself, who merited a very long life.

15. One who truly and passionately loves God—who considers His being above all others—cannot help but be zealous and righteously indignant toward those who abandon Him. His heart is alternately overtaken by peace and disquiet, calm and overwhelming sensitivity to his Lover's "feelings." But this trait can be very dangerous, and the next chapter's subject, the evaluating of piety, must be taken into consideration when obsession is acted upon.

of God and visit His Sanctuary," as well as to receive the reward of the World to Come, cannot be said to be ill-motivated. But he cannot be said to have the best intentions either. As long as someone is moved by selfish reasons he is serving God for self-serving needs. The motivation in serving God found among the truly pious, those who toil and strive in it, is only that His glory grow and spread.

But this only comes after your love of God is developed, and you come to long for the expansion of His honor and suffer with its lessening. Only then will you be motivated to serve God so that His honor grows and enlarges through you at least. And then you would want others to act that way and would grieve over their lessening God's honor (though you would grieve most over your own diminution of it, even if it came about by happenstance or because of a character flaw, which might very well happen, for in truth it is difficult to avoid sin at all times, as the Torah says [Ecclesiastes 7:20]: "There is no man so righteous in the land that he only does good and never sins").[16]

This is all expounded in *Tanna D'Bei Eliyahu Rabbah* (chap. 4), where it says, "The sage of Israel who has honest Torah within him and grieves over the honor of the Holy One (blessed be He) as well as the honor of Israel his whole life; who longs for and worries about the honor of Jerusalem and the Holy Temple, and hopes that salvation will blossom soon and the exiled will be gathered is worthy of Divine inspiration in his words. . . ." We can infer from this that a motivation which is based upon the honor of the Creator and the sanctification of His name (accomplished when His creations do His will) is the best and farthest from being self-serving. Regarding this it is said (*Zohar, Mishpatim*), "Who is pious? One who is pious towards his Creator."

Besides serving God by performing His *mitzvot* with this motivation, the pious person must be in a constant state of agitation about the exile and the destruction of the Holy Temple, because both are the cause of the lessening (so to speak) of God's honor. He should long for the redemption which will bring an uplifting of God's honor. This is what the quote from Tanna D'Bei Eliyahu Rabbah was referring to when it spoke of someone, "who longs for and burdens himself over the honor of Jerusalem and the Holy Temple," and so forth. The pious person should constantly pray for the redemption of Israel and the restoration of the previous glory of Heaven.

Should you say, "Who am I that I should be so esteemed as to pray over the exile and for the sake of Jerusalem, as if the exiled would ever be gathered or salvation blossom because of *my* prayers?" our response would be based on the statement (*Sanhedrin* 37a) ". . . that was why man was created alone, so that each individual should say, 'The world was created for my sake.'" God finds satisfaction in His children's prayers for this. While He may not respond to their prayers because the

---

16. Notice he uses the term, "it is *difficult* to avoid sin" when he quotes the verse that reads (Ecclesiastes 7:20), "There is no man so righteous in the land that he only does good and never sins." He is not saying it is impossible, because it is expected of those rare individuals who will attain to it at this point. Refer to the first note to part 4.

right time has not come, or for some other reason, they should do what they must and God will be happy with that.

The prophet thundered about the lack of this, saying (Isaiah 59:16): "And I saw that there was no man, and I was dumbfounded that there was no interceder"; and (Isaiah 63:5) "I looked and saw that there was no helper, and I was dumbfounded that there was no supporter."

It is also said (Jeremiah 30:17), "It is Zion, for whom no one cares." Our sages explain (*Sukkah* 41a) that we can imply from this that someone must care for it. So we see we are duty-bound in this, and we cannot excuse ourselves by claiming a lack of power, for we have learned (*Avot* 2:16) "It is not for you to complete the task, but you are not free to avoid it." The prophet also said (Isaiah 51:18), "There is no leader for her from amongst the children she has borne, nor a protector from amongst the children she has raised"; and (Isaiah 40:6) "All flesh is like hay and all its kindness is like weeds in the field." Our sages (*Avodah Zarah* 2b) interpret that to mean that all the kindnesses they did were for their own sake, their own good and benefit, and no one was idealistically motivated or wanted the redemption of Israel and the restoration of her glory, though it is impossible for the Divine glory to increase any other way, as one is actually dependent upon the other. As we quoted from Tanna D'Bei Eliyahu Rabbah, one has to "grieve over the honor of the Holy One (blessed be He), as well as the honor of Israel."

We see that there are two aspects to this matter: the motivation behind the performance of *mitzvot* and Divine service (for the elevation of God's glory by bringing satisfaction to Him) and the suffering in demand for the elevation of this glory and the general well-being of Israel.

There is another major object of a pious person's concentrations: the well-being of his generation. The pious should direct their actions toward the good of the entire generation to earn them merit and protect them. This is the point of the verse that reads (Isaiah 3:10), "Praise the righteous for they are good—they eat the fruits of their deeds," signifying that the entire generation eats of their fruits. Our sages say about the verse (Numbers 13:20), ". . . (see) if there are any trees . . . (in the land)"—"(see) if there is anyone who can protect the generation like a tree" (*Baba Batra* 15a).

So you see, it is God's will that the pious of Israel atone for and make worthy all sorts of people of the nation. And our sages used the *lulav* and its co-components as an example, saying (*Vayikra Rabbah* 30:12) "These will come and atone for those." God does not want the destruction of the evil. The saintly have been commanded to try to make them worthy and to atone for them. And that has to be done with certain concentrations in worship and prayers. The pious person should pray for his generation to atone for whoever needs atonement, to return in repentance whoever needs that, and to act as an intercedent for the entire generation.[17]

17. So the pious person must be intensely aware of three things at all times: the presence of God, the state of exile and the subsequent destruction of the Temple, and the well-being of his generation.

Our sages said (*Ein Yaakov, Yoma,* chap. 8) about the verse (Daniel 10:12), "And I have come because of your words," that Gabriel did not go through the curtain again until he acted as an intercedent for Israel. It is said (*Yalkut Shimoni*) that Gideon was allowed to (Judges 6:14) "go with this, your strength" because he had acted as an intercedent for Israel.

God only loves those who love the Jewish nation, and He enlarges His love for someone who enlarges his own love for them. Those kinds of individuals, the true shepherds—the ones who sacrifice themselves for Israel, who ask and strive for their welfare and well-being in all ways, who stand by the breach to pray for them so any edicts against them would be nullified and so that the gates of blessing would be open for them—are the ones whom the Holy One (blessed be He) desires so much. Toward them He is like a father who cannot love anyone more than the person he sees faithfully loving his child, which is only natural. This is in fact the whole matter of the High Priest, about whom is written (*Makkot* 11a), "(They) should have asked for mercy for their whole generation, but they did not." We find that (*Makkot* 11a) "a certain man was eaten by a lion a distance of three parsangs from Rabbi Joshua ben Levi. (Because of that) Elijah did not appear to (Rabbi Joshua ben Levi) for three days (in a vision)" and that shows the responsibility a pious person has to ask and strive for, for the sake of his generation.

What we have done is explain the major aspects of piety. The particulars are left to the thinking person with a pure heart to come to so that he can go on the honest path based upon them at the proper time.

That is to say, he must be aware of the ever-present, represented by God; the past, represented by the exile and destruction; and the future, represented by his generation, the seed of the future of the Jewish nation.

20

The Evaluating Needed for Piety

What has to be explained now is the process of evaluating that is involved in piety. It is a very, very essential matter as well as the most difficult and subtle element of piety. The *yetzer hara* has a lot of input in it, so there is a lot of danger, because the *yetzer hara* can have you avoid many good things as if they were bad, and draw you into many transgressions as if they were great *mitzvot.*

In truth, the only way a person can succeed in this evaluating process is by these three means: his heart must be the most forthright of hearts; his only motivation should be to bring satisfaction to his Creator, nothing else, and he should reflect deeply upon his actions and try to rectify them toward this end; and after all this he should cast his burden upon God so that it may be said of him (Psalms 84:6–12), "Happy is the man who places his strength in You. . . . There is no lack of good for those who go about wholeheartedly."

You will never reach wholeness if you lack one of these conditions and will be dangerously close to stumbling and falling instead. If your motivations will not be the highest and purest, or if you slacken off from thorough reflection, or if, after all this, you do not place your trust in God, it is unlikely that you will not fall. But if all three conditions—purity of thought, analysis, and trust—are met, you can truly go safely and no misfortune will come upon you.[1]

---

1. There is an inclination to overdo anything we have invested a lot of time or self in. We worry about it, fret over its turns and changes, and fear for the worst. While that can certainly be said about our material concerns, though it is not often perceived as being so, it is true of our spiritual investments as well.

Nearly everyone can be made to see how he has perhaps put too much weight on his social standing, wealth, athletic ability, physical appearance, and the like. And a pious individual would have come to realize that such a trap is to be avoided at all costs, and would have spent the better part of his preparation to come to this point doing just that.

But the *yetzer hara* is exceedingly creative. The very person who will have come to the point of realizing the fallaciousness of all of the above obsessions could be guilty of his own

This is what Channah was prophetically referring to when she said (1 Samuel 2:9), "He will watch over the feet of His pious." David alluded to this as well when he said (Psalms 37:28), "He will not abandon His pious; they will always be protected."

What you have to understand is that you cannot judge matters relevant to piety by first impressions. You must reflect and analyze their ramifications. Sometimes an act may appear to be good, but it must be abandoned because what would come out of it would be bad, and if you were to do it you would actually be a sinner, not a pious person. The actions of Gedaliah ben Achikom (Jeremiah 40:16) bespeak this. Because of his overpiety and his unwillingness to adjudge Ishmael guilty or to hear out slander, he said to Yochanan ben Koreach: "You are lying about Ishmael." What happened because of that? He died, Israel was dispersed, and their last dying ember

---

form of the same error. Let us call it "overpiety." There are times when it is wrong to act piously, as Luzzatto will point out, simply wrong. It is obsessional at those times, in poor taste, and counterproductive. It detracts from the Glory of God, which is essential, and evidences an exceedingly fine and pale gray form of arrogance. As Luzzatto says near the end of this chapter, "so many great, pious people abandoned their saintly practices when they were among the common people when such acts would appear to be rooted in pride." In fact, that is why the trait to be studied immediately following this one is modesty, to prevent that.

One who has come so far in his evolution does not want to fall back. His whole being has been dissected, re-ordered, and infused with goal, and he is surging onward. The natural inclination is to go further. But it must be kept in mind that the person who has come so far is capable of great wrong simply because he is so great. That is so because few if any around him are that great or anywhere near it, and he is responding to a call they cannot hear and which they think odd. If they were to hear his call or come to understand what he has understood they would probably act the same way, but they do not. In their eyes he is fanatical. And when they perceive that, they want nothing to do with him, and his actions foster animosity, avoidance, and rebelliousness.

There is so little piety in the world as is. Too much of it in one individual is so powerful and overwhelming to encounter that at times it might be misunderstood and might cause a negative reaction on the part of the observer. To use an old image: Could anyone ever endure the full light of the sun and not wither and die? So in order for it to be effective and act as an agent of rectification (which it is meant to do), piety must be tempered at times and screened. The pious individual's true piety may be dependent upon a willingness to let go of it from time to time so as to let it shine when it must and not shine when it must not.

It also should be pointed out that there are times when the pious, saintly man must just be a *man*, so others can see that he is not an angel and that they too can attain his rank. For if they consider him to be an angel and unearthly, they will assume that piety and nearly all that precedes it are beyond their reach. And that would be tragic and against the best interests of the generation.

For the pious person to come to that he must be honest with himself ("his heart must be the most forthright of hearts"), he must realize his ultimate goal ("to bring satisfaction to his Creator, nothing else"), focusing entirely upon it (by "reflect[ing] deeply upon his actions and try[ing] to rectify them toward this end"), and he must have trust enough in the success of his own quest ("he should cast his burden upon God").

was extinguished. The Torah credits him with the death of those who were killed as if he himself had killed them, as our sages explained (*Niddah* 61a). They based their proof on the verse (Jeremiah 41:9), ". . . all of the corpses of the men struck by the hand of Gedaliah."

The Second Temple was destroyed because of this kind of piety—piety not weighed on the scales of balanced insight. It involved the actions of Bar Kamsa (*Gittin* 56a): "The Rabbis wanted to offer the animal, but Rabbi Zechariah ben Evkolas said to them, 'People will surmise that blemished animals can be offered on the altar.' The Rabbis then wanted to kill Bar Kamsa, but Rabbi Zechariah ben Evkolas said to them, 'People will surmise that whoever wants to offer a blemished animal will be killed by the Rabbis.'" All the while the evil-doer was slandering Israel, and Caesar came to destroy Jerusalem. Rabbi Yochanan said that Rabbi Zechariah ben Evkolas's caution caused the destruction of his household, the burning of the Sanctuary and our exile amongst the nations.

So you see that you cannot make judgments relevant to piety according to how they first appear. You have to turn it over in your mind a number of times until you can judge what would be most fitting—to act, or to refrain from acting.

The Torah commands (Leviticus 19:17), "You shall surely rebuke your companion." How many times does a person start to rebuke a sinner at a time or place he would not be listened to? He actually causes the person to advance in his bad ways, to profane the name of God, and to add rebelliousness to his transgressions. In this instance the pious thing to do would be to remain silent. This is what our sages meant when they said (*Yevamot* 65b), "Just as it is a *mitzvah* to say something when it would be listened to, so too is it a *mitzvah* sometimes to not say what would not be listened to."[2]

---

2. The tradition is as against listening to slander as it is speaking it, if not more so, as listening renders it credible and tends to cause more of it. The sanctity of the Temple was to be maintained at nearly all costs, as it stood for the Divine Presence. And when done correctly, rebuke evidences a great love for another person and a deep concern for his spiritual well being.

So while it might seem that Gedaliah was acting with compassion toward Ishmael by not hearing out slander against him, in fact he was acting in a way that proved to be cruel to many others who died because of Gedaliah's overpiety. He should have taken that all into consideration before he acted. And while it might seem that Rabbi Zechariah ben Evkolas's caution was in keeping with the sanctity of the Temple and its sacrifices, and that when someone rebukes his friend he can only be having his best interests in mind, we see that that is often not the case, and that the person is doing much more harm than good.

The tradition tells us that once there was a man on a journey who came to a fork in the road and was puzzled. He wanted to get to the capital city, but did not know which path to take. A child passed by, and he asked him.

"Do you want to take the long road which is the short road, or the short road which is the long road?"

"I certainly want to take the short road," the man replied.

Obviously, it is proper for a person to be eager and run to do a *mitzvah* and try to be one of those who busies himself with it. But sometimes controversy can result from this, and you would thereby more likely shame the *mitzvah* and profane the name of God than honor it. In such a case the pious individual has the responsibility to abandon the *mitzvah* rather than pursue it. As our sages said in regard to the Levites (*Bamidbar Rabbah* 5:1), "Because they knew that whoever would carry the Ark would get the greater reward, they left the table, Menorah, and altars behind, and ran to carry the Ark instead to get the reward. They would argue back and forth saying to each other, 'I'll carry the Ark!' As a result of that they were disrespectful, and the Divine Presence struck them. . . ."

You are duty-bound to follow the *mitzvot* as strictly as possible, no matter who is watching you as you do, and are to neither be afraid nor embarrassed. This is what the Torah means when it says (Psalms 119:46), "I will speak of Your ordinances (even) before kings and will not be ashamed," and (*Avot* 5:23) "Be as strong as a lion. . . ." But even this requires discrimination and forethought, as it refers to those *mitzvot* which we are absolutely obligated to do. In regard to them you have to be as hard as flint. But as to those extra flourishes of piety which, when done in front of most people would cause laughter and mocking, and would have them sin and be punished because of the pious person's extra measures—the pious person should abandon such things, as they are not an absolute obligation upon him. The prophet referred to this when he said (Micah 6:8), "Walk humbly with your God." So many great, pious people abandoned their saintly practices while among the common people when such acts would appear to be rooted in pride.

The child directed him toward one of the two roads on the fork, and the man proceeded. After a short time he came to the gate of the capital city. He was stunned at the immediacy with which he had reached his destination. "Why would the child have thought I would ever have wanted to take another route?" he wondered.

At the gate stood a guard who demanded the man's official papers and a letter of entry signed by the prince of the man's province. He had none of that. There were ways to work around those requirements, he knew, primarily by being in contact with the official he meant to see in the capital city in the first place, so he asked the guard to contact that man. Contacting the official in the capital city and having him arrange entry for the man took a very long time—several weeks—but the man finally gained entry, and accomplished what he wanted.

One his way home he decided to retrace his steps so as to take the other route at the fork in the road the child had described as the "long road that is the short road."

He found that it was a long road indeed that required a week of traveling. But at the end of the road there was an unused and unlocked gate to the capital city through which the man could have gone in. He would have saved weeks of time if he had taken this "long road" as it was indeed the short road.

So we see that there are times when a short road can actually be a long one, and a long road can be a short one. So too, there are times when compassion is cruelty, or sanctification is profanation. The pious person must arrive at the fork of each road and consider.

The crux of the matter is that you should do any essential, obligatory *mitzvah* when its time comes, no matter who may mock you. But you should not do anything which is not essential and which will cause laughter and mockery.

We can infer that one who would truly be pious must evaluate all of his actions in light of their results, and according to the concurrent conditions: according to the company he finds himself to be in, the circumstances, and the physical location. If refraining will result in further sanctification of the name of God and satisfy Him more than the performance of the act, you should refrain rather than do.

If an act appears to be good but is actually bad in its results or its ramifications; or if another act seems to be bad, but is actually good in its results—you are to act in consideration of the ultimate effect and outcome, as that is in truth the fruit of all actions.

These words are passed on only to the understanding of heart and the ready of mind, because it is impossible to enunciate the endless particulars. (Proverbs 2:6) "God will give wisdom from His mouth, knowledge, and understanding."

The story of Rabbi Tarphon (*Berachot* 10b) goes to prove that. Because he was strict and acted in accordance with the decisions of the House of Shammai[3] he was "deserving of corporal punishment, because (he) went against the words of the House of Hillel"—even though he was more stringent—because the controversies between the House of Hillel and Shammai were a burden upon Israel, as they were numerous. It was finally decided that the *Halachah* would always follow the decisions of the House of Hillel. The upkeep of Torah demanded that this decision stay in place ad infinitum and never weaken so that Torah should never, God forbid, become divided. Therefore, in the opinion of this *Mishnah* it would have been the better part of piety to enforce the rulings of the House of Hillel even when that would mean a certain leniency rather than to be stringent and follow the decisions of the House of Shammai.[4] This should indicate to us the path the light of truth actually and faithfully dwells upon so that we might do what is correct in the eyes of God.

---

3. . . . after the House of Hillel's decisions had been accepted as *Halachah*.

4. The reason Luzzatto is so wordy in his explanation here is because he wants to show that—though it would seem to contradict what he said at the beginning of chapter 14—stringency is not proper in this instance.

21

The Means of Acquiring Piety

A lot of introspection and profound reflection especially helps in the acquisition of piety. The more you reflect upon the exalted nature of God, the infinite nature of His perfection, and the great and unfathomable difference between His greatness and our lowliness, the more will you be filled with trembling and reverence before Him. When you reflect as well upon the great goodness He has provided us with, His vast love for Israel, the closeness to Him the righteous enjoy, the excellence of Torah, *mitzvot*, and other learned matters—an intense and powerful love will arise within you, and you will want nothing but to attach yourself to Him.[1]

When you will see that He is literally a father to us, and has compassion upon us as a father has compassion upon his children, the desire and longing to reciprocate, as a child would want to do for a father, will constantly be aroused in you.

To do this, you have to sequester yourself in your room and collect your thoughts for the introspections and considerations of these truths. What will certainly help in all this is a thorough familiarity with and profound understanding of the Songs of David, and a reflection upon their statements and main points. As they are full of love, reverence, and all manner of piety, there cannot help but be aroused in you a

---

1. As has been said above, God is both transcendent and approachable, that is, He is both distant and near, removed and intimate. When we revere Him, we recognize His distance and transcendence; when we love Him, we recognize His approachability and His intimacy with us.

Luzzatto is referring to that when he says that "the more you reflect upon the exalted nature of God, the infinite nature of His perfection, and the great and unfathomable difference between His greatness and our lowliness, the more will you be filled with trembling and reverence before Him," and that "when you reflect as well upon the great goodness He has provided us with, His vast love for Israel, the closeness to Him the righteous enjoy, the excellence of Torah, *mitzvot*, and other learned matters, an intense and powerful love will arise within you, and you will want nothing but to attach yourself to Him."

great urge to follow in David's footsteps and to go on his path when you reflect upon them.[2] It also helps to read the stories of the pious in the *Aggadot* they are found in. Obviously, they excite the mind to take note and follow their noble deeds.

What deters from piety are preoccupations and worry. When the mind is preoccupied and is stewing in its worries and external concerns it is impossible for it to reflect. And without reflection you will never obtain piety. Even if you will have already obtained it, preoccupation will compel and confuse your mind, and will not allow you to grow in your reverence, love, and the other matters relevant to piety we have mentioned. That is why our sages said (*Shabbat* 30b), "The Divine Presence does not dwell in the midst of sadness. . . ."[3]

All the more so is piety deterred by the delights and pleasures that are literally the opposite of piety, which flirt with the heart and draw it after itself rather than anything relevant to abstinence and true knowledge.

The only thing that can stand guard over a person and save him from these deterrents is trust—casting your lot upon God completely. That comes about with the knowledge that it is utterly impossible to lack what is already determined to be yours. As our sages have put it (*Betzah* 16a), "All of one's sustenance is fixed on Rosh HaShanah . . ."; and (*Yoma* 38b) "One person cannot have as much as a stringsbreadth worth of what is another's."

It would have been possible for you to simply sit back and do nothing and still be provided for were it not for the fact of the penalty exacted from all people, which

---

2. Luzzatto said very bluntly in his introduction that "it has come to appear to most that piety is dependent merely upon the recitation of many Psalms." So why the sudden introduction of such a need?

The truth of the matter is that he is saying here that among the things that will help you acquire piety is a "thorough familiarity with and profound understanding of the Songs of David, and a reflection upon their statements and main points," that is, a studied and inspired reading and taking-to-heart of the Book of Psalms rather than a blind, lifeless recitation of it. After all, has not he himself quoted from the Book of Psalms an innumerable amount of times to prove certain points? And that is how he expects us to benefit from it as well: by using it as a wisdom text.

3. We said earlier on (see part 2) that "worry is a state of being that comes about when you are unsure of your future and realize that you cannot know its outcome. All humans suffer from it, and that should not be denied. . . . The advantage [the full of understanding] enjoy is that they have come to realize the nature of things and our roles in life, and they are able to sublimate their natural human fears into fears about things that matter. We worry about and fear for things that do *not* matter, and that is what has us suffer and grope in the dark."

So too here Luzzatto is saying that the thoroughly disadvantageous kind of worry— the kind that keeps you back from piety—is the kind that is a sort of preoccupation that has you stew in your "worries and external concerns" so much so that it is impossible for you to reflect and grow. It is also a form of sadness rather than a natural concern and wonderment, hence the quote, "The Divine Presence does not dwell in the midst of sadness. . . ."

is enunciated in the Torah by the phrase (Genesis 3:19), "You will eat bread by the sweat of your brow," because of which man is obligated to attempt one way or another to procure a livelihood. Thus did the Great King decree. It is an unavoidable tax that is incumbent upon all human beings to pay.

Our sages put it thusly (*Sifre*), "I might think that you could even get by sitting and doing nothing. But the Torah tells us (Deuteronomy 14:29), '. . . with all the products of your hand which you make.'" But it is not so much that the effort will produce results but that the effort is necessary. By producing the effort you meet the requirement, and there comes to be a place for the blessings of heaven to dwell, so you need not spend your life in diligence and effort.[4]

---

4. Earlier on (chap. 9) Luzzatto spoke about trust. He said there that it should be understood that "there.is trust and there is naivete," that is, there are times when it is wise to trust in God and cast your lot upon Him, and there times when to do so would almost be foolhardy, so to speak.

But in truth, in the earlier citation he is speaking against naively trusting in God to protect you from an immediately threatening situation. An intelligent, thinking person would not walk out into a busy city street without looking out for traffic, for example. He would never say, "God will protect me, so I can do anything!" That would be the epitome of naivete, and he would have no one to blame for his injuries but himself. A thinking person would watch out for his well-being where there is a possibility of danger. As Luzzatto says there, "this sort of self-protection is . . . warranted, sensible, and wise. . . ."

But he is saying here that when it comes to food and shelter, you can depend upon the share of it that God will provide you with, and you should trust in His provision. We must learn the lesson the animals can teach us: that if we allow Him to, God will provide us with food and shelter, and we can depend upon that. We of an era of wealth and abundance have forgotten that lesson and will settle for nothing less than glory and exaggerated comfort. We overestimate our bare necessities. In fact, we can do with very much less than we think we can, and we would probably be much happier.

So when Luzzatto says that "it is utterly impossible to lack what is already determined to be yours" that is to be taken literally—remembering that you can very well do with less than you think you need.

And when he says, "It is not so much that the effort will produce results but that the effort is necessary," he means to say that you will certainly be provided for, but you must initiate an effort—but the effort is not one to procure food itself, but to make sure there "comes to be a place for the blessings of heaven to dwell." That alludes to the statement of Rabbi Natan (the principle student of Rabbi Nachman of Breslov) that by our efforts we erect conduits for "the blessings of heaven," and those conduits directly attract the food and shelter we need, making our receiving of them *easier*, not possible. And we should have that in mind when we toil: that we are erecting conduits for God's blessings of food and shelter; we are not directly bringing about our food and shelter. Anyone can see how a lot of effort oftentimes results in no gain or even loss, and that sometimes no effort at all will result in great and abundant profit. All is in the hands of God; our task is to struggle and produce, and He determines the success or failure of that effort.

This is what David was referring to when he said (Psalms 75:7–8), "Growth does not come from the east, from the west, or from the desert; God adjudges that this one will be demeaned and another will be advanced." King Solomon said (Proverbs 23:4), "Do not toil to grow wealthy; do not try to understand."

The true path is that taken by the early pious ones who would make their Torah study primary and their occupations secondary, and were successful at both. Once you work just a little, all you need further do is trust in God and you will never be concerned about worldly matters. Then your mind will be free and your heart readied for true piety and complete service to God.

Summation of Part VII

Chapter 18

1. Piety has come to be a misunderstood trait because there are so many people who have not bothered to think about what it means, and they act oddly and absurdly trying to live up to their own conception of it. As a result, false impressions of what it requires are common, and there is a prevalent notion that it involves either life-threatening or extreme acts.

2. In fact, piety requires great wisdom because it is based upon the ultimate repairing of your ways. It is rooted in toiling in Torah and bringing utmost satisfaction to God.

3. One who wants to be pious and truly love God would not be satisfied with accomplishing the minimum required of him by Torah. Like a loving and loyal son, he would do all his Father would intimate He would like to have done, and he would deduce and accomplish all that his Father *might* like done as well just to satisfy him.

4. While it can be said that abstention is related to negative *mitzvot*, piety is related to the positive ones, and hence they are opposites, in truth they are one and the same thing and are essentially means of going beyond the letter of the law as much as necessary to bring satisfaction to God.

Chapter 19

5. There are three primary factors to be considered in the analysis of piety: your deeds (both interpersonal, and between yourself and God), how your deeds are done, and what the motivations behind them are when you are doing them.

These are the general principles from which particulars are to be extracted by the individual.

6. Piety in deeds in the realm of those between yourself and God involves keeping the *mitzvot* with as much exactitude and care as is humanly possible.

7. Piety in deeds in the realm of those between yourself and others involves bettering the lot of others as much as is humanly possible, and it can be done corporeally (by easing others' physical burdens), monetarily (by being sure that you do not cause financial loss), and psychologically (by bringing satisfaction to others by being benevolent to them, and striving for peace).

8. Piety in terms of *how* deeds are performed involves reverence for God (which includes submission to His will, humility in service to Him, and honoring his *mitzvot*), and love for God (which is composed of three subdivisions: attachment to Him, happiness, and vengeance for Him).

9. Reverence for God is being in awe before God's grandeur and considering the fact that you are literally standing before Him and conversing with Him when you pray. It also involves thinking of *mitzvot* as precious, and honoring God through them as much as you can by ornamenting and glorifying them.

10. Love of God involves desiring and longing for closeness to Him and pursuing His Holiness as much as you would pursue anything urgently longed for. It is not dependent upon His actions toward you, and does not diminish in times of sorrow or woe.

11. The first subdivision of love of God—attachment to Him—involves clutching onto His Name with all of your heart and caring for nothing else. The second subdivision—happiness—involves serving God with joy by being happy for the privilege to pray to and serve the Master of the Universe. And the third subdivision—obsession with Him—involves being zealous for His Name and hating and obstructing those who hate Him.

12. Piety in your motivations involves altruism, as it was delineated in the last section, which only comes after a full love for God is fostered in your heart. The pious person must also be in a constant state of agitation over the exile of the Jewish nation and the destruction of the Holy Temple because they bring about a diminution of God's honor (so to speak), and he should long for the redemption. And finally, he should be concerned for the well-being of his generation as well as atone for their transgressions.

Chapter 20

13. To be truly pious, you have to learn to evaluate your actions. And the only way you can do that is by having an honest and forthright heart, wanting

nothing but what is best for God while reflecting deeply upon your deeds and repairing them with this in mind, as well as trusting in God and casting your burden upon Him.

14. Evaluation is necessary because you often cannot quite grasp the full ramifications of an act when it comes upon you to do it. Sometimes what might appear to be a good thing to do will result in bad, and should not be done. Many tragic things have come about because of such errors.

15. This also includes not being extra stringent, above and beyond your obligations, in *mitzvot* before people who would mock you for doing that. While you certainly must do what you are commanded to do no matter what the consequences, you must *not* be extra stringent if that will defile the *mitzvot* in the eyes of others. The pious person should evaluate his actions before doing them and determine if their being done will further sanctify the Name of God or desecrate it.

Chapter 21

16. The best way to acquire piety is to be profoundly introspective and reflective about God's grandeur, His goodness to us, His love for us, how close to Him the pious are, and the excellence of His Torah—until an intense and mighty love for Him will arise in you, and you will want nothing else but to attach yourself to Him. Such introspection is only possible with seclusion and meditation upon the truth.

17. Preoccupations and worry keep you back from being pious because they make it difficult for you to reflect upon all this. The way to save yourself from all that is to trust in God. It is best in fact to follow the path of the early pious ones who would concentrate upon their Torah study and make their monetary concerns secondary. They were successful at both and enjoyed the peace of mind necessary for complete service to God because they did the little they had to do to earn their living and trusted in God that He would provide for them.

VIII

HUMILITY

Introduction to Part VIII

The eighth part comprises two chapters (22–23) and it concerns itself with the trait of "humility." The chapters are entitled, "An Explanation of the Trait of Humility" (chap. 22) and "The Means of Acquiring Humility" (chap. 23).

The matters aside from the essential one discussed in this section include: our inherent human imperfections, failings in our understandings, personal talents as part of your nature, taking credit for your actions, timidity, enduring insult, the dangers and burdens in the assumption of power, according honor to others, how modest people are loved and fortunate (chap. 22); and force of habit, existential reflection, change of circumstance, human fallibility, deprivation, ignorance and arrogance, flatterers, and the choice of friends (chap. 23).

We are aware by this point that we are approaching the end and that we have to eradicate as many deterrents to holiness as possible. That brings us to the exceedingly difficult requirement of being humble. While humility has been discussed somewhat in chapter 11, it is discussed fully here, and brought out as being in essence the metaphysical loss of self, rather than a mere, pedestrian non–self-centeredness.

Luzzatto describes the essence of humility as not thinking of your own needs or wants, and of not imagining praise and honor are due you in any way. The Hebrew for humility is *anavah*. Besides meaning modesty, or humility, it also indicates a Divine response to prayer, as well as agricultural yield and fertility (cf. *Mishnah, Pe'ah* 1:2, based upon Hosea 2:23–24). That implies a selfless allowance of others, and an essential richness. As such, it does not have the connotations of underestimation, servility, disinterestedness, inferiority, abasement, or disappointment as we would assume it would in the English.

22

An Explanation
of the Trait of Humility

We have already spoken of the disgrace of arrogance,[1] from which you can infer the praiseworthiness of humility. We will now focus more on humility itself and will, as a result, come to understand arrogance.

The general rule in regard to humility is that you should not consider yourself important for whatever reason whatsoever. That is the very opposite of arrogance. What results from it will be diametrically opposite to what would result from arrogance as well.[2]

---

1. See chapter 11 for a full discussion of arrogance and the difference between arrogance and pride.

2. In chapter 11 Luzzatto said arrogance is evidenced by your "consciously or unconsciously thinking yourself worthy of praise. . . ." Here he infers that it is the considering of your own needs before those of others. In fact, both elements are there in the egocentric, and they are interrelated.

Egocentricity is rooted in a misconception of the place of the individual in the grand scheme of things. The truth of the matter is that everyone plays a serious and alternately constructive and destructive role in the machinations of the universe. One person ticks, and everyone else resonates to that tick, which causes further resonance that goes round and round until it comes full circle to the original person who ticked, and it causes him to resonate as well and tick once again. And when that person ticks a second time, he does so more strongly for the fact that he ticked the first time, and he causes yet a stronger chain reaction, ad infinitum.

But oftentimes, that person comes to be impressed and touched by his tick, and overlooks the full process with all of its actors. He forgets as well that even his first tick was not entirely originated by himself and that he was given the power to tick and the greater part of the impetus to do so by a Cause behind himself, God.

So when you misconstrue your place in the drawn out and interlocked process of getting anything done, and you think that you tick of your own volition and follow no one, you

Careful scrutiny will further reveal that humility is dependent upon both thought and action. You must first be humble in thought, and only then can you act humbly. If you are not humble in thought and you want to act humble, you will wind up being one of the previously referred to "so-called humble"—the hypocrites who are the worst of all.[3] We will now explain the various categories of being humble in thought and in action.

Humility in thought involves your reflecting upon and coming to realize the fact that praise and honor, and all the more so aggrandizement above other people, are not due you,[4] for two reasons: because of what is necessarily imperfect in you, and because of things you have done in the past.

---

come to assume the attitude that since you are so potent and matter so much, you are very important. That is, you think yourself worthy of praise, to use Luzzatto's phrase.

Such an important person, you think, should have his needs met sooner than anyone would have theirs met (for the general good of all, you rationalize). One who has his needs met before anyone else, you then come to think, is worthy of note, standing away from the crowd as he does, and must be special and worth more. And you then come to be arrogant, seeing to it that such a one as yourself gets all he has coming to him, which is a lot. At that point you come to consider "your own needs before those of others."

3. He is referring to his previous discussion of the supposedly modest who are in fact self-centered, found in chapter 11. He says there that because these sorts of people are not internally and thoroughly humble, their real arrogance could not help but evidence itself sooner or later. The only way to avoid that, he tells us now, is to internalize and actualize real modesty, and it will imbue itself into all you do. So in order to have you come to modesty in your actions, he tells you how to foster it in your being.

4. There is a natural inclination toward the seeking out of praise. It comes from the very real and central sense we have of self-worthlessness, which, we feel, can only be denied if others tell us we are worth something. The more they tell us we are worth something, in fact, the more that seems to be so, and the more clearly and strongly we sense we *are*.

But it goes without saying that the assurances such praise carry are very, very short-lived. Yet from force of habit we continue on "fishing for compliments," hoping that one day we will come to believe it all, but we never do. The pious take that to heart, and learn to live without praise or aggrandizement. They are none the worse for that, and are in fact liberated by the loss of the need to be corroborated by others. That is the simple truth, and it is the spirit in which Luzzatto's revelations seem to have been made.

It must be realized, though, that this chapter seems to have been written for two audiences: first, the newly-become-pious who will have read this book any number of times, worked at the processes for years, then come to this point ready for its taking-on; and then, the lesser souls who will have come to this point for the first time and sensed that there is a lot to be learned from it even now, which is of course true. And while that could be said about any chapter, and would be correct, it especially seems to be so for this chapter, because it is concerned with the very vital and pivotal matter of self-worth.

So when Luzzatto says point-blank at the beginning of this chapter that "you should not consider your own needs for whatever reason whatsoever," and when he says here that "praise and honor, and all the more so aggrandizement above other people, are not due you,"

As to what is lacking in you, it is obvious that it is impossible for a person not to have many faults, no matter how perfected he may be. Those faults may either be a result of his nature, because of family influence, because of circumstances, or because of certain of his own actions. For (Ecclesiastes 7:20), "No man is so righteous that he would do good and never sin." All these are inherent blemishes in a person that could never

---

the natural inclination of the normal and well-balanced person would be to say, "No thank you. That's not for me, because I could never live like that," and he would be right.

It should be recalled at all times that a healthy and robust sense of ego-worth (as opposed to arrogance) is human, and it is even to be striven for—in most lives—while arrogance is never good and it is invariably indicative of a deep wound. A person who is reading this for the first time who inclines toward unhealthy, neurotic timidity will claim to agree with what is being said in the text right away, and will assume that he has acquired something only the very most pious will have attained to, and he will assume as well that he is to keep on in such a path—when the contrary is true.

There are people who believe they are best satisfied when they are doing only what others would want them to do. They invariably come to suffer because of that when they burn with an unconscious and galloping need to speak out and assert themselves. But they have been taught that they are never ever to assert themselves, and are only and always to do what others say. Their "teachers" will cite writings such as this text and others as proof, and will reiterate over and over again that the best of people (i.e., the pious and the holy) are egoless and servile.

The poor souls hearing that, being good people, will learn early on that humility, meekness, and timidity (phrases used throughout this chapter and the next) are desirable traits, and they will assume those traits. In fact simply because, as we said, there is a natural inclination to seek out praise and assurance from others of our self-worth, such poor souls—wanting to please their teachers—would assume such a stance in the hopes that it will bring them satisfaction as well.

But such an assumption of humility, meekness and timidity so early on in life or in spiritual development is not only undesirable—it is ruinous. It is bound to make itself known, and sure to shake the very ground below the person practicing it. Understand, that while it is true that, as we expressed in the second note above, too often we misunderstand our place in the universe and overassume importance, it is also true that a too early wiping away of ego is crippling. There is a time for timidity; it is all so very, very lovely and so very, very beneficial for the true and fundamental well-being of the soul; but it is nonetheless horrendous for lesser souls.

True and pious humility is the result of a long, studied, and excruciatingly thorough process of dissolution of self, nothing less. The reward for it is the replacement of God's Self for your self (so to speak), and it is the essence of attachment to Him. But it is not a simple matter of denying yourself or clamping yourself down until that self disappears. It is a matter of serious evolution and of transcendence of self. And that can never be taken lightly, as doing so is fraught with threat and danger to the health of the individual. Understand that one has to *have* a being before he can transcend it; and one can never "skip steps" along the way, because to do so is too risky.

So when Luzzatto says here that "praise and honor, and all the more so aggrandizement above other people, are not due you" he is addressing the person who will have come

allow for self-aggrandizement.[5] Even if you were an otherwise extraordinary person, your imperfections would be enough to overshadow your other traits.

The trait that would most likely bring you to arrogance and self-aggrandizement would be wisdom, as it is a personal trait that is in a special part of yourself, your mind. Yet there is no wise man who never makes a mistake and could not learn from his colleagues or even from his students often enough. In that case, how could you ever boast of your wisdom? Anyone with a good mind—even one who merits to be a great and famous sage—must admit, upon honest reflection and consideration, that there is no room for pride or self-aggrandizement.[6]

One whose intellect is greater than someone else's is only acting in a way that comes naturally to him, as a bird would just naturally fly and an ox would naturally be able to pull with his brute strength. If you are wise it is because you are that way by nature. And those who are not as natively wise as yourself at this point could very well train themselves to be as wise as you if they were of that nature. As that is the case, you have no reason to be proud or to boast.[7]

If you are a great sage, it is incumbent upon you to teach whoever may need your knowledge. And, as Rabbi Yochanan ben Zakkai has said (*Avot* 2:9), "If you have learned a lot of Torah, do not laud yourself with it—that is why you were created." If you are wealthy, you should be pleased with your good fortune and come to

---

along very far, and who will have come to realize this as truth. Such a person would only have to be reminded of this and he would want to go on. "Mere mortals," those lesser souls who will come to this statement and the one at the beginning of the chapter for the first time, would react to it in one of two ways: with guilt and unhealthy remorse, or with disgust.

Please understand, dear soul, that the holy author, Moshe Chaim Luzzatto, understands your natural, God-given need for occasional corroboration and recognition, but he means for you to take stock along the way and envision greatness. Take this to heart when you read further about the subject at hand.

5. This is a remarkable statement of fact that both humbles us and sets us free. Who could deny his own occasional degradations and failures? And who could not admit to moments of deeply felt shame? Not a single human being. Needless to say for most healthy and productive people, such moments are rare and they pass quickly, but they always leave an echo behind that humbles and that nudges at your ears at even the best of moments.

But this realization is also a liberation in that it reminds us of our true natures. We are each imperfect and faulty in one way or another. Even the person who will have evolved to this point in his reading and working on this book cannot deny that he too has "many faults, no matter how perfected he may be." And with such a realization we can worry less, can ease off a bit in our hard drive to rectify, rectify, rectify, and can settle into our role as pious though so-very-human beings.

6. It is the *honesty* in the reflection and consideration that allows for such a realization. Most people lie to themselves and continue on in the delusion that they are solely responsible for what they do when they in fact stand upon the proverbial shoulders of the countless generations that preceded them and laid groundwork for their deeds.

7. What gifts we have we are born with; what we do with them we die with.

the aid of one who does not have. If you are strong, you must help the defenseless and rescue the oppressed. To what is this analogous?—to houseguards who are assigned to specific assignments. It is only right that they guard what they have been appointed over so as to be a part of the general well-being of the whole household. In truth, there is no place for personal pride on their part.

This is the kind of contemplation and reflection that is fitting for everyone that is rightminded and not misguided. And it is only when this has become clear to you that you may be called truly humble. For in your heart and in your inner being you will be humble.[8] This is what David was referring to when he said to Michal (2 Samuel 6:22), "And I have been lowly in my own eyes."

Our sages have said (*Sotah* 5b), "How great are the humble. When the Holy Temple yet stood, a person would offer an *olah* sacrifice and he would receive the merit of having offered that *olah* sacrifice. And if he would offer a *minchah* sacrifice, he would receive merit for that. But one who is humble is considered to have offered all of the sacrifices. As it is written (Psalms 51:19), 'God's offering is a contrite spirit.'" This is a praise for those who are humble in their hearts and in their thoughts.

Our sages have further said (*Chullin* 89a), "It is written (Deuteronomy 7:7), 'Not because you are greater in number than all the other nations did God send His love upon you or choose you, for you were the fewest of all people . . .' God said to them, 'I long for you, My son. Even when I attribute greatness to you, you humble yourself before me. I attributed greatness to Abraham and he said (Genesis 18:27), "I am dust and ashes." I attributed greatness to Moses and Aaron and they said (Exodus 16:7), "What are we?" I attributed greatness to David and he said (Psalms 22:7), "I am a worm, not a man."'"

All this comes about if you are honest and will not allow yourself to be seduced by any advantages you might enjoy. You would know that in truth with all of the imperfections you undoubtedly have, you have not outgrown your lowliness. You should also not evidence pride in the *mitzvot* you have performed, for just by having done them you will not have necessarily reached their ultimate goal.[9] Even if you had no fault other than that you were flesh-and-blood and born of a woman—that should

8. Notice he says that it is only "when this *has become clear to you* that you may be called truly humble," not when you start to act humble. That would agree with his statement earlier on in this chapter that "you must first be humble in thought, and only then can you act humbly."

9. The greatest irony is the one that involves the admixture of arrogance and personal nature. Only a moron would be proud of his breathing and his ability to grow hair, just as only a blind and unthinking Jew could ever be proud of the *mitzvot* he has done. It is absurd for a Jew to be proud of having been part of the process of God's will because it is in his nature and part of his heritage.

But "reaching the ultimate goal" which comes about through the doing of those *mitzvot* is not natural and not a heritage. It is fulfilled by a conscious effort of the self. The danger of arrogance lies in that especially so, and it must also be watched out for.

be more than enough to indicate your lowliness and imperfection and the fact that you need not at all be haughty. For, whatever advantages you might possess were given to you by God who wants to be gracious to you because of your piteous and humble corporeality. You can only acknowledge Him who is so gracious to you and be even more submissive to Him.

This is comparable to a pauper who receives a gift out of the goodness of someone else's heart. It is impossible for the pauper to take the gift without being embarrassed. The more generous the giver is to him, the more embarrassed will the pauper be.[10] Such is our case, which is obvious to anyone whose eyes are open to perceive that whatever advantages you enjoy come to you from God. As King David put it (Psalms 116:12), "How can I respond to all the generosity God has bestowed upon me?"

We have seen many greatly pious people who have suffered retribution because, despite of all of their piety, they took some of the credit for themselves. This is what Nechemyah ben Chachalyah did, for example. Our sages said (*Sanhedrin* 93b), "Why wasn't his book called by his name?—because he attributed certain things to himself." Chizzkiyah said (Isaiah 38:17), "Behold—in peace I have great bitterness . . . ," because God said to him (Isaiah 37:35), "I have defended this city so as to rescue it for My sake and for the sake of David, My servant." Our sages said further (*Berachot* 10b), "Whoever attributes some merit to himself has his merit attributed to someone else." From all this we can infer that you are not even to assume goodness in your goodness. All the more so are you not to grow haughty and proud over it.

But all that has been said and that is so fitting to reflect upon is for one who is like Abraham, Moses, Aaron, David, or the other saintly ones mentioned. But as for us—orphans of orphans—we have no need for this. We so clearly have so many faults that we do not need to reflect very deeply to recognize them. All our wisdom is nothing. The greatest of our sages is nothing but a student of the students of the early ones.[11] It is proper to understand and know this so that our hearts not swell vainly. We should recognize that, overall, our minds are superficial, and our perceptions very limited. Foolishness is rampant amongst us and error is triumphant. Whatever we do

---

10. This analogy is often used by the kabbalists to explain why God gave us "tasks," that is, *mitzvot*, to do in this world. The question that is often raised is, "Why didn't God make us perfect from the start rather than demanding that we attain perfection?" The standard response is that, like the "pauper who receives a gift out of the goodness of someone else's heart," who would be embarrassed by his donor's largesse and would not come to be his true self—we would feel undeserving and not come to be our true selves if we would not have to assert ourselves and actively earn our perfection.

But why is the parable brought in here? Because the trouble with your earning your own perfection is that often you become self-centered in the process, and that has to be watched out for, which is the subject at hand.

11. See note 6 above.

know is only the very minimum.[12] It is certainly therefore inappropriate for us to be at all haughty. Instead, we should be humble and lowly—but that goes without saying.

To this point we have spoken about humility in our thoughts. We will now concentrate upon humility in our actions, which can be divided into four subsections: conducting oneself in a humble manner, enduring insults, detesting power and avoiding honor, and attributing honor to others.

The first—conducting oneself in a humble manner—should show in your speech, the way you walk, the way you sit, and in all of your movements. Regarding how it should show in your speech our sages said (*Yoma* 86a), "One's speech with others should always be gentle." The Torah explicitly says (Ecclesiastes 9:17), "The words of sages will be heard when said gently." Your words should be words of respect rather than castigation. So too it says (Proverbs 11:12), "One who castigates his neighbor is heartless," and (Proverbs 18:3) "When an evil person comes, castigation comes with him."

Regarding the way you walk, our sages said (*Sanhedrin* 88b), "Who is a person of the world to come?—the humble and bent-of-knee who enter humbly and exit humbly," who do not walk with a haughty stance or with great dignity, heel to toe, but rather like those who just go about their business. They also said (*Kiddushin* 31a), "Whoever walks with a haughty stance is considered to be one who pushes away the feet of the Divine Presence." It is written (Isaiah 10:33), "The high ones of stature shall be hewn down."

Regarding the way you sit—your place should be amongst the lowly and not amongst the proud. Here too we find an explicit verse in the Torah that says as much (Proverbs 25:5–6): "Do not give yourself airs before a king, and do not stand in the place of the greats. . . ." Our sages said (*Vayikra Rabbah* 1:5), "Move two or three places down from your regular place and then sit so that they would sooner say to you, 'Move up!' rather than, 'Move down!'"

Our sages said about those who humble themselves (*Baba Metzia* 85b), "Whoever humbles himself for the sake of Torah in this world is made great in the World to Come." Corresponding to this they said (*Yalkut Yechezkel* 361), "It is written (Ezekiel 21:31), 'Take off our turban, and lift off your crown . . . ,'[13] which is to say, whoever is great in this world is lowly in the World to Come." From this we can extrapolate the opposite, that whoever is lowly in this world will enjoy his hour of greatness in the World to Come.

It has been said (*Sotah* 5a), "Man should always learn what to do from the reasoning of his Maker. The Holy One (blessed be He) rejected all the other mountains and hills, and had His Divine Presence dwell on Mount Sinai (because of its humble

---

12. Our age especially, which is so privileged as to have clear and laid out data as to just how *much* it does not know, should be humble with the realization of all it lacks.

13. ". . . this will no longer be the same—what is low will be exalted, and what is high will be debased."

stature)." Our sages also said (*Rosh HaShanah* 17b), "It is written (Micah 7:18), '. . . of the remnant of His inheritance' refers to one who considers himself to be scattered remains."

The second aspect is the endurance of insult. That just mentioned verse from Micah begins with, "Whose transgressions does He bypass?—those of the ones who overlook transgressions against themselves. . . ." It is also said (*Shabbat* 88b), "It is written regarding those who take insult but do not insult back, who are abused and do not respond in kind (Judges 5:31), 'So may Your enemies, God, be destroyed, while those that love You come to be like the sun in full strength . . . .'"

It is said regarding the humility of Baba ben Butah (*Nedarim* 66b), "A man of Babylon left to go to Israel to get married. He told his wife to cook something for him and to break it over the top of the gate (the *baba* in Aramaic). Baba ben Butah was presiding over the court at the time. The woman came to him and broke what she had over his head. He said, 'What have you done!?' And she said, 'My husband told me to do that!' To that he responded, 'Since you are doing the will of your husband, may God provide you with two sons like Baba ben Butah.'"

Our sages spoke as well about the humility of Hillel (*Shabbat* 30b): "Our Rabbis taught that one should always be as humble as Hillel. . . ." With all of his modesty, Rabbi Abahu found that he could not in all honesty be called modest. He said (*Sotah* 40a), "I used to think that I was modest, but when I saw Rabbi Abbah from Acco not get angry when he said one thing and his spokesman said another instead, I realized that I was not humble."

Regarding detesting power and avoiding honor the *Mishnah* explicitly states (*Avot* 1:10), "Love doing the work but detest the power." It is also said (*Avot* 4:9), "One who swells with pride upon tending legal decisions is a fool, an evil person and a braggard"; (*Eruvin* 13b) "Honor flees from whoever goes after it"; (*Pesikta Rabbati*) "It is written (Proverbs 25:8), 'Do not fall into argumentation easily,' and that means to say do not run after power. Why? Because what will you do after that?—they will come to you the next day with questions and you will not have answers for them"; (*Pesichta Rabbati*) "Rabbi Menachamah said in the name of Rabbi Tanchum, 'Whoever assumes power in order to derive personal benefit from it is like an adulterer deriving pleasure from the woman's body alone'"[14]; and, (*Pesichta Rabbati*) "Rabbi Abahu said in the name of God, 'I am called Holy. You should not accept authority upon yourself if you do not have all the traits attributed to Me.'"

The students of Rabbi Gamliel are a case in point. Because of their poverty they were very needy, yet they never wanted to assume roles of authority. This is what was being referred to in the section called "The annointed priest" (*Horayot* 10a): "Do

---

14. That is to say, whoever assumes power for the external trappings alone, the personal benefits that accrue with it, is likened to someone who engages in the act of sex for the physical pleasure alone, without consideration of the spiritual benefits (which cannot be derived in an adulterous relationship).

you imagine I am giving you authority? I am giving you servitude!" Our sages also said (*Pesachim* 87b), "Authority is woesome—it buries its carriers." (*Berachot* 55a) "How do we know that authority buries its carriers?—from Joseph's case: he died before his brothers because he conducted himself with authority."

The point of the matter is that authority is nothing but a great burden on the backs of those who bear it. While you are an individual among many, you are subsumed in the many, and are only responsible for yourself. But when you are put into a position of authority and power, you are in the clutches of everyone under you, for you have to be responsible for them—to show them the way and to correct their actions, for if you do not (Deuteronomy 1:13), "The sin is on your heads,"[15] as our sages point out (*Devarim Rabbah* 1:10).

Honor is vanity of vanities, and has a man challenge his own judgments as well as those of his Creator, and forget his obligations (*Devarim Rabbah* 1:10). One who recognizes this will certainly be disgusted by it and grow to hate it. The very praises lauded on him by others will burden him. He will see them lavish praise upon him inappropriately, and he will be abashed and full of grief not only for the fact that his many faults so outnumber his good points, but that he is being further burdened with false praise so that he might be even more embarrassed.[16]

---

15. It must be realized that, out of context, this statement seems not only to be cold and heartless, but maniacally self-centered as well. It says that leadership should be avoided at all costs because it "is nothing but a great burden on the back of those who bear it," and that a leader would be better off somewhere in the background, responsible only for himself rather than "in the clutches of everyone" else for whom he would have to be responsible.

But it must be recalled that this chapter was immediately preceded by the one that relates the responsibilities of the pious person in profound depth. And included among them is the pious person's concerns for the well-being of his generation. If the pious person is the sort who is not a leader, such care for his generation's well-being would involve prayer, selfless dedication to good and righteous deeds, and self-sacrifice. If, however, he is the sort of person who tends toward leadership (which is a natural, God-given inclination with which you are born) then the course he should follow is that of a leader, which does not necessarily imply a position of power, because one can inspire and guide others to the right path from whatever position he might occupy. But he must be especially careful not to assume that with leadership comes control, because with that comes arrogance (as has been explained above).

16. As Luzzatto said in chapter 11, arrogance is "outside the realm of the intellect and wisdom" and it can "lead you on to grave sins." The wise and pious person will come to realize that, will realize as well his small and cog-like part in the spin of the great machines, and he will "be disgusted by it and grow to hate it."

Having arrived at such a point he would find it difficult to be anything but abashed at the inappropriate praise others might lavish upon him, and he would be burdened by the bitter-sweet sight of their trying so hard to find the presence of God, but settling for his presence instead. "If only they knew how they misread me!" he would sigh. "If only they knew how small a part I play in it myself."

The fourth subsection involves attributing honor to others. And so we learn (*Avot* 4:1), "Who is honorable?—one who honors others." Our sages also said (*Pesachim* 113b), "From where do we learn that if you know that your friend is greater than you in some way that you must pay him homage? . . ."; (*Avot* 4:15) "Be the first to say hello (when meeting with others)"; and they said (*Berachot* 17a) that no one— not even a non-Jew in the marketplace—ever had a chance to say hello to Rabbi Yochanan ben Zakkai before he said it first. The point is, you have to honor others, whether you do it through speech or action. Our sages warned us (*Yevamot* 62b) that the 24,000 students of Rabbi Akiva died because they did not honor each other.[17]

Just as castigation is connected with evildoers, as the aforementioned verse says (Proverbs 18:3), "When an evil person comes, castigation comes with him," honor is connected with the righteous. Honor dwells with them and never leaves them. The verse reads (Isaiah 24:23), "Honor faces His elders."

We have explicated the general aspects of modesty, but their particulars are so numerous that you must use your own judgment about them as the situation would indicate. (Proverbs 1:5) "Let the wise listen and take more."

One thing is sure—modesty removes many stumbling blocks along the way, and brings you closer to the great good. The modest person is little concerned for matters of this world, and he is not envious of its vanities. Also, the friendship of a modest person is very wonderful—people enjoy his company. Of a necessity he does not come to anger or argumentation—everything he does is done peaceably and serenely.[18] One who merits this trait is fortunate. As our sages put it (*Shabbat* 1:3), "The very thing wisdom made a crown for its head, humility has made a heel for its sandal," because wisdom cannot compare to it, but that goes without saying.

---

17. See chapter 19, note 3.

18. The humble, selfless person is free and has nothing to lose. He is an agent of God in life. His mission is clear and his distractions are slight. He is the one the wise seek, the one fools overlook.

23

The Means of Acquiring Humility

There are two things that bring you to humility: force of habit, and reflection.[1]

Force of habit involves your slowly[2] habituating yourself to act humbly along the lines we have delineated—by sitting in a less than auspicious place, by walking at the back of a company of people, and by dressing in modest clothing[3] (clothing that is respectable, but not outstanding).[4] By habituating yourself in this path you will find that humility will slowly enter and penetrate your heart as it should.

As it is in our heart's nature to swell and grow haughty, it is difficult to uproot this natural inclination at its source. The only way anything like it can be accomplished is by your taking control of the external actions that are available to you. Thus

---

1. That is, action and thought. But that is not to say simple thought and simple action, but rather reflection, which is deep thought about yourself in relation to things, and habit, which is thorough and ingrained action, brought about consciously and deliberately.

There is of course light reflection, which we would call "rumination" or "fantasy," just as there is light habituation, which does not come about with deliberation, but rather as a result of the *lack* of it. Neither of those is at all acceptable or implied here.

2. *Very* slowly, and purposely . . .

3. See chapter 13 where it is written, "as everyone realizes, the wearing of fine embroidered clothing and accessories is bound to encourage arrogance."

4. It should be noted that Luzzatto says that you are to wear "clothing that is respectable," though "not outstanding." That is, as was stated in chapter 20 when the subject of the evaluation the pious have to be involved in was discussed, you should not assume too much piety when that will lead others to laugh and scoff.

So while you might reason that clothing is the mere outer shell, the husk, and the essence of superficiality, and as a result you would be inclined to wear whatever will cover your nakedness, no more, and you would not care what you look like because appearance is all a sham—it is incumbent upon the pious person to nonetheless dress "respectably" so that others will not laugh at him, and to impress upon them the honor due to piety itself. After all, humility does not require that you make a fool of yourself.

you can slowly affect the internality of it, which you do not have as much control over, as we explained in the chapter on enthusiasm.[5]

All of this is expressed by our sages as (*Berachot* 17a), "Let a man always be creative in his reverence."[6] That means to say that you should always look for some special means of going against your nature and inclination so that you may succeed in subduing them.

Reflection involves various things. The first is as indicated in the statement of Akavyah ben Mahalalel (*Avot* 3:1), "Know where you have come from—a putrid drop; and where you are going—to a place of dust, vermin and worms; and before Whom you are destined to give an account and reckoning—the King of kings, the Holy One (blessed be He)."[7]

---

5. Refer to chapter 7, where it is written: "The best advice for the person in whom this desire does not burn is that he consciously enthuse himself so that it might eventually become second nature to him. External movement arouses the internal, and you certainly have more of a command over the external than the internal. So if you make use of what you have command over, you will eventually take control over what you do not. Great inner joy, desire, and longing will come about as a result of your conscious igniting of your movements."

6. See chapter 19 where this quote is discussed in relation to *Shabbat*-observance.

7. The *Mishnah* quoted here starts out with, "Look upon three things and you will not come to sin: Know where you have come from, where you are going, and before Whom you are destined to give an account and reckoning." It then continues with what Luzzatto quotes, which amounts to the answer.

But if I were to read just the opening sentence, "Look upon three things and you will not come to sin: Know where you have come from . . . ," I would come to react in a different, rather more positive way. Reacting to the first statement, "Know where you have come from," I would say forthrightly, "I come from Abraham, Isaac, Jacob, and other holy ones who have served God selflessly and piously!" In response to "[Know] where you are going," I would say, "I am going to the World to Come!" And to the last statement's declaration, "[Know] before Whom you are destined to give an account and reckoning," I would immediately say, "Why, to God, of course!"

I would think that such a series of responses would be healthy and constructive, and that the responses offered in the *Mishnah* ("a putrid drop," "a place of dust," and "the King of kings, the Holy One blessed be He," a title for God that alludes to His aspect of strict Justice) would be indicative of a decidedly negative, piteous, and woesome attitude toward God and the tradition. So why would the humble, pious person be expected to reflect upon such a response at this point in the book?

The answer lies in the fact that there are two basic ways of serving God: with love, or with fear. The advanced soul serves God with love, because that is a very delightful, enriching means of service to Him, whereas fear is a relatively low way of serving Him, in that it involves more primitive and somewhat base emotions.

But love of God, as it has been explained in part 7 of the book, is an exalted and exceedingly transcendental means of service that is very difficult to come to. It has to be preceded by fear of Him. Because love of God (and its concurrent emotion, attachment) is spo-

In truth, these realizations stifle all arrogance and help foster humility. When you will face the imperfection inherent in your humanity and the lowliness of your origins, you will find that you have no reason to be proud at all. On the contrary—you would be abashed and mortified. To what can this be compared?—to a pig-herder who becomes a king. It is impossible for him to become too proud if he remembers his origins. He will likewise be humbled when he would reflect upon his current greatness's ultimate destiny—the return to dust and the becoming food for worms—and all the more so when he will consider the fact that his reign will be eventually be undone, and all the uproar of his personal pride will be forgotten. What, after all, is his goodness, what his greatness, if he is destined to shame and mortification?

If you will reflect further and try to imagine for just a moment your appearance before the great angelic Court, when you will stand before the King of kings, the Holy One (blessed be He), who is the ultimate in holiness and purity, thick in the mystery of the Holy Ones, the mighty servants who are great in power, who do His will without a blemish—you: lowly, imperfect, and inherently shameful, impure, and sullied because of your actions. . . . Could you even lift your head? Is there anything you could say?

If they were to ask you, "Where's your tongue? Where's the power and honor you bore in the world?" what would you say? How would you respond to their reproofs? If you were to honestly and convincingly impress this scene upon your mind for just one moment, all of your arrogance would surely flee, never to return.

The second object of reflection involves the consequences of the changes that come about through the passage of time. The rich can easily become poor; the ruler can easily become the ruled; the honored the despised. Since it is so easy to transform into something which is so abhorrent to you at this point, how can you possibly be proud of your current, so tenuous situation?

An illness may strike you (God forbid) that will force you to seek someone's help so that you can be a little relieved. Pains and sorrows of all sorts could come your way (God forbid) that would force you to seek out certain people for help whom,

---

ken of again in the last chapter of this book, it is obvious that it is not expected that the reader will have thoroughly attained it by this point. And the reader will have been expected to have gone through a level of fear of God before he can hope to foster thorough love of Him in his heart. That is why the part immediately following this one and immediately preceding the very last one involves fear—fear of sin: so the reader can wrench out the last drop of nudging impediment on his way to holiness and the absolute love of and attachment to God spoken of in the last chapter.

So when the *Mishnah* seems to lean toward the fear of God, that is because it is more attainable for most people.

It should be understood that Luzzatto draws upon this *Mishnah* to make another point: that even a person at this stage of development is still susceptible to some degree of arrogance. These reflections will help obviate that.

at this point, you would just hate to offer a hello to in the street. You see these sorts of things happening every day. They are enough to wipe out arrogance from your heart, and envelop you in humility and submission.

When you will further reflect upon your obligations to God, and of how often you disregard them or are lax in them, you can never grow haughty—you will certainly be embarrassed rather than proud. So the verse says (Jeremiah 31:17–18), "I have surely heard Ephraim lamenting. . . . For after I turned away I repented; after I was made to know, I smote my thigh. I was ashamed and confounded. . . ."

What you should ultimately do is recognize the fallibility of human knowledge and of how liable it is for error and untruth. It is more likely to be wrong than right. You should therefore constantly be afraid of the dangers inherent in this situation, and try to learn from all people and take advice so that you will not stumble. This is what our sages were referring to when they said (*Avot* 4:1), "Who is a sage?—one who learns from all." And the Torah says (Proverbs 12:15), "One who takes advice is a sage."

What deters from this trait is the overabundance of and the being full of the good things in this world. As the verse clearly states (Deuteronomy 8:12–14), "(Beware, lest) you eat and grow full (and forget God) and your heart be made proud." The pious find it better to deprive themselves sometimes, so that they might subdue the inclination towards arrogance, which prospers in a climate of plenty.[8] Our sages have said along these lines (*Berachot* 32a), "A lion does not roar over a basket of straw, but, rather, over a basket of meat."

What is most likely to deter is ignorance and lack of true knowledge. As can be seen, arrogance is most often found in the more ignorant. As our sages put it (*Sanhedrin* 24a), "A sure sign of haughtiness is poverty in Torah learning"; (*Zohar, Balak*) "A sure sign that someone knows nothing is bragging"; (*Baba Metzia* 85b) "A single coin in a bottle makes a loud clanging sound"; and (*Bereishit Rabbah* 16:3) "They asked the barren trees why their voices were heard, and they responded, 'We only wish our voices would be heard. That way we would be remembered.'" And we see that Moses, the best of men, was the most modest of men.

Another deterrent to humility is the association with flatterers who steal your heart away with their praise. They will praise and exalt you for their own ulterior motives by expanding upon the good points you possess to the hilt, then praise you unjustifiably in addition. And sometimes the very thing you are being praised for is what you should not be praised for.

The point of the matter is that human intelligence is actually quite weak, and human nature is gullible and easily swayed—especially when it comes to something it just naturally leans toward. When you hear those sorts of things being said about you by someone you trust, a certain poison enters into you, you fall into the trap of arrogance, and are captured.

---

8. Arrogance "prospers in a climate of plenty" because it is the psychological equivalent of it, in that it is an abundance of self.

We find this to be the case with Yo'ash (2 Kings 12:3), who was virtuous as long as he studied with his master, Y'hoyadah the Cohen, but who, after Y'hoyadah's death, listened to and took in what his servants said when they flattered and lauded him, and likened him to a god. This sort of thing is clear in the case of most kings, lords, and people of stature. No matter where they stand spiritually, they still stumble and suffer ruination as a result of the flattery of the people who surround them.

Therefore, the intelligent person will be more careful and scrutinizing of the person he would want to befriend, be counseled by, or oversee his household than he would of what he eats or drinks. Food or drink could only harm his body, but bad friends and associates could ruin his soul, his possessions, and his honor. King David said (Psalms 101:6–7), "The one who goes along the honest way will serve me. A deceiver will not dwell in the midst of my house."

There is nothing better for you than to make friends with honest people who will open your eyes to matters you are blind to and reproach you lovingly. They will save you from all evil. For what you cannot see (when you overlook faults, as we all do) they can, and they will warn you about it so that you will be protected. Regarding this it is said (Proverbs 24:6), "Salvation comes about through a lot of counsel."

Summation of Part VIII

Chapter 22

1. The essence of humility is never considering yourself important. It removes many stumbling blocks from along your path, brings you to a state of not being overconcerned for matters of this world nor envious of its vanities, and it has others enjoy your company because you will inevitably be neither angry nor argumentative, but rather peaceful and serene.

2. There is humility in thought, and humility in action, and you must be humble in thought before you can be humble in your actions or else you will in fact be a hypocritical egotist.

3. Humility in thought involves realizing that honor and glory are not due you both because of what you inherently are (due to your personality, upbringing, or as a result of circumstances) and what you have done (i.e., your transgressions). You are to come to realize that we are each given natural gifts (such as wisdom, wealth, or strength), and that when we make use of those gifts we are only doing what comes naturally, and should not be self-centered about them.

4. Humility in actions involves timidity (by speaking gently and respectfully, walking in an unhaughty manner, sitting among the lowly), enduring insult (by overlooking personal degradation or others' lack of respect for you), detesting power while avoiding honor (by realizing that prominence is a great burden and a detriment to growth), and attributing honor to others (by considering their honor over your own).

Chapter 23

5. You acquire humility through force of habit (by routinely sitting amongst the lowly, dressing inauspiciously, and the like) and reflection (upon your humble, mortal roots; upon the impression you would make before the Heavenly Court; upon the often tragic consequences of change of circumstance; upon how you so often disregard or are lax in your obligations to God; and upon how fallible we all are, and how likely we are to err).

6. What keeps you back from this trait is overattachment to the good things of the world, lack of true knowledge, and associating with flatterers rather than with honest and lovingly reproachful friends.

IX

FEAR OF SIN

Introduction to Part IX

The ninth part comprises two chapters (24–25) and concerns itself with the trait of "fear of sin." The chapters are entitled "An Explanation of Fear of Sin" (chap. 24) and "The Means of Acquiring Fear of Sin" (chap. 25).

The topics discussed herein include: the fear of punishment, self-preservation, God's Grandeur, pious fears of failure, and the agitation of the angels (chap. 24); God's involvement in the world, meditation and contemplation, and our natural disinclination toward the Divine (chap. 25).

The book returns to a theme that had been found in earlier parts but that had been left unreiterated for some time: the difficulty of the tasks being spoken of. Luzzatto says (chap. 24), "Only Moses found it easy to obtain this sort of fear, thanks to his great clinging to God, while others were certainly held back. . . ," and that (chap. 25) "King David would pray for this and say (Psalms 86:11), 'Teach me Your ways, God, so that I may walk in Your truth; unite my heart so that I might fear Your Name,'" implying that even he might not have arrived at it were it not for the power of his prayers and that acquiring it involves constant study and diligence.

As Luzzatto says in the body of this part, the "fear" (*yirah*) being spoken of here can be understood in two ways: as rank fear of punishment, or reverence for something's exaltedness, as the Hebrew connotes both. The latter, which is the subject at hand, constitutes being in a state of awe and being overwhelmed by something or someone (in this case, God), which is akin to fear. As such the word *yirah* does not carry the connotation of doubt, cowardice, faintheartedness, defeatism, hopelessness, flinching, or deserting; nor does it connote in its other sense shock, surprise, bewilderment, stupefaction, or bafflement. But it does connote purposeful shirking, discretion, and caution, as well as wonder, marvel, astonishment, and amazement.

24

An Explanation of Fear of Sin

You will notice that this trait is placed after all of the exalted traits we have discussed to this point. That should be enough to point out to us its importance. It is only fitting that it would be a very special and essential matter which is difficult to obtain, as would be expected of a trait that could only be reached by one who has obtained those already discussed to this point.[1] We must however start off by saying that there are

---

1. Luzzatto is intimating that we might have thought that fear of sin would be a long gone prerequisite, and that there would be no need to even mention sin by this point, as it would have already been eradicated. But the *beraita* upon which this book is based is informing us that it is necessary to speak of it at this point in the development of our piety.

There are two reasons for that: (1) because, as Luzzatto stated in the previous part, everybody transgresses, if only by happenstance and accident, hence there are still sins to be undone (albeit negligible, minuscule, and whisper-like ones), and a pertinent fear of sin to be concentrated on; (2) and, because it also refers to the "higher" sort of fear of sin.

The reader who is coming across this part for the first time (see n. 4, chap. 22) will have to know about the more coarse and superficial fear of sin before he can go on to the finer, more subtle form of it, which Luzzatto speaks of as "reverence for God's Grandeur." Such a reader will in fact have to initiate such a lower fear of sin in his heart long before he can ever hope to love God. And when Luzzatto speaks here of this trait as being "a very special and essential matter which is difficult to obtain" he is referring to the *higher* and subtler form of it which can indeed "only be reached by one who has obtained those already discussed to this point."

It has been our contention all along that each of these traits leads into the one following it, and that no one could ever hope to move along until he has mastered what was already discussed. That point is being especially underscored here by Luzzatto, because we might not understand it, and we might assume that we can work on a sense of fear of sin before we do anything else. But that would be dangerous, out of place, and detrimental to our development. True fear of sin, that "reverence of God's Grandeur," cannot even be *grasped* by one who is still enveloped in sin and desires, and is still bound by the laws of self and personal

two sorts of fear that are actually three, the first of which is very easy to obtain—there is nothing easier than it—and the second of which is the hardest. When you have perfected it, you have perfected a lot.

The first category is fear of punishment. The second is fear of, or reverence for, God's Grandeur, of which fear of sin is the subcategory. We will now explain their essences and how they differ.

Fear of punishment is when you are literally afraid of transgressing the dictates of God because of the punishments (either corporal or capital) that are due transgressors. This is certainly very easy to come to because everybody has an instinct for self-preservation and is concerned for his well-being, and there is nothing that is more likely to keep you away from doing something harmful to yourself than fear of its consequences. But this sort of fear is only fitting for illiterates and for simpleminded women—not for sages and intellectuals.[2]

---

need. In other words, this is no mere "Watch out and don't sin!" which came long ago in the work. This is another, more transcendental indication of the attitude to be fostered in the individual who is selfless.

2. The essence of Torah is that (1) God exists, (2) He involves Himself in the world, (3) He communicates with it, and (4) He has let His will be known to that world so that it may act on it. It follows logically that something has to result from keeping or abandoning that revealed will of God.

But that result has to affect two parties: the person doing the action himself and the world in general. So, for example, if I feed the hungry, I am affected for having done that, and the world is affected for my having done that, too. What I did by feeding the hungry was to bring something called "good" into the world, and I receive something called a "reward" for having done it.

If when given the opportunity to feed the poor I do *not*, the effect I have on the world by acting that way is to bring "bad" into the world, and I receive something called "punishment."

It simply makes sense that you would not want to suffer anything negative, let alone God's "punishment." After all, as Luzzatto puts it, "everybody has an instinct for self-preservation and is concerned for his well-being." So why is such concern "only fitting for illiterates?"

And why do so many of our contemporaries have trouble with the notions of "reward" and "punishment" and "good" and "evil" as it worded here?

Luzzatto answers those questions elsewhere. If you will recall, in chapter 4 he spoke of three classes of people: those of complete understanding, those of lesser understanding, and the multitude. What sets those three groups apart from each other is not their moral or spiritual stature, or even their actions. It is their ability to come to realize a basic truism of the universe: that "wholeness alone is the thing that should be longed for, nothing else; that nothing is worse than the lack of wholeness and what keeps it back from us" (chapter 4).

Those of complete understanding come to realize that truism, those of lesser understanding do not, but may come close, and the multitude never realize it at all. Luzzatto goes on to explain there that once the people of complete understanding come to realize the truism, "and it likewise becomes clear to them that the means to wholeness are good deeds and

The second category is fear of, or reverence for, God's Grandeur. This holds sway when you keep away from transgressions and do not commit them, for the sake of God's great Glory.[3] After all, how can it ever occur to the lowly and despicable

---

good personality traits . . . ," then "they would certainly never want to diminish or make light of them."

Once the people of complete understanding come to this series of realizations, something else also becomes clear to them: that the "good" they bring into the world and the "reward" they receive from their acts of following the Divine will are actually different aspects of *wholeness.*

That is to say, such people come to realize that "good" and "reward," or "bad" and "punishment" are no longer terms that describe the *person* who acts that way, but rather the actions themselves. And they describe the wholeness that was brought into or removed from the world.

In other words, when I feed the poor, I bring wholeness into the world, and I enjoy more wholeness as a "reward." If I resist that opportunity to feed the poor I *remove* wholeness from the world, and I cause some element of wholeness to be removed from me.

Those of lesser or no understanding never come to perceive that. They tend to believe that the person is changed from "good" to "bad" and vice versa, and that that is where "reward" and "punishment" come in, which is not so.

And while fear of punishment (the lower-level fear) is not rooted in wisdom, because it does not recognize that "good" equals more wholeness, and "bad" equals less, it is nonetheless important because it has the multitude *act* "good" (and since actions are of the utmost importance, one is allowed misunderstandings that do not cause misdeeds). It also might lead to an understanding of and a desire for the "good." That is why, as Luzzatto puts it here, fear of sin is "only fitting for illiterates"—that is, the multitude.

What our contemporaries evidence when they become bothered by "reward" and "punishment" and "good" and "evil" is their failure to understand the need to address the group to which this sort of vocabulary is directed in this manner. They fail to realize that sometimes such terms have to be used to accomplish a particular end.

As we said in our commentary to chapter 2 (see n. 3, chap. 2), "The differentiation of Luzzatto's perceived 'audience' must be kept in mind when we study from this work. We must recall that there will be times when he will address the baser fears and anxieties, and other times when he will address the loftier, more transcendent drives, depending upon the circumstances and the point he wants to make." At this point in the book he is addressing both those who will have advanced and those who will not have. Let the reader be honest with himself as to where he stands at each reading and come to understand the work from that vantage point so as to come to growth.

3. This fear or reverence (*yirah* in Hebrew, connotes both, and Luzzatto is playing with both meanings in this section) is an utterly different kind of "fear." It is not based upon personal consequences. The person who has this sort of "fear" is not cognizant of his own needs, but rather of God's, so to speak. This will bring him to a state of rapture, in which he is filled with a sort of metalogical lust and longing, where he can think of nothing but his beloved, God. Such a person can barely sense his own being; he is walking in the sea and inhaling mountains, as far as he is concerned, because he is with his Lover. He is like

heart that is man's to do something that runs counter to God's will? This sort of fear (or reverence) is not so easy to obtain. It only comes about through a knowledge and understanding that are brought on by the contemplation of the Grandeur of God and the markedly lower state of mankind. These are the sorts of realizations that come to those who understand and delve into these matters, and are like the reverence we noted earlier on in the second section of one of the subcategories of piety.[4]

A person in this category would be abashed and would tremble when standing before, praying to, and serving his Maker. This is the most praiseworthy of fears for which the pious of the world are most exalted. This is what Moses was referring to when he said (Deuteronomy 28:58), ". . . to fear this glorious and fearful name, God your God."

This, the fear we are explaining now, that is, the fear of sin, is both a subcategory of fear of, or reverence for, God's Grandeur and a category in its own right. It essentially involves your constantly fearing and worrying that your actions might contain a trace of transgression, or that there might be some small or even large thing therein that is not fitting for the Glory and Grandeur of God.

You can see the obvious relationship between this sort of fear and the aforementioned fear of, or reverence for, God's Grandeur. Their common denominator is that you do nothing against God's lofty Honor. But what makes them different enough that they are two separate sorts and require two different names is the fact that the fear of, or reverence for, God's Grandeur pertains only to when you are either doing something or are in the midst of serving God, or you are at the crossroads of a possible transgression. Because when you are worshiping or serving, and a transgression is set before you which you recognize as such, you should be abashed and ashamed, should shake and shiver for the loftiness of God's honor, and not do it, so as not to (God forbid) rebel before God.

But fear of sin should be a constant thing. You should always be afraid of stumbling and doing something or some half of something that is against God's honor. That is why this trait is called "fear of sin," because its essence is the fear that sin might enter into or mix in with your actions due to some negligence, weakness, or one or another unconscious reason. It is said regarding this (Proverbs 28:14), "The

---

the person who is afraid to lisp when making a public address not because it will embarrass him, but because it would cause his lover pain to see that. This is a fear that is based on a hounding and vigilant need to express love rather than a small and strangling need to preserve it.

4. It is written in chapter 19: "The main aspect of reverence is reverence for God's grandeur. . . . To obtain this sort of reverence you will have to consider and reflect upon three things: that you are quite literally standing before God and involved in a give-and-take with Him, . . . (the fact of) God's grandeur, . . . (and) the low state of mankind. . . . Taking all this into consideration, it would be impossible for your heart to not tremble or be moved when you speak to God, mention His name, or attempt to fulfill His wishes."

man who is constantly afraid is fortunate," which our sages explained refers (*Berachot* 60a) "to matters of Torah."[5]

Even at those times when you do not see the stumbling block before your eyes you should be anxious that it might be hidden and you are not being careful enough. Regarding such a fear our master Moses said (Exodus 20:17), "God has come to test you so that His fear may be on your faces, and you will not sin."

This is the sort of fear a person should have. He should be agitated at all times and never allow this fear to leave him, for he will thusly never come to transgress. And should he transgress, it will be considered to have been done under duress.[6] Isaiah said in his prophecy (Isaiah 66:2), "but I will look to this man—to him that is poor, broken of spirit, and trembles at my word." King David praised this trait when he said (Psalms 119:161), "Princes pursued me unjustifiably, but my heart feared only Your word."

We find that the great and awesome angels constantly shiver and tremble for the Majesty of God. Our sages said parabolically about this (*Chagigah* 13b), "From where does the River of Fire emit? From the perspiration of the Chayot Angels," all of which comes about from the great terror the angels experience at all times in regard to God's Grandeur. They fear that they might overlook some small aspect of the honor and holiness due Him.

Whenever or wherever the Divine Presence is revealed there is shaking, shivering and trembling. The Torah refers to this when it says (Psalms 68:9), "The earth shook, and the heavens dropped at the presence of God"; and (Isaiah 63:19) "Would that you would tear the heavens and come down, that the mountains would melt at your Presence."

This goes even more so for humans. It is only right that we should tremble and shiver in the knowledge that we are constantly standing in the Presence of God, and that it is so easy for us to do something that is not fitting before God's exaltedness. This is what Eliphaz was referring to when he said to Job (Job 15:14–15), "What is man that he should be worthy, that one born of a woman should be righteous?

---

5. That is to say, if there ever comes a time when you might either not be serving God excellently well, or might even come to sin, you should arouse "the fear of, or reverence for, God's Grandeur" by reflecting upon the three things mentioned in note 4 above. But you should *always* concentrate upon avoiding the loss of wholeness in the world.

6. You are considered to have committed a transgression under duress, and are hence not to suffer the consequences of having done it, if you do so in a situation that was beyond your control. If, for example, you were in prison and could eat nothing but pig's meat with milk or starve, your act of eating it under those circumstances would not be considered a transgression, when it would normally be considered a severe one.

Someone who has persevered so intensely and so forthrightly in his attempt to not transgress can never be said to *purposely* transgress; he can only be said to have *accidentally* transgressed due to circumstances. The human situation necessitates transgression; what matters is your compliance with it.

Behold he has no faith in His holy ones, and in his sight, the heavens are not worthy"; as well as (Job 4:18–19) "Behold, he does not have faith in His servants, and he charges His angels with foolishness. How much more those who live in houses of clay. . . ." Therefore every person must certainly tremble and shiver at all times.

Elihu then said (Job 37:1–2), "My heart trembles and is moved out of its place at this as well; listen closely to the noise of His voice." This is the sort of fear that the truly pious should have on their faces at all times.

There are two subdivisions of this sort of fear: the first is in regard to the present moment and the future, and the second is in regard to the past. In regard to the present it implies that you should fear and worry about what you are doing or are about to, lest there be or come to be something in it that is not fitting for God's honor, as we have explained above.

In regard to the past, you should constantly think about what you have already done, and fear and worry that some transgression might have unknowingly come your way. This was the case with Baba ben Buttah (*Keritot* 25a), who used to offer a suspected guilt offering every day, and with Job, who arose early in the morning after his sons' parties, and (Job 1:5) "offered burnt offerings according to the number of them, for Job said, 'It may be that my sons have sinned'. . . ."

Our sages pointed out (*Horayot* 12a) that in regard to the anointing oil with which Moses anointed Aaron as High Priest it is said (Exodus 30:32), "it shall not anoint human flesh." Yet it was explicitly commanded that Aaron be anointed with it! Moses and Aaron were afraid they had misappropriated its use in some way, and had gone against a commandment.

Moses was worried and said, "Maybe I have misappropriated the anointing oil!" But a voice was heard to say (Psalms 133:2–3), "'As the good oil that is upon the head descends upon the beard, the beard of Aaron . . . as the dew of Hermon'—just as the dew of Hermon is not misappropriated, the anointing oil on Aaron's beard is not misappropriated." But Aaron was still worried. Maybe Moses had not misappropriated, but *he* had, he wondered? But a voice was heard to say (Psalms 133:1) "'How good and how pleasant it is when brothers sit together in unity'—just as Moses had not misappropriated, you have not misappropriated, it explained."

Here you see the ways of the pious. They would even worry about some small measure of impurity creeping (God forbid) into the *mitzvot* they have done.

After Abraham finished coming to the rescue of his nephew who had been abducted, he was worried and wondered if perhaps all of his actions had not been completely meritorious. Our sages made reference to this in their explanation of the verse (Genesis 15:1), "Do not be afraid, Abraham," when they said in the name of Rabbi Levi (*Bereishit Rabbah* 44:4), "Because Abraham was afraid that somehow, between all of the soldiers that he had killed, there might have been a righteous or God-fearing man, he was told, 'Do not be afraid, Abraham (—there was not).'" It is said in *Tanna D'Bei Eliyahu Rabbah* (chapter 25), "'Do not be afraid,' as in, 'Do not be afraid, Abraham' is only said to one who is truly God-fearing."

This is the kind of fear about which it is said (*Berachot* 33b), "The Holy One blessed be He only has His treasure-chest of God-fearers." Only Moses found it easy to obtain this sort of fear, thanks to his great clinging to God, while others were certainly greatly deterred by their corporeality.[7] However, every pious person should try to attain to this as much as possible, as it is said (Psalms 34:10), "His holy ones will fear God."

---

7. This is being said at this point to lead us on to our discussion of clinging to God versus corporeality, which we will come to in the last part.

25

The Means of Acquiring
Fear of Sin

The only way to acquire this sort of fear is to contemplate two truisms: that God's Presence is found everywhere,[1] and that He involves Himself in everything, great and small.[2]

Nothing is hidden from Him, either because of its vastness or its insignificance. Whether a thing is great or small, scant or imposing, He constantly sees and understands it. This is what the Torah refers to when it says (Isaiah 6:3), "The whole world is full of His Glory"; (Jeremiah 23:24) "Do I not fill heaven and earth?"; (Psalms 113:5–6) "Who is like God our God, who dwells on high—who lowers Himself to look upon the heavens and the earth?"; and (Psalms 138:6) "Though God is high up, He nonetheless notices the lowly. . . ."[3]

---

1. Refer to the fourth note of the previous chapter.

2. The word we have translated as "involves Himself in" is usually translated as "oversees," "monitors," or "supervises." We have translated it as we have by taking into account the fact that the root verb (*shagach*) is most often taken to mean "to mind," "pay attention to," "look at," "care for," and "consider," none of which carries the connotation of a one-way relationship.

What we mean to say is that God is not to be thought as One who distantly and uncaringly "oversees," "monitors," or "supervises" us and our world. In truth, He "minds," "pays attention to," "looks at," "cares for," and "considers" us, which allows for us to react in our own way. That action-reaction process is what we have described as an "involvement in" on the part of both God and us. To think that God merely "oversees," "monitors," or "supervises" is to deny His closeness to us.

3. Why would God Almighty care to involve Himself in everything, "great or small, scant or imposing"? Does He really care about and follow my insignificant deeds? See our discussion on that at the end of note 6, chapter 19.

When it will become clear to you that wherever you are, you are standing before the Divine Presence, you will arrive at the fear and dread of stumbling in actions that would not be fitting before God's profound Glory. This is what is indicated by the teaching (*Avot* 2:1), "Know what is above you—a seeing eye, a hearing ear—and that all of your actions are recorded in a book." Since the Holy One (blessed be He) involves Himself in everything, and He sees and hears everything, you can be sure of the fact that all actions make an impression and are recorded in a book for merit or blame.[4]

But this only touches you personally if you constantly reflect upon and observe it. This sort of thing is beyond our ordinary perceptions, and the mind can only grasp it after much meditation and contemplation. And even after it will have made an impression, that impression will be easily lost if you do not constantly work at it. Just as a lot of contemplation is the only way to attain constant fear of heaven, diversion of attention (either purposeful, or because of external interference) or lack of concen-

---

4. Many times we find that the Torah uses human terms to describe God's involvement in the world. In this case, God is said to have a "book" before Him in which He records all of our actions. The obvious questions to be raised are, "Why would God need to record His thoughts in a book? Doesn't He remember? If God cannot be said to be imperfect in anything, how can he have a faulty memory?"

But it must be recalled that (as Maimonides reminds us very often in *The Guide for the Perplexed*) the Torah is said to speak in the language of mankind. That means that the Torah expresses God's ways in human language and imagery. There is no better way to do that, for if the Torah were to describe God's ways as they are, we could never understand or relate to them, as God's ways are beyond our ken. We must recall that when we read something the Torah says about God.

But another principle must be borne in mind at the same time: that the Torah, which is eternal, was transcribed at a certain point in time. And because it was handed down at a particular point in time but it was meant for *all* time, it must speak paradigmatically, using terms that represent the essence and that will not limit themselves to a particular era. So when the Torah refers to the "books" that God keeps before Him to record our deeds, it might have referred to the "computer" he stores His data upon if the Torah were to have been revealed to us today, and we would still be faced with the same problem of anthropomorphism.

But we must analyze the notion of "writing" in the abstract and look for the paradigm within it that can have us understand what is really being said. Doing that we find that "writing" is the paradigmatic act of leaving permanent "impressions" (Luzzatto's own word) behind, on paper. That being so, we can be said to "make an impression" in the universe when we act one way or another. That means to say that everything we do affects the world in one way or another, and we "impress" ourselves upon the world by our actions. So everything we do is symbolically said to be "recorded in a book for merit or blame" because there is no act, or thought of an act, or intention to act that does not leave its own permanent impression on the world. And that is what the Torah is implying in paradigmatic terms.

tration is the way to lose it. And all diversion of attention is a taking away from the state of constant fear of heaven.[5]

This is why the Holy One (blessed be He) commanded all kings of Israel (Deuteronomy 17:19) to have the Torah "with him and to read it all the days of his life so that he might learn to fear God his God." This comes to teach that fear of heaven can only be learned with constant study. A careful analysis of the verse further indicates that it reads, "so that he might *learn* to fear God his God" rather than, "so that he might fear God his God." That is so because the fear of heaven does not come naturally.

In fact, it is very unnatural to us, because of the limited, this-worldly nature of our senses. It only comes to us with study. And the only kind of study that brings it to us is constant diligence in Torah and its path, which involves reflecting and meditating upon this at all times—when you are relaxing, traveling, lying down, and awakening.[6]

The veracity of this—that the Divine Presence is everpresent, and that we stand before God each and every moment—must be set in your mind. Only then can you truly fear and revere God. King David would pray for this and say (Psalms 86:11), "Teach me Your ways, God, so that I may walk in Your truth; unite my heart so that I might fear Your Name."

---

5. There are moments when almost everyone senses the Presence of God in a very palpable, awe-inspiring way. Those are moments of high drama and music, and they are invariably short-lived, though sweeping. And while the sense and memory of such moments may last for a while and may carry us along for weeks or months, the kind of endurance and electricity we would need to remain faithful to an invisible and too often hidden Master of the Universe at the level being spoken of here requires more.

It requires disciplined meditation and reflection, which will bring us to higher perceptions and understandings, rather than just allow us to hold on to those precious rare moments. The pious person has to maintain his passion and project it onto his mind's eye at all times without yielding. Some do that by taking the verse that reads, "I have placed God before me at all times" (Psalms 16:18) literally, and set the four-letter Hebrew word for God at all times in their mind's eye. Others reflect deeply and constantly upon God's name in other, less pictorial ways. And yet others dwell upon other verses from Torah or statements from the sages.

We are not just naturally inclined toward dwelling upon God. We are easily distracted, swayed, and filled with doubts and diversions. So it is imperative that we regularly enunciate an order of truisms so that the soul can be reminded of its source and its goal. Only then can it take itself seriously, and be touched to the point where it will crack its own bounds and alight.

6. As it is written in the first paragraph of the *Shema Yisrael* (Deuteronomy 6:5–7), "Love God your Lord with all your heart, with all your soul, and with all your might, and keep these words which I am commanding you today on your heart. Teach them to your children, and talk about them when you *relax* in your home, *travel, lie down*, and *awake*." This statement hereby acts as a bridge toward the next and final part, which (as was indicated above) also concentrates upon love of God and associated attainments.

Summation of Part IX

Chapter 24

1. There are two sorts of fear: fear of punishment and fear of or reverence for God's Grandeur. A subcategory of the latter is fear of sin. Fear of punishment involves being frightened of going against God's will because of the punishment that will come to you if you do. It is a fear that is easy to come by, but not fitting for sages.

2. Fear of or reverence for God's Grandeur essentially is not wanting to go against God's will for the greater good of His Glory. This sort of fear does not come easily, and requires knowledge and understanding of God's Grandeur itself. Such a person would tremble while standing in prayer or in service to God. He would constantly worry that some action of his might contain some trace of sin or might have in it something that would not do for the glorification of His Name.

3. While fear of or reverence for God's Grandeur is occasional and dependent upon your being involved in an action or service to God, or in your being approached with the possibility of doing a transgression—when you should tremble and desist— fear of sin is constant: you should always be afraid of stumbling and going against God's Honor, even when you do not clearly have a reason to be afraid. And you should even fear that your past actions (even the *mitzvot* you did) might not have been worthy.

4. Moses was the only person to find this sort of fear easy to come to, because he clung to God and was transcendent. However, every pious person should try as much as possible to attain to this.

Chapter 25

5. To come to this sort of fear you must contemplate that fact that God's Presence is found everywhere, that He is cognizant of everything, the vast and the minute, and that He involves Himself in each and every thing. You will then come to know in fact that all of your actions make an impression and are recorded in a book.

6. But realizations such as these do not come easily to humans, and only after a lot of meditation and reflection. Even if they come, they can too easily leave if you are distracted from them for one reason or another. The best way to avoid that is to be diligent and utterly constant in your Torah study, and to set in your mind the fact that God is everpresent.

X

HOLINESS

Introduction to Part X

The tenth part comprises one lone chapter (26, the last) and ostensibly concerns itself only with the trait of "holiness." In fact it is concerned with other traits as well (though briefly): "holy inspiration," and "the resurrection of the dead." The chapter that comprises this part is entitled, "An Explanation of the Trait of Holiness."

There is not too much left to be said at this point in *The Path of the Just* that a mere mortal would understand. How speak outright of the central and most radical longing of the soul, which is attachment to God? What can one say any longer about that exquisite and most elemental need, the need for magnificence?

Themes that have appeared before appear again in this chapter, but in grander, bolder form. Examples of that are the removal from physicality, true love and reverence for God, setting your thoughts on God's greatness and exaltedness, abstention, reflecting upon how God involves Himself in the world, solitary meditation, and the dangers of overassociation with others. Other, new topics are discussed as well, such as the sanctification of all deeds, making the effort despite the near impossibility of it, the indwelling of the Divine Presence, the spiritual elevation of all mundane things, what the *Kohanim* would concentrate upon when offering sacrifices, the various and indescribably subtle shades of attachment to God, and everyone's unique and individual path to God.

Holiness, *kedushah*, is not explicitly defined in this chapter. But we are told two essential things about those who attain to it: that they "constantly attach themselves to God" (so much so that they "never separate nor even move from Him no matter what [they] are doing"), and "(that their) souls move about in the true notions of love and reverence for the Creator."

As in the English, the Hebrew word implies sanctification, sacredness, dedication, consecration, spiritual excellence, guiltlessness, perfection, and impeccability.

A last note: Though we will continue to use the "second person" case ("you" rather than "he") in this chapter as we have done throughout the book, because it was assumed that that would make the work more accessible to the modern reader, it should nonetheless be self-evident to that same reader that this chapter discusses levels of holiness which are not at all easily attainable and which are largely—sadly—out of our experience.

26

An Explanation of the Trait of Holiness

Holiness is a twofold matter: it begins in effort, and ends in recompense; and it begins in striving, and ends in being given as a gift. That is to say, its beginnings are your sanctifying yourself, and its conclusions are your being sanctified.[1] Our sages referred to this when they said (*Yoma* 39a), "A person only has to sanctify himself a little and he is sanctified a lot—he need only sanctify himself down here and he is sanctified up above."

What all of your efforts should be directed toward is the utter separation and removal of yourself from all physicality, and the constant attachment to God.[2] Because of their practice of this, the prophets were referred to as angels. As it was said of Aaron (Malachi 2:7), "For the lips of the priest should guard knowledge, and Torah should be sought from his mouth, for he is an angel of the Lord of Hosts," and as it is written (2 Chronicles 36:16), "And they would mock the angels of God. . . ."

Even when you are embroiled in matters of the world for the sake of the well-being of your body, let your soul not be moved from its state of great attachment.[3]

---

1. As Luzzatto says later on in the chapter, "it is impossible for a human to place himself in this state. . . . All you can do is make the effort of seeking the true knowledge, and try to constantly give thought to the sanctification of actions," and only then will "a spirit from on high . . . descend upon you, and (will) the Creator . . . dwell upon you as He does for all of His holy ones."

2. That is to say, your focus should be on the charged and thorough moving away from matters of this world, and on entrance into the realm of God Himself and the World to Come.

3. Allow your soul its restless urgings, and spoil it in its need to transcend. Let it be free to commune with and wrap itself about God Almighty in fullness.

As it is said (Psalms 63:9), "My soul attaches itself to You, for Your right arm supports me."

I said that holiness ends up being a gift to you. That is necessarily so, because it is impossible for a human to place himself in this state which—because he is in truth physical, and flesh and blood—is so difficult for him. All you can do is make the effort of seeking the true knowledge, and try to constantly give thought to the sanctification of your actions. Ultimately, God alone can direct you in this, the path you would like to follow, and can have His holiness dwell upon you and sanctify you.[4] Only then can you succeed, and only then will you be able to constantly attach yourself to God. God will help you and see to it that you get what your native being would detain from you.[5] As it is said (Psalms 84:12), "No good will be held back from those who walk uprightly." As was said in the above-quoted statement of our sages, "A person only has to sanctify himself a little . . ."—because that is all he *can* do by his own efforts—"and he is sanctified a lot," which is God's help to him, as I have explained.

Even the mundane actions of the person sanctified in the holiness of His Creator are turned around to actual holiness. This can best be illustrated by the eating of sacrificial offerings (which is a positive commandment), about which our sages said (*Pesachim* 59b), "Those who offered them would be atoned for as the priests would eat of the sacrifices."

You can see now the difference between purity and holiness. The pure only do those physical things that are absolutely necessary, meaning to derive no benefit from them other than what is absolutely necessary. They are thus freed from any sort of harm from the physical world and remain pure. But they have not reached the level of holiness, because it would have been better for them to have been altogether without those things. But the holy—those who constantly attach themselves to God, and whose souls move about in the true notions of love and reverence for the Creator—are considered to be walking before God in the land of the living while they are in this world.

The very person of this sort of human being is considered to be a tabernacle, sanctuary, and altar. As our sages said about the verse (Genesis 35:13), "And God alighted from him"—"this indicates that the patriarchs were a vehicle of God" (*Bereishit Rabbah* 62:6). They also said, "The righteous are a vehicle of God." What they meant was that the Divine Presence dwells upon them as it did in the Holy Temple.[6] The

---

4. That is, all you can hope for is the dream of delight in God, and the ram-strength of determination to carry on in the effort. With that comes the great and effervescent gift from God Himself.

5. The "native being," that is, the body and personality, is frightened to the core of dissolution of self and utter attachment to the Master of the Universe. It is desperate for self and dominance. But it can be bound, it can be swept away in the night so that your essence can have its way.

6. That is, just as a tabernacle, sanctuary, and altar are the podiums upon which the offerings were made, where the Divine Presence dwelt, and which also served as means to the desired end, and just as a vehicle is a means through which movement is accomplished,

food that such a person would eat would be like a burnt offering brought upon the fires of the altar. And what was offered upon the altar was considered to have enjoyed a great spiritual elevation, because it was brought before the Divine Presence, and would also enjoy the advantage of having all of its kind blessed throughout the world, as our sages explained in the Midrash (*Tanchuma, Parshat Tetzavah*). So too, the food and drink the holy person would ingest would enjoy a spiritual elevation as if it were actually being offered upon the altar.

This is what our sages were referring to when they said (*Ketubot* 105b), "Whoever brings a gift to a Torah scholar is likened to one who brings a firstfruit offering"; and (*Yoma* 71a), "Let them fill the gullets of the Torah scholars with wine (in the place of libations)." This does not mean to say that the Torah scholars should be encouraged to chase after food and drink, God forbid, and that they should fill themselves like gluttons. But the matter is as we have indicated: Torah scholars who are holy in all of their ways and deeds are considered to truly be like a Temple and an altar, because the Divine Presence dwells upon them as it actually did in the Holy Temple. Something that is offered to them is likened to something offered upon the altar; and filling their gullets is comparable to filling the Temple basins. Therefore, the things of this world they make use of after having attained the level of attachment to God's holiness are elevated because they enjoyed the advantage of having been used by a righteous person. Our sages made reference to this in the case of the rocks that were found in the area, which Jacob took to put around his head.[7] They said (*Chullin* 91b), "Rabbi Yitzchak said . . . they joined together and said, 'Let the righteous man lay his head on me!'"

The general principle behind holiness is that you remain so attached to God that you never separate nor even move from Him no matter what you are doing. Then the physical things you make use of will have had a greater spiritual elevation for your having used them than whatever spiritual descent you would have suffered for having used physical things. But such a state can only come about when your mind is set constantly on God's greatness, exaltedness, and holiness. Then you will be as one who joined the ranks of the angels while yet in the world.

We have already pointed out, however, that you cannot manage to do this on your own. You can only be expected to be attracted to it and to attempt it. And even that can only come about after you will have attained all of the traits we have mentioned thus far, from the initial promptings of caution to the fear of sin. Only then can you approach holiness and be successful at it. If you lack the other traits, you will be a foreigner and a cripple. And as it is said (Numbers 18:4), "a foreigner shall not draw near."[8]

---

the patriarchs in their age and the righteous in ours are the means through which the will and convictions of God are carried out in this world. To be sure, *all* of us are just that. But the patriarchs and the righteous do so willingly, consciously, and rapidly, and that is their greatness. And it is thanks to them that the Divine Presence dwells in our midst.

7. See Genesis 28:11ff.
8. Refer to the end of the first note to part 9.

But after you will have readied yourself in all the ways mentioned, and after you will have further attached yourself to God with a strong love and a powerful reverence by recognizing His vast exaltedness, then disattach yourself from material matters, step by step,[9] and direct all of your movements and actions to the truly hidden aspects of attachment to God. A spirit from on high will descend upon you, and the Creator will dwell on you as He does all of His holy ones. Then you will actually be like one of the angels, and all of your actions—even the most common and corporeal—will be part of your offering and your service.

So you see, the way you obtain this trait is by a lot of abstention, by serious reflection upon the mysteries of God's great involvement in the world and the secrets of creation,[10] and by the sure knowledge of God's exaltedness and praise. Only then will you have become attached to Him strongly and know how to concentrate your thoughts while moving through the world and making use of it. This was the way the priest was supposed to concentrate in order to draw down God's blessing of life and peace as he ritually slaughtered sacrifices and received and sprinkled their blood upon the altar.[11]

Without all this it is impossible to reach this great height. You would remain corporeal and of-the-earth like all other people.

What helps in the attainment of this level is a lot of solitary meditation and abstinence. With this lack of distractions, your soul can more easily strengthen and attach itself to God. What detracts from attaining this trait is a lack of knowledge of the truth and the overassociation with others. Materiality is attracted to its kind and is energized and made stronger by association with it. The soul that is seized by it cannot escape from its trappings. But when it is separated from it, the soul can stand alone and ready itself for the indwelling of holiness. It will be accompanied upon the path it wants to take.[12]

With the help God gives you, your soul can be strengthened and made to grow victorious over physicality, attach itself to God, and grow whole within you.

From there you can grow to an even higher level, "Holy Inspiration," where your intellect will rise above all human capabilities. That will allow you to enjoy a yet higher form of attachment to God. Then the keys to the "Resurrection of the Dead"

---

9.   . . . as that is the only way it can be done. . . .

10.   The discipline of the true study of Kabbalah comprises the "serious reflection upon the mysteries of God's great involvement in the world and the secrets of creation." Kabbalah is not "white magic" or phantasmic meditation. It is the physics of God's creation of the world, and the chemistry of His involvement in it.

11.   What appeared to be so brutal and primitive a series of "cult acts" was actually the score and choreography for God's will on earth. The priest was to engage in a magnificent attachment to God as he was to perform his often-referred-to-as "rites of slaughter and blood-spilling." That is to say, his intentions and concentrations were to be in direct contradistinction to what we would expect them to be.

12.   Refer to the fifth note above.

will be passed on to you as they were passed on to Elijah and Elisha. That would indicate the great degree of attachment to God you would experience. As God is the source of all life, the one who gives life to the living (as our sages say [*Taanit* 2a] "Three keys were not given to tributaries[13]—the keys of the Resurrection of the Dead . . .") one who utterly attaches himself to God can elicit from Him life itself, which is the one thing that is attributable to Him more than anything else. That is how the *beraita* of Rabbi Pinchas ben Yair ends: "holiness brings you to Holy Inspiration, and Holy Inspiration brings you to Resurrection of the Dead."[14]

Precious reader—I realize that you know as well as I that I have not exhausted all the requirements for piety in my book, and that I have not said all that can be said about the subject. But that is because there is no end to the matter, and we cannot fathom the extent of it.

What I have done is mentioned some small part of all the particulars of the *beraita* upon which I have based this book. It is a beginning which will allow for further investigation into these matters. Their paths have therefore been charted, and their ways exposed to our eyes so that we might go on the righteous path. As it is said (Proverbs 1:5), "The wise man will hear and will increase learning, and the man of understanding shall obtain devices"; (*Shabbat* 104a) "One who tries to purify himself is helped"; and (Proverbs 2:6), "For God gives wisdom, and out of His mouth

---

13. . . . but were left in God's hands alone.

14. The original *beraita* reads (*Avodah Zarah* 20b), "Rabbi Pinchas Ben Yaer derived that Torah study brings you to caution, caution to enthusiasm, enthusiasm to innocence, innocence to abstinence, abstinence to purity, purity to piety, piety to modesty, modesty to fear of sin, fear of sin to holiness, holiness to holy spirit, and holy spirit brings you to the resurrection of the dead."

We see that in fact there are *twelve* traits discussed in the original *beraita*: (1) Torah study, (2) caution, (3) enthusiasm, (4) innocence, (5) abstinence, (6) purity, (7) piety, (8) modesty, (9) fear of sin, (10) holiness, (11) holy spirit, and (12) resurrection of the dead, while Luzzatto has apparently only analyzed nine of them, traits 2–10.

In truth, though, he has analyzed Torah study in his introduction, when he directed us toward the form that study should take, but he did not deem it necessary to dwell upon it further, as it is mentioned in various places in the book, and it is not so much a trait as a mechanism to bring about traits (though it is still in the same milieu). And he has not analyzed the last two traits, holy spirit and the resurrection of the dead, because they are not in fact traits, but rather elements of pure angelics, and radical, metahuman tools of the soul.

It can be said that in analyzing ten elements, Luzzatto is likening the human personality to the ten Divine *Sefirot* of the kabbalists; by doing it in 26 chapters, he is expanding upon that relationship, because 26 is the numerical value of the Hebrew four-letter name of God; and he is following in the footsteps of the master kabbalist, Moshe Cordevero, who indicated in his work, *Tomer Devorah* (The Palm-Tree of Deborah), that the rectification of the human personality corresponds to alignment with the ten *Sefirot*.

comes knowledge and understanding" to guide each and every person on his path to his Creator.

It is obvious that each person must be directed and guided according to his own field of endeavor and his concerns. The path to piety for the one whose whole occupation is Torah scholarship is different from the one for the laborer, which is itself different from the one for the professional person. And that goes as well for all the other differentiating factors between people, each of which is its own path to piety. But that is not so because piety changes—it is the same for everybody: it involves doing what brings satisfaction to your Creator. But since the individual participant changes, the means to bring him to that end must necessarily be particular to him. A humble laborer could be as thoroughly pious as someone who never stops studying Torah. As it is said (Proverbs 16:4), "All that God does He does for His own sake," and (Proverbs 3:6) "Know Him in all of your ways, and He will straighten your path."[15]

May He, in His great compassion, open our eyes to His Torah. May He teach us His ways, lead us upon His path, and make us worthy to bring honor to His name and satisfy Him.

(Psalms 104:31) "May the Honor of God endure forever; May God be pleased with His creations"; (Psalm 149:2) "Would that Israel be happy in its Creator; that the sons of Zion rejoice in their King."

Amen, amen, and amen.

I thank God now, I sing and chant to Him whose compassion has helped me until now to bring my book, *The Path of the Just*, into print, which I wrote to teach myself, and which I give over to the many like myself for their elevation.

Perhaps I may merit to have others accrue merits and to improve through my work, thus bringing satisfaction to my Creator. May that be my consolation in the land of great drought (cf. Hosea 13:5), and may I "call it *Rechovot*" (cf. Genesis 26:22). So too may God say that my portion will be in His Torah: to study, teach, observe, and follow His will successfully.

Amen, may that be His will.

---

15. Your activities, concerns, and fields of endeavor illustrate your self in this world. They are your personality's clothing and your soul's voice. And as each individual is a challenge to, a record of, a threat, and a supplement to the status quo, as well as a complex of possibilities for full change, it is incumbent upon each one of us to strive for our own self's excellencies our own ways.

As Luzzatto points out, "All that God does He does for His own sake," which is to say, there is nothing in the world that is so useless that it is irredeemable—certainly no person. But the path to arrive at that redemption and to make full use of the self is the one that embodies "knowing Him in all of your ways" so that He may "straighten your path."

Summation of Part X

Chapter 26

1. Holiness begins in sanctifying yourself and ends in being sanctified, and it involves utterly removing yourself from all physicality and completely attaching yourself to God.

2. Because it is inherently impossible for mere flesh and blood to attain to such heights on its own, all one can ever hope to do is search for the true knowledge and give constant thought to the sanctification of deeds. Then God Himself will have holiness dwell upon you.

3. When you are holy and utterly attached to God (concentrating at all times upon His greatness, exaltedness, and holiness; loving and revering Him mightily, recognizing His vast exaltedness; slowly, gradually detaching yourself from all materiality; and concentrating upon the mysteries of attachment to God), whatever you do becomes sanctified, and you are no longer defiled by the things of this world. At that point you join the ranks of the angels.

4. In order to do this you must practice a lot of solitary meditation and abstinence, because the lack of the knowledge of these truths and the overassociation with others detract from all this. The very obtainment of all this brings with it levels that are yet higher: holy inspiration, and the resurrection of the dead.

5. In summation, it must be said that this book cannot hope to present all you would need to know to become pious, for while it is true that anyone can become pious, nonetheless no two people become so the same way, and each and every person has his own path to piety. The point to be made is that you are to (Proverbs 3:6) "Know Him in all of your ways, and He will straighten your path."

Index

Aaron, 213
Abbahu, Rabbi, 161
Abraham, 213
  eagerness of, 63
  judgment of, 38
Abstinence, 111–129
  acquisition of, 125–127
  bad, 122, 129
  definition of, 116–117
  explanation of, 114–122
  food and, 128
  Halachah-based, 123, 129
  holiness and, 228
  innocence vs., 114n–115n
  personal habit–based, 123, 124,
    129
  piety and, 114–115, 114n–115n
  pleasure-based, 129
  purity and, 135, 143
  sages on, 118, 122
  seclusion in, 124, 126
  sexual relations and, 128
  slow acquisition of, 127
  subdivisions of, 123–124, 129
  three levels of avoidance for, 117

Actions
  analysis of, 30–31
  between a person and God, 154
  definition of, 27n
  humility in, 194–197
  between one person and another,
    154–155
Advice, honest, 92
Akavyah ben Mahalalel, 199
Al moot, 62
Amai, Rabbi, 161
Angels, fear experienced by, 212
Anger, 75
  sages on, 98, 101
  types of, 100–101, 109
Annan, Rav, 162
Antonious, 120
Arrogance, 75, 188, 200
  sages on, 98, 99
  types of, 98–100, 109
  wisdom and, 191–192
Arts and sciences, 21
  Divine service vs., 3–4
  modern preoccupation with, 6–7, 21
Assa, 80

Assai, Rabbi, 161
Astronomy, 7
Attachment, 163, 165–166, 177, 223
    in holiness, 223, 225–226, 227, 230
Authority, 195–196
Awareness, definition of, 27*n*

Baal teshuvah, xi
Baba ben Butah, 195, 213
Bad companionship, 202
    caution and, 42
    and loss of caution, 45–46, 48
Bar Kamsa, 174
Benayahu, 61
Benevolence, piety and, 156–157
Ben Yaer, Rabbi Pinchas, 11, 20, 114*n*

Caution, 23–49
    acquisition of, 34–41, 46
    burdening self with tasks vs., 29, 47
    common sense and, 27–29
    definition of, 26
    enthusiasm and, 53, 55, 65, 66, 70,
        115
    explanation of, 27–29
    innocence and, 79, 105
    resisting loss of, 42–46
    self-mastery and, 25, 27–29, 30–31
    subdivisions of, 30–33
    Torah study and, 34–41, 46
Change
    pitfalls of, 25, 42–46
    Torah study and, 25, 34–41
Chaninah ben Dosah, Rabbi, 166
Chaninah ben Tradyon, Rabbi, 136
Channah Bar Chanilai, Rav, on piety,
    156
Chasid, 117*n*
Chisda, Rabbi, 91, 161
Chizkiyah, 80, 120
Chushai the Arkite, 92
Clothing, sin and, 120

Common sense, caution and, 27–29
Compassion
    of God, 40, 41, 157
    piety and, 157–158
Consciousness, definition of, 27*n*
Conversation, sin and, 120
Cosmogony, 7
Counsel, 32, 33
Coveting, 75, 89, 98, 102–103, 109

David, 61, 103, 164, 177–178, 193
    on bad companions, 45–46
    on closeness to God, 14
    on Divine judgment, 157
    on enthusiasm, 60, 64
    on fear of sin, 212
    on happiness, 166, 167
    on innocence, 80
    judgment of, 39
    on piety, 180
    on purity, 134, 138
    solitude of, 126
    on vengeance, 167
Day of judgment, 38, 48
Deceit, 84–85, 91, 108
Delay, enthusiasm and, 61–62
Delight, 6*n*
Desecration of Divine name, 91, 96
Destruction, 25
Dinah, 339
Divine service
    easy-going nature and, 37–38
    love and, 158
    man's duties and, 12–20, 21–22
    perfection of, 138
    preciousness of, 19–20
    purity in, 138, 144
    reverence and, 158
    subdivisions of, 10–11, 21–22
Drama, 14*n*–15*n*
Duties, Divine service and, 12–20, 21–
    22

Eagerness
of Abraham, 63
enthusiasm and, 62–64, 71
sages on, 63
Solomon on, 63
Effort, 225
Elazar, Rabbi
on benevolence, 157
on oaths, 94
Elazar ben P'dat, Rabbi, 166
Eliezer, Rabbi, sexual abstinence of, 135
Elihu, 213
Elijah, 121
solitude of, 126
on vengeance, 167
Eliphaz, 212–213
Elisha, solitude of, 126
Elitzaphan ben Uziel, 103
Enthusiasm, 49–72
acquisition of, 65–66
caution and, 53, 55, 65, 66, 70, 115
David on, 60, 64
definition of, 53–54, 55–57
eagerness and, 62–64, 71
explanation of, 55–60
fear and, 68, 72
loss of, 67–70
present dearth of, 62
and reflection on God, 65–66
subdivisions of, 61–64
Esau, 39
Ezekiel, 123

Fear
enthusiasm and, 68, 72
of God, *see* Reverence
sages on, 69
Solomon on, 36
warranted vs. senseless, 69–70
Fear of sin, 78n, 205–219
acquisition of, 215–217, 219
constant nature of, 211

David on, 212
explanation of, 208–214, 218
Isaiah on, 212
Moses on, 212
sages on, 36, 212
Fences, 86n, 117
sages' instituting of, 120–121
Food
abstinence and, 128
sin and, 118–119
unkosher, 75, 89–90, 108
Freedah, Rabbi, on piety, 156

Gamliel, Rabbi, 195–196
Gedaliah ben Achikom, 173–174
Glory, desire for, 104
God
actions between a person and, 154
compassion of, 40, 41, 157
David on closeness to, 14
as God of truth, 40
love of, *see* Love of God
Moses on reverence of, 10
presence and involvement of, 215–217, 219
reflection on, *see* Reflection
reverence for, *see* Reverence
Solomon on reverence of, 9
soul's craving for, 6n
true love of, 151–152
trust in, 179n
world as distancing from, 14–16, 16n, 22
see also Love of God; Reverence
Greatness, 25

Halachah, 34n, 105
Halachah-based abstinence, 123, 129
Happiness, 163, 165, 166–167
David on, 166, 167
Solomon on, 166
Hashpah, 152

Hate, 91, 92–93
Hearing, promiscuity through, 88
Hezekiah, judgment of, 39
Hillel, Rabbi, 122, 195
Hitler, Adolf, 25
Holiness, 221–231
    attachment in, 223, 225–226, 227,
        230
    definition of, 223–224
    explanation of, 225–231
    as gift, 225, 226
    modern loss of, $6n$–$7n$
    sages on, 226–227
    twofold nature of, 225
Holy inspiration, 228–229, 230
Honor, 159–163, 196–197
    righteousness and, 197
Human beings
    duties of, Divine service and, 21–
        22
    greatness vs. destruction in, 25
    imperfections of, $9n$, 189–191, 200
    perfection in, 25
    spirituality and, 11
Humility, $78n$, 185–204
    acquisition of, 198–202, 204
    in actions, 194–197
    definition of, 187
    deterrents to, 201
    explanation of, 188–197, 203, 204
    false, 189
    force of habit and, 198
    praise and, 201
    proper time for, $190n$
    reflection and, 198
    sages on, 192, 194–195
    in thought, 189–194, 204
    world and, 201
Hunah, Rav, 97, 156, 161

Illness, 65–66
Inconvenience, dislike of, 68, 72

Innocence, 73–110
    abstinence vs., $114n$–$115n$
    acquisition of, 105–106, 110
    aspects of, 81–104
    caution and, 79, 105
    of character vs. action, 97–98
    David on, 80
    definition of, 76
    difficulty of, 80–81, 107
    explanation of, 77–80, 107
    forbidden traits vs., 75–76
    in honoring of Torah, 162
    self-mastery and, 79–80
Insults, enduring of, 195
Interests, definition of, $27n$
Isaiah, 46, 102
    on fear of sin, 212
    on mockery, 45

Jacob, judgment of, 39
Jealousy, 75, 98, 101–102, 109
Jehosephat, 163
Jeremiah, on closing eyes to own
        actions, 28–29
Jeroboam ben Nevat, jealousy of, 103
Jerusalem Talmud, 88, 97
Jewelry, 120
Jews
    forgotten identity of, x
    present privileges of, ix–x
    primordial dream of, x–xi
Joseph, judgment of, 39
Judah the Prince, Rabbi, 118
Judgment, 39–41
    God's compassion and, 41
Just, definition of, $149n$

Korach, 103

Laziness, 56–57, 71
    rationalizations for, 59, $59n$, 71
    slow destruction of, 57–59, $57n$–$58n$

Levity, 42
and loss of caution, 44–45, 48
sages on, 44
Solomon on, 44
Lies, 91
Loans, 84–85
Love, 10–11, 21
Divine service and, 158
piety and, 151
Love of God, 163–169
piety and, 163
sages on, 164
subdivisions of, 163, 165–169
during troubles and sorrows, 164–165
Lying, 95
degrees of, 94–95

Malachi, 160
Mar Ukva, 123–124
Mashpiah, 152
Mathematics, 7
Methods, definition of, 27*n*
Michal, judgment of, 39
Mitzvah
honoring of, 160
immediate delight in, 16*n*–17*n*
keeping of, 10, 11, 13, 22
keeping of, precision required in, 19
levels of nonaltruistic performance
of, 136–137
piety in, 175–176
preparation for, 141
presentation of, 62*n*–63*n*
pride in, 192–193
purity and widening possibilities of,
152, 181
spoiling of, *see* Delay, enthusiasm
and ulterior motives for, 136
during work hours, 83
Mockery, 42
Isaiah on, 45
and loss of caution, 44–45, 48

Moral scrutiny, meticulous, 75
Mortal desires, removal of, 75
Moses, 16*n*, 40, 213, 218
on fear of Sin, 212
on reverence, 10
Musar, 3, 105
misunderstanding of, ix, xi

Nachman, Rav, 161
N*azir,* wine forbidden to, 85–86
Nechemyah ben Chachalyah, 193
Nechuniah, Rabbi, on piety, 156
Nicknames, 155, 156
Nishpah, 152

Oaths, 91, 94

Path of the Just, The
end result of, 5*n*–6*n*
essential teaching of, 25
patterns in, 114*n*–115*n*
purpose of, 5–6, 11, 21
title of, 149*n*–150*n*
transcendental in, 77–78
Personal behavior–based abstinence,
123, 124, 129
Physical sciences, 7
Piety, 78*n*, 113, 145–183, 211
abstinence and, 114–115, 114*n*–
115*n*
acquisition of, 177–180, 183
benevolence and, 156–157
and capability for wrong actions,
173*n*
compassion and, 157–158
David on, 180
definition of, 147
deterrences in development of, 178
evaluating need for, 172–180, 182–
183
explanation of, 148–153
false, 148–150, 181

Piety (*continued*)
  love and, 151
  in *mitzvah*, 154, 155–156, 175–
    176
  nature of, 7–8, 7*n*, 21
  in prayer, 141–142
  and preoccupations and worries,
    178
  reflecting on God in, 177
  righteousness vs., 115*n*
  sages on, 150, 151, 155–157
  Solomon on, 180
  and spiritual level of people, 121,
    121*n*
  subdivisions of, 154–171
  Temple and, 169
  true, as acquired need, 8
  well-being of own generation in,
    170–171
  the wise and, 7, 7*n*, 21
Pilpul, 8, 8*n*, 34*n*
Pinchas, Rabbi, 11, 20, 43, 100
Pleasure-based abstinence, 129
Pleasures, 140–141, 143
  falseness of, 125–126
  love of, 67, 72
  sin and, 118–119
Poor, indebtedness to God of, 65
Praise, 189, 196
  humility and, 201
Prayer, pious, 141–142
Preoccupations, piety and, 178
Pride, 192–193
Profanity, 88–89
Promiscuity, 44, 75, 80, 82, 85–89,
    107, 108
  sages on, 86–87
  through speech, *see* Profanity
  in thought, 89
  types of, 86
Protective fences, *see* Fences
Psalms, recitation of, 7, 7*n*

Punishment, fear of, 209, 218
Purity, 78*n*, 114*n*, 131–144
  abstinence and, 135, 143
  acquisition of, 140–142
  David on, 134, 138
  definition of, 133
  of Divine service, 138, 144
  explanation of, 134–139
  in honoring of Torah, 162
  problems in acquisition of, 142
  Solomon on, 136
  and widening possibilities of *mitzvot*,
    152, 181

Rachel, 39
Reflection, 199–201
  enthusiasm and, 65–66
  piety in, 177
Relationships, perverse, 75
Relaxation
  desire for, 72
  yearning for, 67
Respect, coveting of, 103, 104
Resurrection of the Dead, 228–229,
    230
Revenge, 91, 92–93
Reverence, 10, 21, 209, 210–211,
    218
  Divine service and, 158–159
Rich, indebtedness to God of, 65
Righteousness, 121
  honor and, 197
  piety vs., 115*n*

Sabbath, *see Shabbat*
Safeguards, 117
Safra, Rav, 95–96, 161
Sages, 170, 201
  on abstinence, 118, 182
  and acquisition of innocence,
    105
  on anger, 98, 101

on arrogance, 98, 99
on attachment, 166
on bad form of abstinence, 122
on day of judgment, 38
on Divine kindness, 41
on eagerness, 63
on enthusiasm, 56
on fear, 69
on fear of sin, 36, 212
fences instituted by, 120–121
on holiness, 226–227
on honoring *mitzvah*, 160–161
on honoring the Torah, 162
on humility, 192, 194–195
on laziness, 57
on levity, 44
on love of God, 164
on lying, 95
on piety, 150, 151, 155–157
on promiscuity, 86–87
on sin, 40, 82, 89
on spiritually whole people, 79
on thievery, 82, 84
on toil in the world, 67–68
on Torah study, 43
on unkosher food, 90
on verbal abuse, 91
Saul, 103
Seclusion
in abstinence, 124, 126
holiness and, 228
Seduction
of the heart, 75
sin and, 125
Self-analysis
mockery and, 45
self-mastery and, 25, 30–33, 34–41
setting aside time for, 31, 33, 47
Self-mastery, 16*n*–17*n*, 29, 41, 47
caution and, 25, 27–29, 30–31
innocence and, 79–80

maze metaphor about, 32–33
self-analysis and, 25, 30–33, 34–41
Selling, deceit in, 84
Senses, holy capabilities of, 87*n*
Sex
abstinence and, 128
sin and, 119
Shabbat
honoring of, 161, 162–163
keeping of, 97, 108
Sheshet, Rav, 87
Shimon ben Lakish, Rabbi, 166
Shonim, 45
Simlai, Rabbi, on benevolence, 157
Sin
clothing and jewelry and, 120
conversation and, 120
difficulty of obtaining freedom from, 80
fear of, *see* Fear of sin
food and drink and, 118–119
God's compassion and, 40–41
pleasure and, 118–119
sages on, 40, 82, 89
seduction and, 125
sex and, 119
of workers, 83
Sitting, humility in, 194, 204
Slander, 80, 92, 174*n*
Solomon, 61, 118, 126, 138, 165–166, 168
on bad companions, 45
on caution, 29
on eagerness, 63
on easy-going nature, 37–38
on fear, 36
on God-reverence, 9
judgment of, 39
on laziness, 56–57, 58
on levity, 44
on lying, 95
on piety, 180

Solomon (*continued*)
    on purity, 136
    on worldly trials, 14
Soul
    craving of, 6*n*
    exercising of, 89*n*
    levels of, 115*n*–117*n*
    world abhorred by, 19
Speech, promiscuity through, *see*
        Profanity
Spirituality, contemporary questions
        about, 5*n*
Striving, 225
Study as expertise, 75

Talebearing, 91, 92
Talmud, *see* Jerusalem Talmud
Tarphon, Rabbi, 176
Temple, piety and, 169
Ten commandments, 35*n*
Teshuvah (repentance), 29
Thievery, 75, 80, 82–84, 107
    rationalizations for, 83
    sages on, 82, 84
    Torah on, 82
    of workers, 82–83
Torah
    affecting in, 152*n*–153*n*
    honoring of, 162
    on necessity of Divine service, 3
    and overinvolvement in world, 43
    on thievery, 82
    writing in, 216
Torah study
    caution acquired by, 34–41, 46
    change and, 25, 34–41
    coveting and, 102–103
    Divine service and, 7, 7*n*
    glory and, 104
    for great majority of people, 38–40
    pilpul vs., 8
    sages on, 43

setting aside time for, 42
for those of lesser understanding,
        36–38
for those who fully understand, 35–
        36
types of, 34
Trials, 14–16, 19, 22
Tsopher the Namasite, 85
Tzaddik, 117*n*
Tzitzit, 120

Ulah Bar Koshev, 121

Vengeance, 163, 165, 167–168
Verbal abuse, 91
Vision
    clouded, 75
    promiscuity through, 85–89

Walking, humility in, 194, 204
"Walking in His ways," 10, 21
Wealth, worry and, 103
Weights and measures, honest, 84
Wholeheartedness, 10, 11, 22
Wholeness, 35–36
Wine, 119
    forbidden to *Nazir*, 85–86
Wisdom, arrogance and, 191–192
Wonders, reflection on, 65–66, 72
Work, escape from, 42*n*
Workers, thievery of, 82–83
World
    as darkness, 31–32
    as distancing from God, 14–16, 16*n*,
        22
    effort and toil required in, 67–68
    false and ephemeral pleasures of,
        125–126, 140–141, 143
    God's compassion and, 40–41
    humility and, 201
    overinvolvement in, and loss of
        caution, 42–44

soul's abhorrence of, 19
three aspects of, 152*n*
toil required in, 72
trials of, *see* Trials
as vestibule for World to Come, 13–
    14, 17–19, 22
World to Come vs., 9*n*
World to Come, 17, 22, 66, 91, 103
spiritual levels in, 37, 48
two understandings of, 8*n*
world as a vestibule to, 13–14, 17–
    19, 22
world vs., 9*n*

Worry, 36*n*
    piety and, 178
    wealth and, 103

Yehoshua ben Levi, Rabbi, 121
Yehosophat, 80
Yochanan, Rabbi, 39, 162
Yochanan ben Koreach, 173–174
Yoseph, Rav, 161

Zaira, Rabbi, 156, 163
Zakai, Rabbi, 155–157
Zechariah ben Evkolas, Rabbi, 174

Rabbi Yaakov Feldman

A leader in Jewish outreach, Rabbi Yaakov Feldman was the founder and director of *Machon Binah:* The Center for Understanding, in California, the director of other outreach organizations in New York, and a Hillel director at the State University of New York at Purchase.

Rabbi Feldman serves on the board of directors of *Ohr Ki Tov,* and is chairman of the clergy committee of the Rockland Council on Alcoholism, a member of the clergy and ethics committees of the Rockland County (New York) Hospice Association, and the volunteer Jewish chaplain at Nyack Hospital. He has served for many years as a spiritual and addiction counselor.

Rabbi Feldman has translated and commented on *The Duties of the Heart* by Bachya ibn Pakuda (Jason Aronson, 1996), as well as authoring children's stories, and articles in Jewish journals, magazines, and newspapers. He lives with his wife, Sara, and their three children in Monsey, New York.